George Washington Ball

**General Railroad Laws of the State of Pennsylvania**

And Acts Relative to Corporations Affecting Railroad Companies

George Washington Ball

**General Railroad Laws of the State of Pennsylvania**
*And Acts Relative to Corporations Affecting Railroad Companies*

ISBN/EAN: 9783744696777

Printed in Europe, USA, Canada, Australia, Japan

Cover: Foto ©Suzi / pixelio.de

More available books at **www.hansebooks.com**

# General Railroad Laws

## State of Pennsylvania

and

### ACTS RELATIVE TO CORPORATIONS AFFECTING RAILROAD COMPANIES.

ARRANGED IN CHRONOLOGICAL ORDER, FROM 1820 TO 1874, WITH A COMPLETE ANALYTICAL INDEX.

*COMPILED BY GEO. W. I. BALL.*

PUBLISHED BY ALLEN, LANE & SCOTT,
No. 233 South Fifth Street.
1875.

# General Railroad Laws

OF THE

## STATE OF PENNSYLVANIA.

---

### AN ACT TO REGULATE PROXIES.

*Passed 28th March, 1820.* (*Smith's Laws, vol. 7, page 320.*)

SECTION 1. All power to vote by proxy in any association incorporated by any authority in this Commonwealth, or by the former proprietary government, shall be obtained and dated within six months previously to the time of holding the election or meeting of stockholders at which such proxy shall be presented, and shall not be used for any purpose or purposes except those therein expressed, nor shall any such proxy be given in blank, nor substitution thereof to a third person be admitted, any law or usage to the contrary notwithstanding: *And provided, also,* That nothing herein contained shall be so construed as to alter or affect the provisions of the act entitled "An act regulating banks," so far as relates to the dates of proxies.

SEC. 2. In all elections of officers in an association or company (incorporated as aforesaid) hereafter to be held by virtue of any law of this Commonwealth, whenever any person shall offer to the judges of such election any vote or votes, as attorney, proxy, or agent for any other person, such person being required thereto by any judge of such election, or any stockholder in such association or company, shall, before his vote or votes shall be received, take and subscribe the following oath or affirmation:—" I —— do solemnly swear (or affirm) that I have no interest, directly or indirectly, in the share upon which I shall vote at this election; that those shares are, to the best of my knowledge and belief, truly and in good faith owned by the persons in whose names they now stand, and that in voting at this election I have not transferred any of the said shares, or caused them to be transferred in trust or otherwise, for the purpose of increasing the votes at this election, and that I shall not violate in any manner, directly or indirectly, any provision of the act of incorporation which limits the number of votes a stockholder may give in his own right;" and the judges of such election are authorized to administer the aforesaid oath (or affirmation), and the said oath and all authorities or powers of attorney to vote by proxy, or as agent, shall be filed and preserved in the office of such association or company, and if any person shall willfully and absolutely swear or affirm falsely in taking any oath or affirmation prescribed by this act, such person so offending shall, upon due conviction thereof, be subject to the pains and penalties which are by law prescribed for the punishment of willful and corrupt perjury.

---

## AN ACT REGULATING LATERAL RAILROADS.

*Approved 5th May, 1832.* (*P. L., 1831-2, pages 501 to 506.*)

SECTION I. That if any owner or owners of land, mills, quarries, coal-mines, lime-kilns, or other real estate, in the vicinity of any railroad, canal, or slack-water navigation, made or to be made by any company or by the State of Pennsylvania, and not more than three miles distant therefrom, shall desire to make a railroad thereto over any intervening lands, he or they, their engineers, agents, and artists, may enter upon any lands, and survey and mark such route as he or they shall think proper to adopt, doing no damage to the property explored, and thereupon may present a petition to the court of common pleas of the county in which said intervening land is situated, setting forth his or their desire to be allowed to construct and finish a railroad in and upon the said route, and the beginning, courses, and distances thereof, and place of intersection of the main railroad, canal, or slack-water navigation, which shall be filed and entered of record in the said court, whereupon the said court shall appoint six disinterested and judicious men, resident in the said county, who shall view the said marked and proposed route for a railroad, and examine the same, and if they or any four of them shall deem the same necessary and useful for public or private purposes, they shall report in writing to the subsequent term of said court what damages will be sustained by the owner or owners of the said intervening land, by the opening, constructing, completing, and using the said railroad, and the report of the said viewers and appraisers shall be filed of record in the said court, and if not appealed from, be liable to be confirmed or rejected by the said court, as to right and justice shall appertain; and if either of the parties shall be dissatisfied with said report, he or they may appeal therefrom to the said court of common pleas within twenty days after such report has been filed in the prothonotary's office, and not after; and after such appeal, either party may put the cause at issue, in the form approved of by the court, and the said issue shall be placed first on the trial list of the next regular term of the said court, and be there tried and determined by the court and jury, and the verdict so rendered, and judgment thereon, shall be final and conclusive, without further appeal or writ of error; and it shall be the duty of the said viewers and jury to take into consideration the advantages which may be derived by the owner or owners of land passed by the said railroad when making up their report or forming their verdict thereon.

SEC. 2. That the said court shall tax and allow such fees to the viewers and appraisers and officers of the court as are chargeable for such services under the existing fee bills, which shall be paid by the petitioners for the said railroad, and if necessary, their payment shall be compelled by attachment; and it shall be at the option of the petitioner or petitioners for the said railroad, either after the report filed or after the verdict of the jury, after paying the legal costs to be taxed as aforesaid, to abandon the further prosecution of the said railroad, and, as evidence thereof, shall file his or their declaration of that intent in writing, in the said court, which shall terminate all further proceedings on the said petition.

SEC. 3. That the said railroad shall not exceed in breadth twenty feet, nor pass through any burying-ground or place of public worship, nor any dwelling-house or out-buildings, without the consent of the owner thereof; it shall be of single or double track, and formed of wood, stone, and iron, each or all of them, as the proprietors of the said road shall adopt; the streams of water over which it may pass shall be bridged with stone or wood, and the right of property in the said railroad shall be vested in him or them, his or their heirs and assigns, who shall have subscribed the said petition for the said railroad, and whose funds shall have been contributed and paid for the construction thereof, in such just proportions as each contribution and payment shall bear to the whole amount expended in the formation and completion of the said railroad, and the satisfaction of damages for lands and materials appropriated thereto; and the said railroad shall be jointly and severally enjoyed and used by the proprietors thereof; the proprietors of the said railroad, their workmen and agents, shall not break ground, or commence the construction of the said railroad, until the damages reported by the viewers, or awarded by the verdict of the jury, shall be tendered or paid to the party or parties entitled thereto, except in cases of their being unknown to the petitioners.

SEC. 4. That fifteen days' notice shall be given of the intention to file a petition for a railroad, in the court of common pleas, and of the time of viewing the premises by the viewers, to the owner or owners of the lands over which the route of the contemplated railroad shall pass, if the said owners shall be resident in this Commonwealth; and if in any case the owner or owners of said lands shall be unknown, an affidavit thereof being filed by any petitioner for said road, notice shall be given in one public newspaper, printed in the county where the land lies, for three successive weeks; and if there is no newspaper printed in the county where the land lies, then publication in any newspaper printed in the adjoining county shall be sufficient.

SEC. 5. That he or they who shall construct the said railroad, after having paid the damages ascertained as aforesaid, shall be entitled to use and apply all the said gravel, timber, and other materials on the route adopted, and within the breadth of twenty feet, to and for the formation and completion of the said road and bridges; and it shall be lawful for

the petitioners for, and the proprietors of, the said railroad, his
or their heirs and assigns, and their agents and persons employed by or under him or them, to enter upon any land near
or adjoining said railroad, to search for stone, gravel, sand,
wood, or other materials to be used in the construction of the
said road; but no stone, gravel, sand, wood, or other materials
shall be taken from any land for the purposes aforesaid until
the rate of compensation therefor shall be ascertained and
settled with the owners of the said lands; but if the parties
cannot agree thereon, each party shall choose a man, who, if
they cannot agree, shall choose an umpire, all of whom shall,
under oath or affirmation, fairly and impartially estimate the
same, and such award shall be final and conclusive; but if the
owner or owners of such land, out of which the said materials
shall be designed to be taken, shall be a *femme couverte, non
compos mentis*, out of the State or unknown, the court of common pleas of the proper county shall, in writing, appoint three
impartial men, who, on oath or affirmation, shall fairly and
impartially estimate the same materials, the amount of which
said valuation shall be paid or tendered to the owner or
owners thereof, if within the State and known, before they are
removed or applied to the construction of the said railroad.

SEC. 6. That the proprietor or proprietors of the said railroad, on the completion of the same, shall file in the court of
common pleas a full statement and account of all the expenses
incurred in the formation and completion of the said road,
under the oath or affirmation of some one or more who shall
have had knowledge of the same, within three months after
the same shall be completed and put in use, under the penalty
of one hundred dollars, to the end that the said road, and the
privileges appurtenant thereto, may be resumed by this Commonwealth whenever the legislature shall enact the payment
to the proprietors of such railroad, their heirs and assigns, of
the principal money expended in the construction of the same.

SEC. 7. That the said railroad shall and may be used by any
person or persons transporting anything thereon, in such cars,
wagons, and vehicles as are adapted to and used thereon by
the proprietor or proprietors of the said railroad or their
agents, and no other, he or they using the same paying four

cents per mile on each and every ton weight of the article transported thereon; and on all single articles weighing less than a ton, it shall be lawful to charge and receive an advance not exceeding twenty per cent. on the rate as above established.

SEC. 8. That the said railroad shall be so constructed as not to obstruct or impede the free use and passage of any public road or roads which may cross or enter the same, being now laid out or hereafter to be laid out; and in all places where the said railroad may cross or in any manner interfere with any public road, the proprietors of the said railroad shall make, or cause to be made, a good and sufficient bridge or bridges, causeway or causeways, to enable all persons passing or traveling such public road to cross and pass over said railroad; and if the proprietor or proprietors of said railroad shall refuse or neglect to make such bridge or bridges, causeway or causeways, or when made to keep the same in good repair, they shall be liable to pay a penalty of ten dollars for every day the same shall be so neglected, or refused to be made or repaired, to be recovered by the supervisor of the township, with costs, for the use of the township, as debts of like amount are by law recoverable, and the service of process on any one of the proprietors of the said railroad shall be as good and effectual as if made on all of them.

SEC. 9. That for the accommodation of all persons owning or possessing land through which the said railroad may pass, and to prevent inconvenience to such persons in crossing or passing over the same, it shall be the duty of the proprietors of the said railroad, if required, to make, or cause to be made, a good and sufficient bridge or bridges, causeway or causeways, whenever the same may be necessary to enable the occupant or occupants of said land to cross or pass over the same with wagons, carts, and implements of husbandry, as occasion may require: *Provided*, That the proprietors of the said railroad shall in no case be required to make, or cause to be made, more than two such causeways through each plantation or lot of land, for the accommodation of any one person owning or possessing land through which the said railroad shall pass: and where any public road shall cross the said railroad, the person owning or possessing land through which the said railroad shall pass shall not be entitled to make such requisition on the proprietors of the said railroad; and the said bridge or bridges, causeway or causeways, when so made, shall be maintained and kept in repair by the proprietor or proprietors of the said railroad; and if they shall refuse or neglect to make such bridge or bridges, causeway or causeways, or when made to keep the same in good repair, the said proprietors shall be liable to pay any person aggrieved thereby all damages sustained by such person or persons, in consequence of such neglect or refusal, to be sued for and recovered before any magistrate or court having cognizance thereof, and the service of process on any one of the proprietors of the said railroad shall be as good and effectual as if made on all of them.

SEC. 10. That no suit or action shall be brought or prosecuted by any person or persons, for any penalties incurred under this act, unless such suit or action shall be commenced within twelve months after the offense committed or the cause of action shall have accrued; and the defendant or defendants in such suit or action may plead the general issue, and give this act and the special matter in evidence, and that the same was done in pursuance and by authority of this act.

SEC. 11. That if any person or persons shall willfully and knowingly break, injure, or destroy the said railroad, or any part thereof, or any work or device, or any part thereof, to be erected by the proprietors of the said railroad, or shall willfully place any obstruction in and upon the said railroad, he or they so offending shall forfeit and pay to the proprietor or proprietors of the said railroad three times the actual damages so sustained, to be sued for and recovered with costs of suit, before any justice of the peace or court having cognizance thereof, by action of debt, in the name and for the use of the proprietor or proprietors of the said railroad.

SEC. 12. That the provisions of this act shall extend to the counties of Lycoming, Luzerne, Schuylkill, and Northumberland only: *Provided*, That if any lateral railroad so constructed as aforesaid, shall be disused or suffered to remain out of repair for the space of two years, all right of way or other privilege therein shall cease and revert to the original owners of the land, their heirs and assigns.

SEC. 13. That the legislature reserve the right to repeal or alter this act, either in whole or in part, as may respect any railroad constructed under the provisions of this act. (Limitation to counties repealed 11th April, 1848.)

---

**A SUPPLEMENT TO AN ACT PASSED THE 22d MARCH, 1817, ENTITLED "AN ACT RELATIVE TO SUITS BROUGHT BY OR AGAINST CORPORATIONS."**

*Approved 16th March, 1833.* (*P. L., 1832–3, pages 78 and 79.*)

SECTION 1. That the service of any civil process upon the toll-gatherer of any corporation, in the proper county, and next to the place where the damage or damages shall have been committed, shall be held as good and valid in law as if served on the president or other principal officer, or the cashier, treasurer, secretary, or chief clerk of the corporation, as aforesaid; and upon such service the like proceedings shall be had as is directed by the aforesaid act, to which this is a supplement: *Provided*, That where a suit shall be commenced and the process served on the toll-gatherer, it shall be the duty of the plaintiff, his agent or attorney, to cause reasonable notice to be given to some one of the officers of the company aforesaid of the commencement of any such suit before trial and final judgment.

---

**AN ACT RELATIVE TO SUITS BROUGHT BY AND AGAINST CANAL AND RAILROAD COMPANIES.**

*Approved 14th April, 1834.* (*P. L., 1833–4, pages 395 and 396.*)

SECTION 1. That it shall and may be lawful for either party, in any suit or action now pending or that may hereafter be brought in any of the courts of this Commonwealth, by or against any canal or railroad company, to remove the same into the court of any other adjacent county through which the canal or railroad of such company is not located, which suits, so removed, shall be proceeded in by the proper court, in like manner, and subject to like rules and proceedings as if it had remained in the court in which it was originally commenced, and upon final judgment, *testatem* executions may issue as in other cases: *Provided*, That the party so removing shall first take and subscribe an oath or affirmation, to be filed of record with the cause, that such removal is not made for the purpose of delay, but because he firmly believes a fair and impartial trial cannot be had in the county through which such canal or railroad may pass: *And provided further*, That the provisions of this act shall not be so construed as to interfere with the existing laws relative to the assessment of damages to property, occasioned by the construction of such canals or railroads, nor with the right and privilege heretofore granted to any canal or railroad company, to have suits against them tried in any particular county or counties.

---

## AN ACT RELATING TO INSPECTIONS.

*Approved 15th April, 1835. (P. L., 1834-5, page 399.)*

SECTION 41. Every person who shall unload or discharge any flour, corn, or meal designed for exportation at any landing-place or other place, shall cause the same forthwith to be put in a store, or under a shelter sufficient to keep it dry.

SEC. 42. If the carrier of any flour, corn, or meal, designed for exportation, shall cause or suffer the same to be wet or to take damage for want of due care, or for want of sufficient shelter or covering as before required, such carrier shall forfeit and pay to the owner thereof twenty-five cents for every cask of flour, cornmeal, bread, and biscuit, over and above the damage actually sustained.

## AN ACT FOR THE PREVENTION OF INJURIES TO INDI-VIDUALS BY THE GROSS NEGLIGENCE OR WILLFUL MISCONDUCT OF STAGE-DRIVERS AND OTHERS.

*Approved 1st April, 1836. (P. L., 1835-6, page 427.)*

SECTION 1. That from and after the first day of July next, if any person within this Commonwealth shall become injured, either in person or property, through or by reason of the gross negligence or willful misconduct of the driver of any public stage, mail-coach, coachee, carriage, or car employed in the conveyance of passengers, or through or by reason of the gross negligence or willful misconduct of any engineer or conductor of any locomotive-engine engaged in the transportation of passengers, or of goods, wares, merchandise, or produce of any description, such driver, engineer, or conductor shall be deemed guilty of a misdemeanor, and, on conviction thereof, shall for every such offense be punished by a fine not exceeding fifty dollars, and imprisonment in the jail of the county wherein such offense shall have been committed for any length of time not exceeding six months, at the discretion of the court: *Provided,* That the provisions of this act shall not interfere with the civil remedies against the proprietors or others to which the party injured may by law be now entitled.

(Repealed and supplied 31st March, 1860.)

---

## AN ACT RELATING TO ROADS, HIGHWAYS, AND BRIDGES.

*Approved 13th June, 1836. (P. L., 1835-6, pages 565 and 566.)*

SECTION 74. If any person shall willfully set fire to any wooden bridge within this Commonwealth, with intent to destroy the same, or shall be accessory thereto before the fact, such person shall, for every such offence, be liable to indictment, and to the punishment provided by law in cases of arson, and also shall forfeit and pay a sum not more than two thousand dollars, at the discretion of the court having cognizance of such offence, for the use of the county, township or townships, corporations, or persons aggrieved.

(Repealed and supplied 31st March, 1860.)

## AN ACT RELATING TO THE COMMENCEMENT OF ACTIONS.

*Approved 13th June, 1836. (P. L., 1835-6, pages 579 and 580.)*

SECTION 41. Every corporation, aggregate or sole, shall be amenable to answer upon a writ of summons as aforesaid, and in the case of a corporation aggregate, except counties and townships, service thereof shall be deemed sufficient, if made upon the president or other principal officer, or on the cashier, treasurer, secretary, or chief clerk of such corporation, in the manner hereinbefore provided.

SEC. 42. In actions for damages, occasioned by a trespass or injury done by a corporation, if the officers aforesaid of such corporation, or any of them, shall not reside in the county in which such trespass or injury shall be committed, it shall be lawful to serve the summons upon any officer or agent of the corporation, at any office or place of business of the corporation within the county; or if there be no such office or place of business, it shall be lawful to serve the summons upon the president or other principal officer, cashier, treasurer, secretary, or chief clerk, in any county or place where they may be found.

---

## AN ACT RELATING TO EXECUTIONS.

*Approved 16th June, 1836. (P. L., 1835-6, pages 774 and 775.)*

SECTION 72. All executions which shall be issued from any court of record, against any corporation, not being a county, township, or other public corporate body, shall command the sheriff, or other officer, to levy the sum recovered, together with the costs of suit, of the goods and chattels, lands and tenements of such corporation, and such execution shall be executed in the manner following, to wit:—

I. The officer charged with the execution of such writ shall go to the banking-houses, or other principal office of such corporation, during the usual office hours, and demand of the president or other chief officer, cashier, treasurer, secretary, chief clerk, or other officer having charge of such office, the amount of such execution, with legal costs.

II. If no person can be found on whom demand can be made, as aforesaid, or if the amount of such execution be not forthwith paid, in lawful money, after demand as aforesaid, such officer shall seize personal property of said corporation, sufficient to satisfy the debt, interest, and costs, as aforesaid.

III. If the corporation against which such execution shall be issued be a banking company, and other sufficient personal property cannot be found, such officer shall take so much of any current coin, of gold, silver, or copper, which he may find, as shall be sufficient to satisfy the debt, interest, and costs as aforesaid.

IV. If no sufficient personal property be found, as aforesaid, such officer shall levy such execution upon the real estate of such corporation, and thereupon proceed in the manner provided in other cases for the sale of land upon execution.

SEC. 73. In every case in which judgment shall have been obtained against such corporation, except as aforesaid, and an execution issued thereon shall have been returned unsatisfied, in part or in whole, it shall be lawful for the court in which such judgment shall have been obtained, upon the bill or petition of the plaintiff in such judgment, to award a writ to sequester the goods, chattels, and credits, rents, issues, and profits, tolls and receipts, from any road, canal, bridge, or other work, property, or estate of such corporation.

SEC. 74. The court shall, upon the awarding any such writ, appoint a sequestrator to execute the same and to take charge of the property and funds taken or received by virtue of such writ, and to distribute the net proceeds thereof among all the creditors of such corporation, according to the rules established in the case of the insolvency of individuals, and such sequestrator shall have all the powers and be subject to all the duties of trustees appointed under the law relating to insolvent debtors: *Provided*, That in the case of any work in the maintenance or repair of which the public may be interested, and which may from time to time require a portion of the revenue thereof, as aforesaid, to be expended thereon, the court which awards such writ shall make such allowances for such purpose, and otherwise take such order thereon as the public good shall require.

SEC. 75. The said court shall have power, at the time of awarding any such writ, or afterwards, to make such orders and decrees as may be necessary to carry the same into full and complete effect, and they may also make all such other orders and decrees in the premises, for the purpose of giving full and effectual relief to all the creditors of such corporation, as shall be agreeable to equity, and they may enforce all such orders against all persons neglecting or refusing to comply therewith, or obstructing the execution thereof, or of such writ, by attachment or by a writ or writs to the sheriff or coroner, in aid of the sequestrator, or otherwise, as fully as a court of chancery might do.

---

AN ACT TO AUTHORIZE THE AUDITOR-GENERAL TO INSTITUTE SUIT FOR THE COLLECTION OF ANY BALANCE WHICH MAY BE FOUND DUE FROM LAWRENCE L. MINOR, LATE CLERK OF THE SENATE, AND FOR OTHER PURPOSES.

*Approved 14th April, 1838. (P. L., 1837-8, page 396.)*

SECTION 5. That from and after the passage of this act, all and every suit or action now pending, or that may hereafter be brought by or against any canal or railroad company, in any of the courts of this Commonwealth, and which now are or hereafter shall be removed into a court of any other adjacent county, by virtue of the act of the 14th April, 1834, relative to suits brought by and against canal and railroad companies, the costs and expenses thereof shall be borne and paid by the county in which such suit or action was brought; and that in all cases where the venire of any suit now depending has been or may be changed, and where the venire of any suit hereafter to be instituted may be changed, and where suits are directed to be brought in any particular county, the costs of summoning the jury and the pay of the jurors shall be borne by the county in which the cause of action originated.

SEC. 6. It shall and may be lawful for the county commissioners of the county into which any suit or action now is or hereafter may be removed, by virtue of the above-recited act,

to ask, demand, sue for, recover, and receive of the commissioners of the county from which the same may or shall be
removed, all the costs and expenses incurred by the county to
which the same may have been removed as aforesaid.

---

## A SUPPLEMENT TO THE ACT ENTITLED "AN ACT TO INCORPORATE THE MIDDLEPORT AND PINE CREEK RAILROAD COMPANY," AND FOR OTHER PURPOSES.

*Approved 16th April, 1838. (P. L., 1837–8, pages 462, 463, and 464.)*

SECTION 5. That the president and directors of Philadelphia,
Wilmington and Baltimore Railroad Company, and the president and directors of any other railroad company, are hereby
authorized and empowered to unite such railroads as are
constructed and terminate in the county of Philadelphia, the
location of which is hereby confirmed, by curves, switch,
turning-platforms, or otherwise, so as to form a continuous
line of railroad with railroads of other companies in this
Commonwealth: *Provided,* That each company is entitled to
all the privileges and immunities which such company now
possess, have, and enjoy under their respective charters:
*Provided,* That no change shall be made in the location of the
curves, switches, turning-platforms, or other appurtenances of
said railroads, or any of them, within the county of Philadelphia, without the consent of the judges of the Quarter Sessions
of the County of Philadelphia.

SEC. 8. That if any person shall willfully and maliciously set
fire to, destroy, or injure any part of a locomotive or stationary
engine, engine-house, bridge, culvert, trestle-work, or other
building or structure belonging or appurtenant to any railroad constructed or located by this Commonwealth, or by
any company authorized by law to construct a railroad; or
shall willfully and maliciously obstruct any such railway, or
do any damage to the materials or any part thereof, or shall
put any timber, stone, iron, or other matter thereon, or do any
other act in relation to such railroad, whereby the lives of
persons or property employed or transported on the same

shall be endangered, such person or persons shall, upon conviction of such offense, before any court of competent jurisdiction, be sentenced to pay the damages caused by such offense, and to be imprisoned in the jail of the proper county, or in one of the penitentiaries in the State, for any term not exceeding five years.

(Section eight repealed and supplied 31st March, 1860.)

SEC. 9. That if any person shall wantonly derange or displace the fixtures or machinery of any locomotive or stationary engine or inclined plane, used or employed on any railroad as aforesaid, or shall put in motion any machine, engine, car, or other vehicle, upon or belonging to any such railroad, without the consent of the person having the charge of the same, or shall destroy or injure any fence or wall or crossroad passing over or under such railroad, such person or persons shall forfeit any sum not exceeding one hundred dollars, and pay all damages caused by such offense; such person or persons may also be prosecuted criminally, and on conviction of the said offenses, or either of them, be sentenced to imprisonment, not exceeding twelve months, in the jail of the proper county.

(Section nine repealed and supplied 31st March, 1860.)

SEC. 10. That if any person shall willfully and wantonly, without the consent of the person having charge of any such railroad, lead, drive, or cause to be led or driven, any horse, mule, ox, sheep, swine, or other cattle on such railroad, or upon the banks or sideways thereof, or haul any other vehicle than railroad cars upon any such railroad, except at places constructed for crossing the same, or use any animal or vehicle on such railroad, contrary to the regulations of the canal commissioners, or of the board of managers or directors, as the case may be, such person or persons shall forfeit twenty-five dollars, and pay all damages arising from such offense.

SEC. 11. No person shall construct any building, wharf, platform, switch, sideway, lateral railroad, or crossing-place, or make or apply any device whatever on the ground set apart for, or belonging to or forming part of, or on the banks or excavation of any railroad as aforesaid, without permission given under the authority of the canal commissioners, or of the managers of the proper railroad company, as the case may be, which permission shall only be given in writing, by a person duly authorized for that purpose; and if any person shall commence or make any such construction or device without such permission, or shall not conform to the direction of the proper officer or agent in the case, in the construction of such building, wharf, platform, switch, sideway, lateral railroad, crossing-place, or device, as aforesaid, such person shall, for every such offense, forfeit and pay a sum not exceeding one hundred dollars, and the officer or agent having charge of such railroad may, at the expense of such person, remove and destroy every such structure or device as aforesaid: *Provided*, That nothing in this act shall prevent any corporation authorized to make a railroad, or individual owning land contiguous to a railroad, from laying rails on his or their land and connecting the same with such railroad, in such manner as shall be directed by the managers thereof.

RESOLUTION RELATIVE TO CHANGING THE LOTS AT-
TACHED TO CERTAIN LOCK-HOUSES ON THE JUNIATA
DIVISION OF THE PENNSYLVANIA CANAL, AND RELA-
TIVE TO OTHER PURPOSES.

*Approved 17th April, 1838.* (*P. L., 1837–8, pages 695 and 696.*)

*Resolved*, That all companies hereafter incorporated for the construction of canals, railroads, or other works of internal improvement in the State of Pennsylvania, shall cause correct topographical maps to be made, showing accurately the location of their works, together with accurate profiles of the ground; the said maps and profiles shall be made on a uniform scale, to be designated by the canal commissioners, and shall be deposited in the office of the said commissioners, at Harrisburg; and the said companies shall further cause a complete and correct set of drawings to be made, exhibiting the plans, profiles,' and elevations of all important constructions upon their respective works, accompanied by the proper specifications and bills of materials; the plans shall be of uniform size, and bound together in the form of a book, which shall be deposited in the office of the canal commissioners, and that the canal commissioners be directed to request all canal and rail-road companies heretofore incorporated to furnish and deposit in their office, as far as practicable, similar maps, profiles, and drawings, as is herein provided in relation to companies here-after to be incorporated.

---

A SUPPLEMENT TO THE ACT ENTITLED "AN ACT REGU-LATING LATERAL RAILROADS."

*Approved 28th March, 1840. (P. L., 1839-40, pages 196 and 197.)*

SECTION I. That the several provisions of the act entitled "An act regulating lateral railroads," passed May 5th, Anno Domini one thousand eight hundred and thirty-two, shall ex-tend to the counties of Northampton, Lehigh, and Cambria; also, to the owner or owners of land, mills, quarries, coal or other mines, lime-kilns or other real estate in the vicinity of any railroad, canal, or slackwater navigation made or to be made hereafter by any company, individuals, or by the State of Pennsylvania: *Provided,* That if the parties interested cannot agree upon the mode, manner, or point of connection with such railroad, canal, or slackwater navigation, the same shall be determined by the jury to be appointed by virtue of the pro-visions of the first section of the act to which this is a supple-ment.

SEC. 2. That from and after the passage of this act it shall and may be lawful for any person or persons, company or companies, now or hereafter to be incorporated in this Common-wealth, to construct railroads with one or more tracks, under the surface, over any intermediate lands, not exceeding six miles in length, to or from any coal or iron or other mines, quarries, lime-kilns, or other real estate, and connect the same with any railroad or railroads belonging to any individual or individuals, company or companies, now or hereafter to be incorporated in this State, and also with any highway or public improvement: *Provided,* That the parties interested shall in* cases be subject to the same proceedings required under

---

\* " Such" evidently being omitted from original act.

the act of May 5th, Anno Domini one thousand eight hundred and thirty-two, an act regulating lateral railroads: *Provided further*, That if the parties interested cannot agree upon the mode, manner, or point of connection with such railroad or railroads, the same shall be determined by the jury to be appointed by virtue of the provisions of the first section of the act last aforesaid: *Provided*, That so much of the act to which this is a supplement as prohibits a writ of error or appeal shall be and the same is hereby repealed.

(Repealed as to Cambria county, 21st April, 1846.)

---

## AN ACT TO REPEAL PART OF AN ACT SUPPLEMENTARY TO THE ACT ENTITLED "AN ACT LIMITING THE TIME DURING WHICH JUDGMENTS SHALL BE A LIEN ON REAL ESTATE, AND SUITS MAY BE BROUGHT AGAINST THE SURETIES OF PUBLIC OFFICERS," AND TO RENDER CERTAIN APPEALS FROM AWARDS OF ARBITRATORS VALID, AND FOR OTHER PURPOSES.

*Approved 11th February, 1841.* (*P. L., 1841, page 24.*)

SECTION 3. That so much of the act entitled "An act relative to suits brought by and against canal and railroad companies," approved the fourteenth day of April, 1834, as is applicable to actions brought on contracts, express or implied, be and the same is hereby repealed; and all such actions as have been removed in pursuance of such act and still pending be returned for trial to the court in which they were respectively commenced.

---

## A FURTHER SUPPLEMENT TO THE ACT ENTITLED "AN ACT REGULATING LATERAL RAILROADS."

*Approved 12th February, 1842.* (*P. L., 1842, page 18.*)

SECTION 1. That the several provisions of the act entitled "An act regulating lateral railroads," passed May 5th, Anno Domini one thousand eight hundred and thirty-two, and of the several supplements thereunto, shall extend to the counties of Tioga and Columbia.

AN ACT AUTHORIZING JOHN PRALL TO SELL AND CON-
VEY CERTAIN REAL ESTATE IN BUCKS COUNTY.

*Approved 21st March, 1842.  (P. L., 1842, pages 145 and 146.)*

SECTION 8. That hereafter, when any action is commenced
by any person or persons, or bodies corporate, against an incorporated railroad or canal company, in any county in which
the corporate property of such company is wholly or in part
situated, it shall be lawful, if the president, treasurer, secretary,
or chief clerk of such corporation does not reside or cannot be
found in such county, for the sheriff or other officer to whom
such process is directed, to serve the same on any manager or
director of such company, being in such county, and the service so made shall be deemed sufficient, and in case no director
or manager can be found in the county, it shall be lawful for
such officer to go into an adjoining county to serve the process
as hereinbefore stated.

AN ACT TO AUTHORIZE THE COURT OF COMMON PLEAS
OF LUZERNE COUNTY TO APPOINT AUDITORS IN CER-
TAIN CASES, AND FOR OTHER PURPOSES.

*Approved 16th July, 1842.  (P. L., 1842, page 395.)*

SECTION 13. That in all cases for the assessment of damages
caused by the construction of canals or railroads by incorporated companies in this Commonwealth, if the viewers or a
jury shall find for the plaintiff any sum of damages, such
award or verdict, on the rendition of judgment, shall carry
costs, unless there may be some provision in the act incorporating such company to the contrary.

AN ACT TO INCORPORATE THE LIBERTY FIRE COMPANY,
OF HOLMESBURG, IN THE COUNTY OF PHILADELPHIA.

*Approved 26th July, 1842.  (P. L., 1842, page 434.)*

SECTION 11. That whenever any railroad or canal company
has borrowed money, and given to the lender thereof a bond

or other evidence of indebtedness in a larger sum than the amount actually received, such transactions shall not be deemed usurious, or in violation of any law of this Commonwealth prohibiting the taking of more than six per cent. interest.

---

## AN ACT ANNEXING THE COUNTY OF SCHUYLKILL TO THE EASTERN DISTRICT OF THE SUPREME COURT, AND FOR OTHER PURPOSES.

*Approved 2d August, 1842.* (*P. L., 1842, page 459.*)

SECTION 3. That the Select and Common Councils of the City of Philadelphia be and they are hereby authorized and empowered to pass ordinances to require the owners or agents of cars traveling on the railroads in Broad, High, Third, and Dock streets, in the city of Philadelphia, to deliver a certificate of the contents of each car and the number of passengers conveyed therein and of the distance they have been conveyed on said railroads, and to require the owners or agents of such cars to pay toll for the same : *Provided*, That the toll charged shall be the same toll as may be charged on the Pennsylvania Railroad (and that all distances under half a mile shall be charged as half a mile, and all distances over half a mile and under one mile shall be charged as one mile).

SEC. 4. That it shall be lawful for the mayor, aldermen, and citizens of Philadelphia, to provide for the punishment of any person or persons who shall refuse or omit to comply with the provisions of the ordinances which may be enacted by virtue of this act, by imposing a fine, to be recovered in the same manner as penalties for the violation of the ordinances of the city of Philadelphia are now by law recoverable.

(Mileage changed 13th May, 1856, to actual distance.)

---

## RESOLUTION TO PROTECT LABORERS AND CONTRACTORS.

*Approved 21st January, 1843.* (*P. L., 1843, page 367.*)

*Resolved*, That from and after the passage of this resolution, it shall not be lawful for any company incorporated by the laws of this Commonwealth, and empowered to construct, make, and manage any railroad, canal, or other public internal improvement, while the debts and liabilities, or any part thereof incurred by the said company to contractors, laborers, and workmen employed in the construction or repairs of said improvement remain unpaid, to execute a general or partial assignment, conveyance, mortgage, or other transfer, of the real or personal estate of the said company, so as to defeat, postpone, endanger, or delay their said creditors, without the written assent of the said creditors first had and obtained; and any such assignment, conveyance, mortgage, or transfer shall be deemed fraudulent, null, and void, as against any such contractors, laborers, and workmen, creditors as aforesaid.

---

### AN. ACT TO CONFER UPON THE ORPHANS' COURT OF LANCASTER COUNTY CERTAIN POWERS IN RELATION TO THE REAL ESTATE OF JOHN LINDEMUTH, DECEASED, AND FOR OTHER PURPOSES.

*Approved 4th April, 1843. (P. L., 1843, page 132.)*

SECTION 3. That the several courts of quarter sessions of this Commonwealth are hereby empowered, on petition of the parties in interest, to change the corporate name, style, and title of any corporation within their respective counties. (Repealed 20th April, 1869, and common pleas authorized.)

---

### AN ACT TO INCORPORATE THE BUTLER COUNTY MUTUAL INSURANCE COMPANY, AND FOR OTHER PURPOSES.

*Approved 24th April, 1843. (P. L., 1843, pages 361 and 362.)*

SECTION 10. That when the owners of any railroad, constituted under an act of this Commonwealth, possess the landing at the termination of the said railroad, where it joins any canal or other navigation, and any lateral railroad shall be constructed to connect with said railroad for the purpose of conveying any mineral or other productions to the said navigation, and the owners of the said landing shall refuse to permit the trade of the said lateral railroads to make use of the said landing, upon the payment of a suitable compensation, it shall be the duty of the court of common pleas of the proper county, upon application of the party aggrieved, to direct the sheriff to summon a jury of five disinterested men from the proper county, who, being duly sworn or affirmed, shall examine the premises, and if they shall find that the landings are of sufficient capacity to accommodate the trade of the lateral railroad, in addition to the trade of the main railroad, they shall mark off a portion of the land to be allotted thereto, and fix upon a compensation suitable therefor, either in fee simple or as an annual rent, or a price per ton for the use of the same, and shall make return thereof to the court, who shall thereupon, if the report be approved by them, direct the said landing to be opened to the use of the public, upon the payment of the price assessed by the said jury,—an appeal to the superior [court] being allowed as in other cases; and the jury shall be allowed the same compensation as jury upon county roads, to be paid by the party applying for the landing.

---

AN ACT FURTHER TO REGULATE PROCEEDINGS IN COURTS OF JUSTICE, AND FOR OTHER PURPOSES.

*Approved 6th May, 1844. (P. L., 1844, page 565.)*

SECTION 5. That in all cases where acts creating railroad or canal companies, security to the owners of lands through which any canals and railroads may pass is required to be given, and approved by any of the courts in the counties where such lands lie,—said security may be given and approved of by any two of the judges of said courts during vacation : *Provided,* That at least five days' notice shall first be given to the owners of such lands, or their known agent or attorney, of the time and place of offering such security, and the names of the sureties to be offered.

## AN ACT FIXING THE CONSTRUCTION OF CERTAIN ACTS OF ASSEMBLY IN RELATION TO THE RIGHTS OF PRIVATE PROPERTY.

*Approved 10th March, 1845.* (*P. L., 1845, page 126.*)

SECTION 1. That the fourth section of the seventh article of the Constitution of Pennsylvania, which directs that the legislature shall not invest any corporate body or individual with the privilege of taking private property for public use, without requiring such corporation or individual to make compensation to the owners of said property, or give adequate security therefor before such property shall be taken, shall be deemed to apply to all acts of assembly passed, or that may be passed during the present session of the legislature, as fully and effectually as if the same were incorporated in said act.

## AN ACT CONCERNING BAIL AND ATTACHMENTS.

*Approved 20th March, 1845.* (*P. L., 1845, page 188.*)

SECTION 1. That in lieu of the bail heretofore required by law, in the cases herein mentioned, the bail in cases of appeal from the judgments of aldermen and justices of the peace, and from the awards of arbitrators, shall be bail absolute, in double the probable amount of costs accrued and likely to accrue in such cases, with one or more sufficient sureties, conditioned for the payment of all costs accrued or that may be legally recovered in such cases against the appellants.

## AN ACT CONCERNING BAIL AND ATTACHMENTS.

*Approved 20th March, 1845.* (*P. L., 1845, page 189.*)

SECTION 4. That so much of the act of assembly passed sixteenth day of June, 1836, entitled "An act relating to executions," as provides for the levy and recovery of stock, deposits, and debts due to defendants by process of attachment and *scire facias*, is hereby extended to all cases of attachments to be issued upon judgments against corporations (other than municipal corporations), and from and after the passage of this act all such process which hereafter may be issued may be proceeded in to final judgment and execution, in the same manner and under the same rules and regulations as are directed against corporations by the provisions of the act of 16th June, 1836, relating to executions; and that so much of the thirty-sixth section of the act of 16th June, 1836, as requires service of the attachment on any defendant, be and the same is hereby repealed, except where the defendant is a resident of the county in which the attachment issued.

---

## AN ACT RELATIVE TO THE OBSTRUCTING OF THE CROSSINGS OF PUBLIC ROADS BY LOCOMOTIVES AND CARS.

*Approved 20th March, 1845.* (*P. L., 1845, pages 191 and 192.*)

SECTION 1. That it shall not be lawful for any railroad company to block up the passage of any crossings of public streets or roads, or obstruct the said crossings with their locomotives or cars; and if any engineer or other agent of any such railroad company shall obstruct or block up such crossings, he or they shall be subject to a penalty of twenty-five dollars, to be recovered with costs, in the name of the Commonwealth of Pennsylvania, before a justice of the peace; one-half of such penalty shall be paid to the informer or informers, and the remaining half shall be paid into the treasury of the Commonwealth: *Provided*, That in the event of the said engineer or agent being unable to pay the said penalty, then and in that case the said railroad company employing the said engineer or agent shall pay the penalty aforesaid.

---

## AN ACT TO RELIEVE CANAL AND RAILROAD COMPANIES FROM PENALTIES FOR NOT PERFORMING CERTAIN ACTS ON THE SABBATH DAY.

*Approved 11th April, 1845.* (*P. L., 1845, page 364.*)

SECTION 1. That no part of any act of assembly heretofore passed shall be construed to require any canal or railroad company to attend their works on the Sabbath days, for the purpose of expediting or aiding the passage of any boat, craft, or vehicle along the same; any clause or clauses in their respective charters, imposing a penalty for not aiding boats, crafts, or vehicles to pass within a certain time, to the contrary notwithstanding.

## AN ACT TO INCREASE THE REVENUES AND DIMINISH THE LEGISLATIVE EXPENSES OF THE COMMONWEALTH.

*Approved 16th April, 1845.*   (*P. L., 1845, page 535.*)

SECTION 12. That hereafter it shall be lawful to commence and prosecute to final judgment and execution, in the Court of Common Pleas of Dauphin county, suits against any and all persons who are or may hereafter be officers of any description whatsoever within this Commonwealth, appointed by the governor or by the board of canal commissioners or elected by either house of the legislature or by both houses in joint ballot, and who shall become defaulters in not paying over or accounting for money in their hands due and belonging to the Commonwealth, and against their sureties, in the same manner and with like effect as if the said defaulting persons and officers and their sureties were residents of the said county of Dauphin; and for this purpose, all necessary writs of summons, writs of *fieri facias*, writs of *fieri facias* with clause of attachment, to attach debts owing and stocks, as practiced in other cases, and writs of *venditioni exponas*, and *alias* and *pluries* writs of the same kind, may issue from the said court into any county, and at the same time, if deemed necessary, into the several counties of this Commonwealth, there to be transmitted by mail to the sheriff or coroner, as the case may require, whose duty it shall be to execute the same, and make return thereof in the same manner as is now practiced in relation to *testatum* writs.

## AN ACT FIXING THE CONSTRUCTION OF CERTAIN ACTS OF ASSEMBLY IN RELATION TO THE RIGHTS OF PRIVATE PROPERTY.

*Approved 20th April, 1846.* (*P. L., 1846, page 407.*)

SECTION 1. That the fourth section of the seventh article of the Constitution of Pennsylvania, which directs that the legislature shall not invest any corporate body or individual with the privilege of taking private property for public uses, without requiring such corporation or individual to make compensation to the owners of said property, or give adequate security therefor, before such property shall be taken, shall be deemed to apply to all acts of assembly passed, or that may be passed, during the present session of the legislature, as fully and effectually as if the same were incorporated in said act.

---

## A SUPPLEMENT TO THE LAW RELATING TO DEFAULTING PUBLIC OFFICERS.

*Approved 21st April, 1846.* (*P. L., 1846, page 414.*)

SECTION 4. That in all suits hereafter brought in any court, under the provisions of this act, or the act to which this is supplementary, the attorney officiating for the Commonwealth shall file a declaration along with the *præcipe*, and judgments shall be entered therein, and the sums be liquidated by the respective prothonotaries, as aforesaid, immediately after thirty days from the return of the writ in each case, unless before that time the defendants shall have filed an affidavit of defense and shall have put the cause to issue, as is directed in the second section of this act in suits heretofore brought; and all causes so put to issue shall be put down for trial at the next succeeding court of common pleas in each county, and shall, until the same are tried or ended, be placed on the trial list, and have the preference over all other causes.

## A SUPPLEMENT TO THE ACT ENTITLED "AN ACT RELATING TO ROADS, HIGHWAYS, AND BRIDGES."

*Approved 21st April, 1846.* (*P. L., 1846, page 417.*)

SECTION 3. That the act of the 5th of May, 1832, entitled "An act regulating lateral railroads," and the supplement thereto of March 28th, 1840, be and the same is hereby repealed, so far as they relate to the county of Cambria.

---

## AN ACT RELATING TO ARBITRATIONS.

*Approved 24th February, 1847.* (*P. L., 1847, page 153.*)

WHEREAS, Great inconvenience and embarrassment are often experienced in the trial of suits between contractors and laborers and workmen employed in the construction or repairs of railroads and canals, by companies incorporated by the laws of this Commonwealth and empowered to construct such railroads and canals, and such incorporated companies, by reason of the want of power in arbitrators in actions depending before them, to compel the production of books and papers which contain evidence pertinent to the issue; therefore,

SECTION I. That from and after the passing of this act, arbitrators shall have power in any action depending before them, between any contractors, laborers, or workmen, and any company incorporated by the laws of this Commonwealth, and empowered to construct, make, and manage any railroad, canal, or other public internal improvement, to require either party to produce any books or writing, in their possession or power, which contain evidence pertinent to the issue; and if such party shall fail to produce such books or writings, or to satisfy said arbitrators why the same is not in their power so to do, it shall be lawful for the said arbitrators to find an award against such party, if plaintiff, of no cause of action; if defendant, for such sum as the plaintiff, his agent or attorney, shall make oath or affirmation is justly due, according to the best of his knowledge and belief: *Provided,* That before such requirement shall be made by such arbitrators, it shall be proved to their satisfaction, on oath or affirmation, that clear and distinct notice in writing shall have been given to produce such books or writings at least ten days previous thereto.

---

## AN ACT REQUIRING BANKS AND OTHER CORPORATIONS TO GIVE NOTICE OF UNCLAIMED DIVIDENDS, DEPOSITS, AND BALANCES IN CERTAIN CASES.

*Approved 6th March, 1847.* (*P. L., 1847, pages 222 and 223.*)

SECTION 1. That each of the banks, savings institutions, loan companies, and insurance companies, and each and every other of the companies, institutions, or associations incorporated by or under any law of this Commonwealth, and legally authorized to declare and make dividends of profits amongst the stockholders thereof, shall, in the month of December of the present year, and annually thereafter, cause to be published, for four successive weeks, in one or more public newspapers having the largest circulation, printed in the city or county in which such bank, savings institution, loan company, insurance company, or other company, institution, or association may be located, or in which its principal office or place of business may be situated, a true and accurate statement, verified by the oath or affirmation of the cashier or treasurer thereof, of all dividends or profits declared on its capital stock, which, at the date of such settlement, shall have remained unclaimed by the person, copartnership, or corporation authorized to receive the same for the period of three years then next preceding; which said statement shall set forth the names, and if known, the residence and business of the persons, copartnerships, or corporations in whose favor said dividends or profits may have been declared, the amount of such dividends or profits and the number of shares in the capital stock upon which the same had accrued.

SEC. 2. That each of the said banks, savings institutions, and loan companies, and each and every saving fund society, insurance, or trust company, or other company, institution, or association, incorporated as aforesaid and legally authorized to receive deposits of money, shall, in the said month of December of the present year, and annually thereafter, cause to be published in like manner and for the same period, a statement, verified as aforesaid, of the names, and, if known, the residence and business of all persons, copartnerships, or corporations who have made deposits therein, or have balances due them, and who have not, within the three years then next preceding the date of said statement, either increased or diminished the amount of such deposits or balances, or received any interest thereon, with the dates when such deposits were made or balances accrued, the amount thereof, and the amount of interest, if any, accruing thereon.

Sec. 3. If any such bank, savings institution, loan company, insurance company, or other banking institution or association, incorporated as aforesaid, shall neglect or refuse to publish the statement hereinbefore required to be published, the same, and the cashier or treasurer thereof, in his individual capacity, shall be liable to the party in whose name such unclaimed dividend, profit, deposit, or balance may stand, or to his, her, or their legal representatives for the amount thereof, with interest thereon, at the rate of twelve per cent. per annum from the date of such dividend, profit, deposit, or balance until paid, recoverable by action of debt, as in other cases: *Provided*, That nothing herein contained shall be so construed as to require the publication of any such unclaimed dividends or profits amounting to less than five dollars, nor such unclaimed deposits or balances amounting to less than ten dollars.

Sec. 4. That at the expiration of three years after the first publication of any particular dividend or profits, balance or deposit, with the interest that has accrued thereon, as provided for by the first and second sections of this act, such dividend or profit, balance or deposit, with the interest that has accrued, if not demanded within that time by the rightful owner or owners thereof, or their legal representatives, shall escheat to the Commonwealth, and shall be paid into the treasury thereof, without discount or deduction for commissions, fees, or expenses of any description, by the cashier, treasurer, or other proper officer of said bank, savings institution, loan company insurance company, saving fund society, or other company, institution, or association in which such dividend or profit, balance or deposit, shall have remained without being demanded, as aforesaid, or without being increased or diminished for the length of time aforesaid; and the said bank, savings institution, loan company, insurance company, saving fund society, or other company, institution, or association, as the case may be, shall thereupon be discharged from any obligation or liability to pay over such dividend or profit, balance or deposit, or interest thereon, to the owner or owners thereof; that the said owner or owners, or their legal representatives, upon application to the State treasurer for the time being, and producing satisfactory proof to that officer of his, her, or their right to such dividend or profit, balance or deposit, with the interest thereon, paid into the treasury, as aforesaid, or any part thereof, shall receive from the Commonwealth the amount he, she, or they shall be found legally or equitably entitled to: *Provided*, That the expense of the publication or publications required by this act shall be paid out of such dividend or profit, balance or deposit, so published.

---

### AN ACT RELATING TO CERTAIN CORPORATIONS.

*Approved 13th March, 1847. (P. L., 1847, pages 333 and 334.)*

WHEREAS, Certain corporations deriving their charter from the Commonwealth of Pennsylvania, in cases where a majority of the board of managers are resident out of the State, or the chief officer for the transaction of the business of such corporation is located out of the State, have it in their power to evade, and in some cases have evaded, the laws of this Commonwealth, subjecting the stock and property of such corporations to taxation; and to escape and evade their amenability to the laws of this Commonwealth, for misuser or neglect of their corporate duties and liabilities, and other violations of the provisions of their charters; therefore,

SECTION I. That it shall be the duty of any and every railroad or canal company, incorporated by this Commonwealth, whose works and property are principally located within this State, in all elections for president, managers, directors, or other officers of said companies, having the control and direction of the works or affairs of such company, held at any time after the passage of this act, to hold their elections at some place, to be determined upon by the board of managers, in this State, and to elect a majority of citizens, resident within this State, as managers or directors of their said companies respectively, of which majority the president shall in all cases be one; and it shall be the duty of the respective boards of such corporations so elected to establish their principal office for the transaction of their corporate business in some convenient place within this State, and not elsewhere, within one month after their election as aforesaid; and any election not made in conformity to the directions of this act shall be void.

SEC. 2. That upon the failure of any company, incorporated and situated as aforesaid, to elect officers in accordance with the provisions of this act, and to establish their office as herein directed, it shall be the duty of the governor to nominate to the canal commissioners seven persons, stockholders of such company, resident within this State, fitted to conduct the affairs of the said company failing as aforesaid; and if the said commissioners shall approve of the persons so named, they shall confirm their appointment as directors of such company; and if any of the persons so nominated shall not be approved by the said commissioners, others shall be nominated in such case by the governor aforesaid, till the required number shall be approved; and the like course shall be pursued if any stockholder so appointed shall refuse to serve; in such case a proper person, not a stockholder, may be nominated and appointed as aforesaid in his place; and when the number is complete as aforesaid, the directors so appointed shall elect one of their number president of the board, and shall also elect a treasurer of the said company; and it shall be the duty of the directors aforesaid to take charge of the works and property, books, papers, and documents of the said company, and conduct the business thereof, under the provisions, regulations,

and directions of the charter thereof, and with the same
liabilities, duties, and responsibilities as a board regularly
elected under the provisions of the charter would be liable to
do, and with like powers and authorities; and the said directors
shall continue to hold possession of the works of said company, and to execute their duties as aforesaid, until a board
shall be regularly elected by the company, in accordance with
the provisions of this act; and upon such election, the said
directors appointed as aforesaid, in charge of the works as
aforesaid, shall deliver up to the said board elected as aforesaid,
within one month after they shall, by resolution, have determined to comply with the requirements of this act, a copy of
which resolution shall be delivered to the directors aforesaid,
all and singular the works, property, books, papers, and
documents of the said company, or having any connection
therewith, and all funds not necessarily expended in the discharge of the expenses incident to the conducting of the affairs
of the said company, and in payment of its liabilities: *Provided*,
That the person who shall act as treasurer of such company
shall give bond with security, to be approved by the court of
common pleas of the county in which the works of the company shall be principally situated, in such sum as the said
court shall direct; and shall keep books, in which the whole
receipts and disbursements of the company shall be fully set
forth and exhibited.

---

### AN ACT IN REFERENCE TO RUNNING OF LOCOMOTIVE-ENGINES AND CARS ON CONNECTING RAILROADS.

*Approved 13th March, 1847.* (*P. L., 1847, page 337.*)

SECTION I. That in all cases where two railroads in this
Commonwealth are or shall be connected, it shall be lawful for
the company owning either of the said railroads (with the consent of the company owning the other of the said railroads) to
run its cars and locomotive-engines upon the said other railroad,
and to erect water-stations and other buildings for the due accommodation of the cars and engines employed thereon:

*Provided*, That nothing herein contained shall be construed or interpreted to release or exonerate any company owning a railroad from the obligation and duty which may be now imposed by existing laws, of transporting, subject to the rules and regulations of said companies, by locomotive steam-engines, the cars, whether loaded or empty, of all persons and companies who may require such transportation over and along so much and such parts of their railroad as locomotive ' steam-engines shall be run upon, whether they be run by the company owning the road or by any other company.

---

## AN ACT TO REQUIRE CORPORATIONS TO GIVE BAIL IN CERTAIN CASES, AND RELATIVE TO THE COMMENCEMENT OF SUITS AGAINST FOREIGN CORPORATIONS, TO THE ACCOUNTS OF JOHN SLOAN, LATE TREASURER OF LYCOMING COUNTY, AND PITTSBURG AND CONNELLSVILLE RAILROAD COMPANY.

*Approved 15th March, 1847.* (*P. L., 1847, pages 361 and 362.*)

WHEREAS, Doubts have arisen in regard to the effect of the first section of the act entitled "An act concerning bail and attachments, passed 20th March, 1845, and as to the bail required to be given by corporations in cases of appeal and writs of error since the passage of the said act; therefore,

SECTION 1. That from and after the passage of this act, when any corporation (municipal corporations excepted), being sued, shall appeal or take a writ of error, the bail requisite in that case shall be taken absolute, for the payment of debt, interest, and costs on the affirmance of the judgment.

SEC. 2. That in all cases where any company has been incorporated by this Commonwealth, and the principal office for the transaction of business thereof shall be located out of this State, or where the president, treasurer, cashier, or other principal officer of such company shall reside out of this State, it shall be lawful to sue such company in any county of this State where the works of such company shall be located, or adjoining thereto, or where any director, manager, or other officer of such company shall reside ; and service of legal process upon such director, manager, or other officer shall be valid and effective upon said company, and such company shall be taken, both in law and in equity, for every purpose of legal proceeding, to be located in this State; and shall also be liable to the writs of *quo warranto*, mandamus, attachment, and execution; and service of such writ upon any manager, director, or other officer of such company shall be, to all intents and purposes, as effective as if served upon the president of such company, and he resident of this State, and as if the locality of such company's office were within this State; and any property of any description of such company, which would be liable to attachment or execution, if the same were located in this State, shall be taken to be in this State for such purpose; and shall be liable to levy and sale, in the same manner as if the officers of said company were located in the county of this State in which the same is made liable to be sued by the provisions of this act.

---

A SUPPLEMENT TO THE ACT OF 5th MAY, 1832, ENTITLED " AN ACT REGULATING LATERAL RAILROADS."

*Approved 6th January, 1848. (P. L., 1848, pages 1 and 2.)*

SECTION 1. That the provisions of the act of the 5th of May, 1832, entitled "An act regulating lateral railroads," and the supplement thereto, passed twenty-eighth day of March, 1840, be and the same is hereby extended to the counties of Dauphin, Allegheny, Bedford, Blair, and Washington, and shall be so construed as to authorize the construction of lateral railroads, either under or over the surface of any intervening lands, subject to the restrictions of the act to which this is a supplement.

SEC. 2. The rights and privileges conferred by the act to which this is a supplement are hereby extended to the owner and owners of coal and iron mines, situated in the township of Denison, Luzerne county, more than six miles from the Lehigh navigation, and not more than ten miles from the same.

SEC. 3. The rights and privileges as to the acquisition of landings and wharves conferred by the tenth section of the act entitled "An act to incorporate the Butler County Mutual Insurance Company, and for other purposes," passed the twenty-fourth day of April, Anno Domini one thousand eight hundred and forty-three, upon certain persons therein mentioned or described, shall be extended to all persons proceeding to procure the right to make a lateral railroad under the authority of the act to which this is a supplement, so that they shall be enabled to procure landings or wharves for a compensation, of the owner or owners of land, whether said owner or owners of land have any interest in any railroad or not; and the powers and duties conferred upon the jury authorized by the said tenth section are hereby conferred upon the viewers which may be appointed under the authority of said act, to which this is a supplement: *Provided*, That no landing, wharf privilege, or franchise shall be taken from the owner thereof, if in the opinion of the viewers aforesaid such landing, wharf privilege, or franchise is necessary to the use and enjoyment of the owner of any mill, quarry, lime-kiln, coal-mine, or other real estate adjoining any navigable stream or slackwater navigation.

---

**AN ACT FOR THE RELIEF OF WILLIAM BURNS AND OTHER SOLDIERS AND WIDOWS OF SOLDIERS OF THE REVOLUTIONARY AND INDIAN WARS, AND IN REFERENCE TO ACTS OF INCORPORATION AND SUPPLEMENTS THERETO, PASSED AT THE PRESENT SESSION OF THE LEGISLATURE.**

*Approved 11th April, 1848. (P. L., 1848, page 509.)*

SECTION 7. That nothing contained in any act passed during the present session incorporating any company or extending the powers of any incorporated company, shall be construed to authorize any such company to take private property without making compensation therefor, or securing it agreeably to the provisions of the Constitution; and the said act shall be taken and construed as if the constitutional provision was expressly inserted therein.

38

## AN ACT TO AUTHORIZE MARGARET PARTHEMORE * * AND RELATIVE TO LATERAL RAILROADS, &c.

*Approved 11th April, 1848. (P. L., 1848, page 516.)*

SECTION 4. That so much of the twelfth section of the act regulating lateral railroads, passed the fifth day of May, 1832, as limits the provisions of said act to the counties of Lycoming, Luzerne, Schuylkill, and Northumberland, be and the same is hereby repealed; and the provisions of the act aforesaid, and the several supplements thereto, be and the same are hereby extended throughout the Commonwealth, as well to all lands lying in the vicinity of any navigable river as to lands lying in the vicinity of any railroad, canal, or slackwater navigation.

---

## AN ACT REGULATING RAILROAD COMPANIES.

*Approved 19th February, 1849. (P. L., 1849, page 79.)*

SECTION 1. That whenever a special act of the general assembly shall hereafter be passed, authorizing the incorporation of a company for the construction of a railroad within this Commonwealth, the commissioners named in such act, or any five of them, shall have power to open books for receiving subscriptions to the capital stock of such company, at such time or times, and at such place or places, as they may deem expedient, after having given at least twenty days' notice in one or more newspapers published in the county where books of subscription are to be opened; and at the times and places so designated and named in the public notices to be given, as aforesaid, the said commissioners, or any two of them, shall attend and furnish to all persons duly qualified, who shall offer to subscribe, an opportunity of so doing; and it shall be lawful for all such persons, and for all firms and copartnerships, by themselves or by persons duly authorized, to subscribe for shares in said stock; and the said books shall be kept open at least six hours in every day, for the term of three juridical days, or until there shall have been subscribed the whole number of shares authorized by the special act; and if, at the expiration of three days, the books aforesaid shall not have the number of shares therein subscribed, the said commissioners may adjourn from time to time, and to such places as they may deem proper, until the whole number of shares authorized, as aforesaid, shall be subscribed; of which adjournment, the commissioners aforesaid shall give such public notice as the occasion may require; and when the whole number of shares shall be subscribed the books shall be closed: *Provided always*, That no subscription for such stock shall be valid unless the party or parties making the same shall, at the time of subscribing, pay to the said commissioners five dollars on each and every share subscribed, for the use of the company.

SEC. 2. That when ten per centum on the capital stock, as provided by any special act of incorporation, shall have been subscribed, and five dollars paid on each and every share, as aforesaid, the said commissioners, or such of them as shall have acted, shall certify to the governor, under their hands and seals, the names of the subscribers and the number of shares subscribed by each, and that five dollars on each share have been paid, whereupon the governor shall, by letters patent, under his hand and the seal of the Commonwealth, create and constitute the subscribers, and if the subscription be not full at the time, those who shall thereafter subscribe to the number of shares aforesaid, their successors and assigns, into a body politic and corporate, in deed and in law, by the name, style, and title designated by the special act of assembly; and by the said name, style, and title the said subscribers shall have perpetual succession, with all the privileges, franchises, and immunities incident to a corporation, and be able to sue and be sued, plead and be impleaded, in all courts of record and elsewhere, and to purchase, receive, have, hold, use, and enjoy to them and their successors, goods, chattels, and estate, real and personal, of what kind and nature soever, and the same from time to time to sell, exchange, mortgage, grant, alien, or otherwise dispose of, and to make dividends of such portion of the profits as they may deem proper; and also to make and have a common seal, and the same to alter and renew at pleasure, and also to ordain, establish, and put in execution such by-laws, ordinances, and regulations as shall appear necessary or convenient for the government of said corporation, not being contrary to the Constitution and laws of the United States or of this Commonwealth, and generally to do all and singular the matters and things which to them it shall lawfully appertain to do for the well-being of said corporation and the due ordering and management of the affairs thereof: *Provided*, That nothing herein contained shall be construed as in any way giving to such corporation any banking privileges whatever, or any other liberties, privileges, or franchises but such as may be necessary or convenient to the procuring, owning, making, maintaining, regulating, and using the railroad, the locomotives, machinery, cars, and other appendages thereof, and the conveyance of passengers, the transportation of goods, merchandise, and other commodities thereon: *And provided further*, That such company shall not purchase or hold any real estate, except such as may be necessary or convenient for the making and constructing of their railroad, or for the furnishing of materials therefor, and for the accommodation of depots, offices, warehouses, machine-shops, toll-houses, engine and water stations, and other appropriate appurtenances, and for the persons and things employed or used in and about the same.

SEC. 3. That the commissioners named as aforesaid, or such of them as shall have acted, shall, as soon as conveniently may be after the said letters patent shall be obtained, appoint a time and place for the subscribers to meet to organize the company, and shall give at least two weeks' notice thereof in the manner provided for in the first section of this act; and the said subscribers, when met, shall elect, by a majority of the votes present, to be given in person or by proxy, a president and twelve directors, the president and a majority of whom shall be resident citizens of this Commonwealth, and shall be owners, respectively, of at least three shares in the stock of such company; and the said president and directors shall conduct and manage the affairs and business of said company until the second Monday in January then next ensuing, and until others are chosen; and may make, ordain, and establish such by-laws, rules, orders, and regulations, and perform such other matters and things as are by this act authorized: *Provided*, That in case of the resignation, death, or removal of the president, the directors shall, by a majority of votes, supply the vacancy until the next annual election.

SEC. 4. That the stockholders of such company shall meet on the second Monday in January in every year, at such place as may be fixed on by the by-laws, of which notice shall be given at least two weeks previously by the secretary, in the manner before mentioned, and choose, by a majority of the votes present, a president and twelve directors, qualified as aforesaid, for the ensuing year, who shall continue in office until the next annual election, and until others are chosen; at which annual meeting the said stockholders shall have full power and authority to make, alter, or repeal, by a majority of votes given, any or all such by-laws, rules, orders, and regulations as aforesaid, and do and perform every other corporate act authorized by their charter; the stockholders may meet at such other times and places as they be summoned by the president and directors, in such manner and form, and giving such notice as may be prescribed by the by-laws; and the president, on the request in writing of any number of stockholders representing not less than one-tenth in interest, shall call a special meeting, giving the like notice, and stating specifically the objects of the meeting; and the objects stated in such notice, and no other, shall be acted on at such special meeting.

SEC. 5. The elections for directors provided for in this act shall be conducted as follows, to wit :—At the first election the commissioners shall appoint three stockholders to be judges of the said election, and to hold the same; and at every succeeding election the directors for the time being shall appoint three stockholders for the like purpose; and the persons so appointed by said commissioners and directors shall not be eligible to an election as a director at said election, and shall respectively take and subscribe an oath or affirmation, before an alderman or justice of the peace, well and truly, and according to law, to conduct such election to the best of their knowledge and ability; and the said judges shall decide upon the qualifications of voters, and when the election is closed, shall count the votes and declare who have been elected; and if, at any time, it shall happen that an election of directors shall not be made at the time specified, the corporation shall not for that reason be dissolved; but it shall be lawful to hold and make such election of directors on any day within three months thereafter, by giving at least ten days' previous notice of the time and place of holding said election in the manner aforesaid, and the directors of the preceding year shall in that case continue in office, and be invested with all powers belonging to them as such until others are elected in their stead. In case of the death or resignation of a director, or a failure to elect in case of a tie vote, the vacancy may be filled by the board of directors. At all general meetings or elections by the stockholders, each share of stock shall entitle the holder thereof to one vote, and each ballot shall have endorsed thereon the number of shares thereby represented; but no share or shares transferred within sixty days next preceding any election or general meeting of the stockholders shall entitle the holder or holders thereof to vote at any such election or general meeting, nor shall any proxy be received or entitle the holder to vote, unless the same shall bear date and have been duly executed within the three months next preceding such election or general meeting.

SEC. 6. That the president and directors of such company for the time being are hereby authorized and empowered to exercise all the powers granted to the corporation; they shall meet at such times and places as shall be by them deemed most convenient for the transaction of their business, and when met, seven shall be a quorum to do business; the president, if present, shall preside at all meetings of the board, and when absent, the board shall appoint a president *pro tem.;* they shall keep minutes of their proceedings fairly entered in a suitable book to be kept for that purpose; they shall choose a secretary and treasurer, and may appoint or employ all such officers, engineers, agents, superintendents, artisans, workmen, or other persons, as in their opinion may be necessary or proper in the management of the affairs and business of said corporation at such times, in such manner, and under such regulations as they may from time to time determine; they shall fix the amount of the salaries and wages of such officers and persons employed by them, and they may require bond, with security in such amounts as they may deem necessary, of each or any of said officers or other persons by them appointed or employed, for the faithful discharge of their duties, and generally to do all such other acts, matters, and things as by this act and the by-laws and regulations of the said company they may be authorized to do.

SEC. 7. That the president and directors of such company first chosen shall procure certificates or evidences of stock for all the shares of such company, and shall deliver one or more certificates or evidences, signed by the president, countersigned by the treasurer, and sealed with the common seal of the corporation, to each person or party entitled to receive the same, according to the number of shares by him, her, or them respectively subscribed or held; which certificates or evidences of stock shall be transferable, at the pleasure of the holder, in a suitable book or books to be kept by the company for that purpose, in person or by attorney duly authorized, in the presence of the president or treasurer, subject, however, to all payments due or to become due thereon; and the assignee or party to whom the same shall have been so transferred shall thereupon be a member of said corporation, and have and enjoy all the immunities, privileges, and franchises, and be subject to all the liabilities, conditions, and penalties incident thereto, in the same manner as the original subscriber would have been : *Provided*, That no certificate shall be transferred so long as the holder thereof is indebted to said company, unless the board of directors shall consent thereto: *And provided*, That no such transfer of stock shall have the effect of discharging any liabilities or penalties theretofore incurred by the owner thereof.

SEC. 8. The capital stock of such company shall be divided into shares of fifty dollars each, and shall be called in and paid at such times and places, and in such proportions and installments, not, however, exceeding five dollars per share in any period of thirty days, as the directors shall require, of which public notice shall be given for at least two weeks next preceding the time or times appointed for that purpose, in the

manner above mentioned; and if any stockholder shall neglec
to pay such proportion or installment so called for at the tim
and place appointed, he, she, or they shall be liable to pay, i
addition to the proportion or installment so called for, at th
rate of one per cent. per month for the delay of such payment
and if the same and the additional penalty, or any part thereo
shall remain unpaid for the period of six months, he, she, o
they shall, at the discretion of the directors, forfeit to th
use of the company all right, title, and interest in and to ever
and all share or shares, on account of which such default i
payment may be made as aforesaid, or the directors may, a
their option, cause suit to be brought before any competen
tribunal, for the recovery of the amount due on such shares
together with the penalty of one per cent. per month as afore
said; and in the event of a forfeiture, the share or shares s
forfeited may be disposed of at the discretion of the presiden
and directors, under such rules and regulations as may b
prescribed by the by-laws.. No stockholder shall be entitle
to vote at any election, nor at any general or special meetin
of the company, on whose share or shares any installment o
arrearages may be due more than thirty days next precedin
said election or meeting: *Provided*, That no forfeiture of stocl
shall release or discharge the owner thereof from any liabilitie
or penalties incurred prior to the time of such forfeiture.

Sec. 9. That the dividends of so much of the profits of sucl
company as shall appear advisable to the directors shall b
declared in the months of July and January, in each and ever
year, and be paid to the stockholders or their legal represent
atives, on application at the office of such company, at an
time after the expiration of ten days from the time of declarin
the same; but the said dividends shall in no case exceed th
amount of the net profits actually acquired by the company
so that the capital stock shall never be impaired thereby; an
if the said directors shall make any dividend which shal
impair the capital stock of the company, the directors con
senting thereto shall be liable, in their individual capacities, t
such company for the amount of the capital stock so divided
recoverable by action of debt as in other cases; and eacl
director present when such dividend shall be declared shal

be considered as consenting thereto, unless he forthwith enter his protest on the minutes of the board, and give public notice to the stockholders of the declaring of such dividend.

SEC. 10. That the president and directors of such company shall have power and authority, by themselves, their engineers, superintendents, agents, artisans, and workmen, to survey, ascertain, locate, fix, mark, and determine such route for a railroad as they may deem expedient, not, however, passing through any burying-ground or place of public worship, or any dwelling-house in the occupancy of the owner or owners thereof, without his, her, or their consent, and not, except in the neighborhood of deep cuttings or high embankments or places selected for sidelings, turnouts, depots, engine or water stations, to exceed sixty feet in width, and thereon to lay down, erect, construct, and establish a railroad, with one or more tracks, with such branches or lateral roads as may be specially authorized, and with such bridges, viaducts, turnouts, sidelings, or other devices as they may deem necessary or useful between the points named in the special act incorporating such company, commencing at or within, and extending to or into any town, city, or village named as the place of beginning or terminus of such road; and in like manner, by themselves, or other person by them appointed or employed as aforesaid, to enter upon and into and occupy all land on which the said railroad or depots, warehouses, offices, toll-houses, engine and water stations, other buildings or appurtenances hereinbefore mentioned, may be located, or which may be necessary or convenient for the erection of the same, or for any purpose necessary or useful in the construction, maintenance, or repairs of said railroad, and therein and thereon to dig, excavate, and embank, make, grade, and lay down and construct the same; and it shall in like manner be lawful for such company, their officers, agents, engineers, contractors, or workmen, with their implements and beasts of draught or burden, to enter upon any lands adjoining or in the neighborhood of their railroad so to be constructed, and to quarry, dig, cut, take, and carry away therefrom any stone, gravel, clay, sand, earth, wood, or other suitable material necessary or proper for the construction of any bridges, viaducts, or other buildings which may be required for the use, maintenance, or repairs of said railroad: *Provided*, Tha before such company shall enter upon or take possession o any such lands or materials, they shall make ample compen sation to the owner or owners thereof, or tender adequate security therefor: *Provided further*, That the timber used ir the construction or repair of said railroad shall be obtainec from the owner thereof only by agreement or purchase: *And provided further*, That whenever any company shall locate it: road in and upon any street or alley, in any city or borough ample compensation shall be made to the owners of lot: fronting upon such street or alley for any damages they may sustain by reason of any excavation or embankment made ir the construction of such road, to be ascertained as othei damages are authorized to be ascertained by this act.

.SEC. 11. That when the said company cannot agree with the owner or owners of any lands or materials for the com- pensation proper for the damage done or likely to be done to or sustained by any such owner or owners of such lands oi materials which such company may enter upon, use, or take away, in pursuance of the authority hereinbefore given, or by reason of the absence or legal incapacity of any such ownei or owners, no such compensation can be agreed upon, the court of common pleas of the proper county, on application thereto by petition, either by said company or owner oi owners, or any one in behalf of either, shall appoint seven discreet and disinterested freeholders of said county, neithei of whom shall be residents or owners of property upon or adjoining the line of such railroad, and appoint a time, not less than twenty nor more than thirty days thereafter, for said viewers to meet at or upon the premises where the damages are alleged to be sustained, of which time and place ten days' notice shall be given by the petitioner to the said viewers and the other party; and the said viewers, or any five of them, having been first duly sworn or affirmed faithfully, justly, and impartially to decide, and true report to make, concerning all matters and things to be submitted to them, and in relation to which they are authorized to inquire in pursuance of the provisions of this act, and having viewed the premises, they shall estimate and determine the quantity, quality, and value of said lands so taken or occupied, or to be so taken or occupied, or the materials so used or taken away, as the case may be, and having due regard to and making just allowance for the advantages which may have resulted, or which may seem likely to result, to the owner or owners of said land or materials in consequence of the making or opening of said railroad and of the construction of works connected therewith; and after having made a fair and just comparison of said advantages and disadvantages, they shall estimate and determine whether any and, if any, what amount of damages has been or may be sustained, and to whom payable, and make report thereof to the said court; and if any damages be awarded, and the report be confirmed by the said court, judgment shall be entered thereon; and if the amount thereof be not paid within thirty days after the entry of such judgment, execution may then issue thereon, as in other cases of debt, for the sum so awarded, and the cost and expenses incurred shall be defrayed by the said railroad company; and each of said viewers shall be entitled to one-dollar and fifty cents per day for every day necessarily employed in the performance of the duties herein prescribed, to be paid by such railroad company.

SEC. 12. That whenever, in the construction of such road or roads, it shall be necessary to cross or intersect any established road or way, it shall be the duty of the president and directors of the said company so to construct the said road across such established road or way as not to impede the passage or transportation of persons or property along the same; and that for the accommodation of all persons owning or possessing land through which the said railroad may pass, it shall be the duty of such company to make or cause to be made a good and sufficient causeway or causeways, whenever the same may be necessary, to enable the occupant or occupants of said lands to cross or pass over the same with wagons, carts, and implements of husbandry, as occasion may require; and the said causeway or causeways, when so made, shall be maintained and kept in good repair by such company; and if the said company shall neglect or refuse, on request, to make such causeway or causeways, or when made, to keep the same in good order, the said company shall be liable to pay any person aggrieved thereby all damages sustained by such person in consequence of such neglect or refusal,—such damages to be assessed and ascertained in the same manner as provided in the last section for the assessment of damages: *Provided* That the said company shall in no case be required to make or cause to be made more than one causeway through each plantation or lot of land, for the accommodation of any one person owning or possessing land through which the said railroad may pass; and where any public road shall cross such railroad, the person owning or possessing land through which the said public road may pass shall not be entitled to require the company to erect or keep in repair any causeway or bridge for the accommodation of the occupant of said land.

SEC. 13. That if any such railroad company shall find it necessary to change the site of any portion of any turnpike or public road, they shall cause the same to be reconstructed forthwith at their own proper expense, on the most favorable location, and in as perfect a manner as the original road: *Provided*, That the damages incurred in changing the location of any road authorized by this section shall be ascertained and paid by such company in the same manner as is provided for in regard to the location and construction of their own road.

SEC. 14. That in all suits or actions against such company the service of process on the president, secretary, treasurer engineer, agent, or any director of the same, shall be good and available in law; but no suit or action shall be prosecuted by any person or persons, for any penalties incurred under this act, unless such suit or action shall be commenced within two years next after the offense committed or cause of action accrued; and the defendants in such suit or action may plead the general issue, and give this act and the special matter in evidence, and that the same was done in pursuance and by authority of this act.

SEC. 15. That if any person or persons shall willfully and knowingly break, injure, or destroy any railroad authorized by special act of assembly, or any part thereof, or any edifice device, property, or work, or any part thereof, or any machinery engine, car, implement, or utensil erected, owned, or used by such company in pursuance of this act, he, she, or they so offending shall forfeit and pay to such company three times the actual damage so sustained, to be sued for and recovered, with full costs, before any tribunal having cognizance thereof, by action in the name and for the use of the company.

SEC. 16. That if any person or persons shall willfully and maliciously remove or destroy any part of the road, property, buildings, or other works belonging to such company, or place, designedly and with evil intent, any obstruction on the line of such railroad so as to jeopard the safety of or endanger the lives of persons traveling on or over the same, such person or persons so offending shall be deemed guilty of a misdemeanor, and shall, on conviction, be imprisoned in the county jail or penitentiary, at the discretion of the court, for a term not more than three years: *Provided*, That nothing herein contained shall prevent the company from pursuing any other appropriate remedy at law in such cases.

SEC. 17. That at each annual meeting of the stockholders of any such company, the president and managers of the preceding year shall exhibit to them a full and complete statement of the affairs and proceedings of the company for such year, with all such matters as shall be necessary to convey to the stockholders a full knowledge of the condition and affairs of said company; and the said president and directors of every such company shall, whenever required, furnish to the legislature, or either branch thereof, a full and authentic report of their affairs and transactions, or such information relating thereto as may be demanded of them.

SEC. 18. That upon the completion of any railroad authorized as aforesaid, the same shall be esteemed a public highway for the conveyance of passengers and the transportation of freight, subject to such rules and regulations, in relation to the same, and to the size and construction of wheels, cars, and carriages, the weight of loads, and all other matters and things connected with the use of said railroad, as the president and directors may prescribe and direct: *Provided*, That the said company shall have the exclusive control of the motive-power, and may from time to time establish, demand, and receive such rates of toll or other compensation, for the use of such road and of said motive-power, and for the conveyance of passengers, the transportation of merchandise and commodities, and the cars or other vehicles containing the same, or otherwise passing over or on the said railroad, as to the president and directors shall seem reasonable: *Provided, however, nevertheless,* That said rates of toll and motive-power charges so to be established, demanded, or received, when the cars used for such conveyance or transportation are owned or furnished by others, shall not exceed two and one-half cents per mile for each passenger, three cents per mile for each ton of two thousand pounds of freight, three cents per mile for each passenger or baggage car, and two cents per mile for each burden or freight car, every four wheels being computed a car; and in the transportation of passengers no charge shall be made to exceed three cents per mile for through passengers and three and a half cents per mile for way passengers.

SEC. 19. That if any company incorporated as aforesaid shall not commence the construction of their proposed railroad within three years, and complete and open the same for use, with at least one track, within the term prescribed by the special act authorizing the same, or if after completion the said railroad shall be suffered to go into decay, and be impassable for the term of two years, then this charter shall be null and void, except so far as to compel the said company to make reparation for damages.

SEC. 20. That if any company incorporated as aforesaid shall at any time misuse or abuse any of the privileges granted by this act, or by the special act of incorporation, the legislature may revoke all and singular the rights and privileges so granted to such company; and the legislature hereby reserves the power to resume, alter, or amend any charter granted under this act, and take for public use any road constructed in pursuance of such charter: *Provided,* That in resuming, altering, or amending said charters no injustice shall be done to the corporators, and that in taking such roads for public use full compensation shall be made to the stockholders.

## AN ACT AUTHORIZING THE PAVING OF THE GRAY'S FERRY ROAD, FROM CEDAR STREET TO FEDERAL STREET, PROVIDING FOR THE CONSTRUCTION OF LATERAL RAILROADS, &c.

*Approved 5th April, 1849. (P. L., 1849, page 389.)*

SECTION 2. That it shall be lawful for any individual, or association of individuals, to construct a railroad or plank road from his or their premises, to connect with any railroad or plank road which may be constructed, or to any stream of water which has been or may hereafter be declared a public highway: *Provided*, Such railroad or plank road shall not exceed three miles in length; and any individual or individuals making any such improyement shall be subject to all the provisions and restrictions of an act regulating turnpike and plank road companies, approved the twenty-sixth day of January, 1849: *And provided further*, That this act shall only extend to the counties of Warren, McKean, Elk, and Potter.

NOTE.—The turnpike and plank road act of 26th January, 1849, is given in full on the succeeding pages.

---

## AN ACT REGULATING TURNPIKE AND PLANK ROAD COMPANIES.

*Approved 26th January, 1849. (P. L., 1849, page 10.)*

SECTION 1. That whenever a special act of the general assembly shall be passed, authorizing the incorporation of a company for the construction of a turnpike road, or for the construction of a plank road, within this Commonwealth, the commissioners named in such act, or any five of them, shall have power to open books for receiving subscriptions to the capital stock of such company, at such time or times, and such place or places, as they may deem expedient, after having given at least twenty days' previous notice in one or more newspapers published, or having circulation within the county where books of subscription are to be opened; at which times and places two or more of the said commissioners shall attend, and permit and suffer all persons of lawful age, who shall offer to subscribe in such books, in their own names, or in the name of any other person who shall duly authorize the same, for any number of shares of stock; and the said books shall be kept open, respectively, for the purpose aforesaid, at least six hours in every juridical day, for the space of five days, or until the said books shall have the whole number of shares authorized by such special act therein subscribed; and if, at the expiration of the said five days, the books aforesaid shall not have the said number of shares authorized as aforesaid therein subscribed, the commissioners respectively may adjourn from time to time, and transfer the books from place to place, until the whole number of shares shall be subscribed; of which adjournment and transfer the commissioners aforesaid shall give such public notice as the occasion may require, and when the whole number of shares subscribed shall amount to the number authorized as aforesaid, the same shall be closed: *Provided always*, That every person offering to subscribe in such books, in his own or any other name, shall at the time of subscribing pay to the attending commissioners any sum not less than one dollar nor more than five dollars (as shall be fixed and determined by said commissioners, previously to the opening of books for every share to be subscribed, out of which shall be defrayed such incidental charges and expenses as may be necessary for taking such subscription, and the remainder shall be paid to the treasurer of the corporation, as soon as the same shall be organized and the officers chosen as hereinafter mentioned.

SEC. 2. When twenty persons or more shall have subscribed ten per centum on the capital stock provided for by such special act of assembly, the said commissioners respectively may, or when the whole number of shares authorized as aforesaid shall be subscribed, they shall certify under their hands and seals the names of the subscribers, and the number of shares subscribed by each, to the governor of this Commonwealth, whereupon it shall and may be lawful for the governor by letters patent under his hand and seal of State, to create and erect the subscribers, and if the subscription be not full at the time, then those who shall afterwards subscribe to the

number aforesaid, into one body politic and corporate, in deed
and in law, by the name, style, and title designated by such
special act; and by such name the said subscribers shall have
perpetual succession, and all privileges and franchises incident
to a corporation, and shall be capable of taking and holding
the capital stock, and the increase and profits thereof, and of
enlarging the same by new subscription, in such manner and
form as they shall think proper, if such enlargement shall be
found necessary to fulfill the intent of such special act; and of
purchasing, taking, and holding to them and their successors
and assigns, and of selling, transferring, and conveying, in fee
simple, or for any less estate, all such lands, tenements, and
hereditaments, and estate, real and personal, as shall be necessary to them in the prosecution of their works; and of suing
and being sued, and of doing all and every other matter and
thing which a corporation or body politic may lawfully do.

Sec. 3. That the commissioners aforesaid, as soon as conveniently may be after the said letters shall be sealed and obtained,
shall give notice, in the manner provided for in the first section of this act, of the time and place by them appointed; at
which time and place the said subscribers shall proceed to
organize such corporation, and shall choose, by a majority of
votes of the subscribers by ballot, to be delivered in person or
by proxy duly authorized, one president, five managers, and
one treasurer, and such other officers as may be necessary to
conduct the business of such company until the first Monday
of November next ensuing, and until such other officers shall
be chosen; and shall and may make such by-laws, orders, and
regulations, not inconsistent with the Constitution and laws of
the United States and of this Commonwealth, as shall be necessary for the proper management of the affairs of such company:
*Provided always*, That each stockholder shall be entitled to
one vote for each share of stock not exceeding ten, and one
vote for every five shares exceeding that number: *And provided, also*, That no stockholder, whether the original subcriber
or assignee, shall be entitled to vote at any election or meeting
of said company, unless the whole sum due and payable on
the share or shares by him or her held at the time of such
election shall have been fully paid and discharged.

SEC. 4. The stockholders of such company shall meet or the first Monday in November in every year, at such place as shall be fixed by their by-laws, for the purpose of choosing officers as aforesaid for the ensuing year, and at such other times as they shall be summoned by the managers, in such manner and form as shall be prescribed by their by-laws; at which annual or special meetings they shall have full power and authority to make, alter, or repeal, by a majority of votes all such by-laws, rules, orders, and regulations made as afore said, and to do and perform any corporate act.

SEC. 5. The president and directors of such company first chosen shall procure certificates or evidences of stock, for all the shares of the said company, and shall deliver one or more certificates or evidences, signed by the president, countersigned by the treasurer, and sealed with the common seal of the corporation, to each person or party entitled to receive the same according to the number of shares by him, her, or them respectively subscribed or held; which certificates or evidences of stock shall be transferable, at the pleasure of the holder, in a suitable book or books to be kept by the company for that purpose, in person or by attorney duly authorized, in the presence of the president or treasurer, subject, however, to all payments due or to become due thereon; and the assignee or party to whom the same shall have been so transferred shall be a member of said corporation, and have and enjoy all the immunities, privileges, and franchises, and be subject to all the liabilities, conditions, and penalties incident thereto, in the same manner as the original subscriber would have been: *Provided* That no certificate shall be transferred so long as the holder thereof is indebted to said company, unless the board of directors shall consent thereto.

SEC. 6. It shall be lawful for the said president and managers, their superintendents, surveyors, engineers, artists, and chain-bearers, to enter in and upon all and every the lands, tenements, and enclosures in, through, and over which such intended turnpike road or plank road may be thought proper to pass, and for that purpose to examine the ground and quarries of stone and gravel, and other materials that may be necessary in making and constructing such road, and to cut or open such drains through the same as they shall judge necessary to drain the water from the turnpike road or plank road, with the same rights and under the same penalties as the supervisors of highways; and the said road shall be constructed between the points named in the special act incorporating such company.

SEC. 7. The president and managers of such corporations, three of whom shall for that purpose be a quorum, shall keep minutes of all their proceedings, fairly entered in a book to be kept for that purpose, and shall have full power and authority to appoint, agree, and contract with such engineers, superintendents, artists, laborers, and other persons, as they may think necessary, to make and construct such road, and collect the tolls hereinafter authorized, and fix their compensation.; to ascertain the times, manner, and proportions in which the stockholders shall pay the amount of their respective shares, in order to carry on their work; to draw orders on the treasurer for all debts contracted by them, which orders shall be signed by the president, or, in his absence, by a majority of the managers, and attested by their secretary; and to do and transact all other acts, matters, or things as by the by-laws, orders, and regulations of such company shall be entrusted to them.

SEC. 8. If any stockholder, whether the original subscriber or assignee, after twenty days' notice, as aforesaid, of the time and place appointed for the payment of any installment or proportion of the capital stock, shall neglect to pay such proportion, at the place appointed, for the space of thirty days after the time appointed for the payment thereof, any such stockholder shall, in addition to the installment so called for, pay at the rate of one per centum per month for every delay of such payment; and if the same and additional penalty shall become equal to the sum before paid in part on account of such share, the same may be forfeited by and to the said company, and may be sold by them for such price as may be obtained therefor; or in default of payment of any stockholders of such installments as aforesaid, for the space of sixty days aforesaid, the president and managers may, at their election, cause suit to be brought in the same manner as debts of a like amount are now recoverable, for the recovery of the same, together with the penalties aforesaid.

Sec. 9. It may be lawful for the president and managers of such company, incorporated as aforesaid, by and with their superintendents, engineers, artists, workmen, laborers, their tools and instruments, carts, wagons, and other carriages, and beasts of draught or burden, to enter in and upon the lands contiguous and near to which the said road shall be made or constructed, first giving notice of their intention to the occupiers thereof, and doing as little damage thereto as possible, and making amends for damages upon a reasonable and equitable agreement by the parties; or if they cannot agree thereupon, a just and equitable assessment to be made upon oath or affirmation by three disinterested freeholders, or any two of them, two of whom shall be mutually chosen by the parties, and said two thus chosen shall choose a third; or if either party, upon due notice, shall neglect or refuse to join in the choice, then to be chosen by a justice of the peace of the county wherein the land lies, who shall not be interested therein; and upon the tender of the assessed value, to dig and carry away any timber, stone, sand, earth, or other materials, necessary or suitable for making said road: *Provided*, That no part of this act shall authorize the taking of any property by such company, unless the same be previously paid for, or adequate security given to the owners for the payment thereof.

Sec. 10. The president and managers of every such company, incorporated as aforesaid, shall keep fair and just accounts, as well of all moneys received by them as of those paid out and expended in the prosecution of the work; and shall, at least once in every year, submit their books and accounts to a general meeting of the stockholders; and whenever it shall be ascertained that the capital stock of such company is not sufficient to complete their road, according to the true intent and meaning of this act, it shall and may be lawful for the president and managers, at a stated or special meeting, convened according to the provisions of this act or their own by-laws, to increase the number of shares to such an extent as they shall deem sufficient to accomplish the work, and to demand and receive the moneys subscribed for such additional shares, in like manner and under like penalties as are provided 'by this act in the case of the original subscriptions.

SEC. 11. The president and managers of such company shall have power to erect good and sufficient bridges over all the streams of water crossed by their road, whenever the same shall be found necessary; and shall cause a road, if a turn-pike, to be laid out, not exceeding fifty feet in width, and cause at least eighteen feet of said width to be made an artificial road of wood, stone, gravel, or other proper and convenient materials, such as the nature of the ground may require and will afford, to be constructed in such manner as will admit an even surface, and so nearly level in its progress, that it shall at no place rise or fall more than will form an angle of four degrees from a horizontal line; and if a plank road, the same shall be opened of any width not exceeding forty feet, and shall be graded in such manner as may be necessary for either a single or double track, as may be determined upon by the president and managers of the said company, each track being not less than eight feet in width, and so nearly level in its progress that it shall in no place rise or fall more than will form an angle of three degrees with a horizontal line: *Provided*, That if any part of the ground on the route of said road shall be so hard and compact as to make a good road without any covering of wood, gravel, stone, slate, or other hard substance, the said president and managers are hereby authorized to construct such part of said road without any such covering, and shall forever maintain and keep the same in good repair: *Provided*, That in all deep cuts the said road need not be of greater width on the surface than thirty feet: *And provided*, That said bridges shall not be constructed so as to obstruct the navigation of any stream declared a public highway.

SEC. 12. Whenever such company shall have finished five miles or more of road, the president thereof may give notice to the governor, who shall appoint forthwith three sklilful, judicious, and disinterested persons to view and examine the same, and report, on oath or affirmation, to him whether the said road is so far executed in a competent and workmanlike manner, according to the true intent and meaning of this act; and if their report shall be in the affirmative, then the governor shall, by license, under his hand and the seal of the State, permit and suffer said company to erect and fix such and so many gates upon and across the said road as will be necessary and sufficient to collect from all persons, otherwise than on foot, the same tolls as hereinafter authorized and granted.

SEC. 13. When such company is licensed in manner aforesaid, it shall and may be lawful for them to appoint such and so many toll-gatherers as they shall think proper, to collect and receive, of and from all and every person or persons using the said road, the tolls and rates hereinafter mentioned; and to stop any person riding, leading, or driving any horses, cattle, hogs, sheep, coach, coaches, sulky, chair, chaise, phaeton, cart, wagon, wain, sleigh, sled, or any other carriage of burden or pleasure, from passing through the said gate until they shall respectively have paid the same—that is to say, for every five miles in length of the said road completed and licensed as aforesaid, the following sums of money, and so in proportion for any lesser distance, or for any greater or lesser number of sheep, hogs, or cattle, to wit:—For every score of hogs, five cents; for every score of sheep, five cents; for every score of cattle, ten cents; for every horse and his rider, or led horse, three cents; for every sulky, chair, or chaise, with one horse and two wheels, six cents; with two horses, nine cents; for every chariot, coach, phaeton, or dearborn, with one horse and four wheels, ten cents; for every coach, phaeton, or chaise, with two horses and four wheels, twelve cents; for either of the carriages last mentioned, with four horses, twenty cents; for every other carriage of pleasure, under whatever other name it may go, the like sums, according to the number of wheels and horses drawing the same; for every stage-wagon, with two horses, twelve cents; for every such wagon, with four horses, twenty cents; for every sleigh, three cents for each horse drawing the same; and for every sled, two cents for each horse drawing the same; for every cart or wagon, whose wheels shall be less than four inches, four cents for each horse drawing the same; and for every cart or wagon whose wheels shall be four inches, and not exceeding seven inches, two cents for every horse ·drawing the same; for every cart or wagon, the breadth of whose wheels shall be more than seven inches, one cent for every horse drawing the same; and if any person or persons shall represent to the said company or any of their officers that he, she, or they have traveled a less distance than he, she, or they have actually traveled along said road, with intent to defraud the said company of its toll or any part thereof, such person or persons shall, for every such offense, forfeit and pay to the use of said company the sum of five dollars; and if any toll-gatherer shall demand and receive toll for a greater distance than the person of whom such toll is demanded shall have traveled along said turnpike road or plank road, or shall demand and receive greater toll from any person or persons than such toll-gatherer is authorized to demand and receive by virtue of this act, such toll-gatherer shall forfeit and pay the sum of five dollars for every such offense, to the supervisors of the township in which the forfeiture is incurred, to be expended in repairing township roads, and for the payment of which the said company shall be responsible; and all such penalties and forfeitures shall be recoverable, with costs of suit, before any justice of the peace of the county in which the offense is committed: *Provided*, That no toll shall be demanded from any person or persons passing and repassing from one part of his, her, or their farm to any other part of the same; and all persons, with their vehicles or horses, going to or from funerals or places of public worship, or of military trainings or elections, shall be exempt from the payment of toll when traveling on such turnpike road.

SEC. 14. If such company shall neglect or refuse to keep their road in good traveling order and repair for the space of thirty days, and information thereof shall be given under oath or affirmation to any justice of the peace of the neighborhood and county, designating particularly where and in what respect said road is defective, such justice shall issue a precept to any constable of the county, requiring him to notify the gate-keeper nearest whose gate the part or parts of the road complained of is situate, that on a certain day and at a certain hour therein mentioned, not less than three nor more than six days thereafter, three freeholders will be chosen at his office to hold an inquest to inquire into the truth of the matters specified in said information, an attested copy of which shall be furnished by said justice to said gate-keeper, at the time of serving said notice.

SEC. 15. The three freeholders mentioned in the preceding section shall be chosen as follows:—If the gate-keeper, or any other officer or agent of the company, and the informant, shall attend at the time and place of choosing, they shall commence with the complainant, and nominate alternately to the justice a list of nine freeholders of the neighborhood, from which list the complainant and the officer or agent of the company shall alternately strike out a name until three names are left, which three shall be the persons chosen to hold said inquest. Should either party be unrepresented at the time of choosing said free-holders, the justice shall act for him or them, and should both parties be absent, the justice shall appoint three disinterested freeholders to form said inquest.

SEC. 16. The inquest thus chosen shall, after having been duly sworn or affirmed, proceed to view the parts of the road complained of, and shall report to the said justice, in writing, under their hands and seals, or the hands and seals of a majority of them, within five days after said view, whether the said road be out of order and repair, contrary to the true intent and meaning of this act; and if so found, the said justice shall adjudge the said company to pay a fine of not less than twenty-five nor more than fifty dollars, at his discretion,—one-half thereof for the use of the supervisors of the roads in the township in which the portion of the road so found defective is situate: *Provided*, That the said company shall have the right of appealing, within twenty days after judgment, to the court of common pleas of the proper county, from the finding of said inquest, and the judgment of the justice thereon, as in other cases: *And provided further*, That no proceedings shall be commenced or prosecuted under the last three sections of this act, unless the informant or some other person shall have given twenty days' previous notice, in writing, to the gate-keeper nearest to whose gate the part or parts of the road complained of is situate, specifying particularly the part or parts of the road alleged to be out of repair, and the nature of the defect alleged, and notifying him that unless the proper repairs be made in thirty days after the service of the notice, proceedings will be commenced before a justice and three freeholders.

SEC. 17. Should the said company not appeal from the finding of the said inquest and the judgment of the justice thereon, and continue to neglect and refuse to repair the part or parts of the road thus found out of repair, new proceedings may be commenced and prosecuted against said-company for such neglect or refusal; and should said parts of said road continue out of repair until the holding of the next general court of quarter sessions for the proper county, it shall be the duty of the said justice to certify and send copies of the finding of the said inquests and the judgments thereon to the judges of the said court; and the said judges shall thereupon cause process to issue, and bring in the body or bodies of the person or persons intrusted by the company with the care and superintendence of such part of the said road as shall be so found defective, and shall proceed thereon as in cases of supervisors of highways for neglect of their duty; and if the persons intrusted by the said company as aforesaid shall be convicted of the offense by the said inquisition charged, the said court shall give judgment according to the nature and aggravation of the neglect, as according to right and justice would be proper in the case of supervisors of the highways neglecting their duties; and the fines and penalties so to be imposed shall be recovered in the said court, and shall be paid to the supervisors of the highways of the township wherein the offense was committed, to be applied to repairing the public roads within such township; and like proceedings may be instituted from time to time, until the said road is put into proper repair.

SEC. 18. In all cases of complaint made or suit instituted, under the provisions of this act, against any corporation, if the complainant shall fail to sustain his complaint, or the plaintiff to sustain his suit, as the case may be, the corporation shall be entitled to recover costs as in other cases, from the complainant or plaintiff, as the case may be; and in all cases when any corporation which may have been chartered under and subjec to the provisions of this act, shall be adjudged to pay any penalty, or the cost of any proceedings authorized by this act the party plaintiff or complainant shall have all the remedies for recovering of the same, with costs, against the said corpor ation, that are provided for the recovery of debts or judgment of like amount in other cases; and if the said corporation shall fail to make payment in any case within twenty days after final adjudication, the court of common pleas of the proper county, on application of the plaintiff, or some other person on his behalf, shall direct sequestration, and appoint a sequestrator, who shall have like powers, and be subject to all the regulations and requirements provided in the seventy-third and seventy-fourth sections of an act of the general assembly of this Commonwealth, entitled "An act relating to executions," passed June 16th, 1836: *Provided*, That where the judgment is final before the justice, or is not appealed from as provided in this act, the complainant, before proceeding to sequestration, shall file in the court of common pleas of the proper county a transcript of the proceedings and judgment before the justice, which transcript shall be entered of record in the said court, as under existing laws for the filing and entering of transcripts of judgments in other cases; and from such filing and entering shall have the effect of a judgment originally entered in the said court.

SEC. 19. If any person or persons whosoever, owning, riding in, or driving any sulky, chair, chaise, phaeton, cart, wagon, sleigh, sled, or other carriage of burden or pleasure, riding or leading any horse, mule, or gelding, or driving any hogs, sheep, or other cattle, shall therewith pass through any private gates or bars, or along or over any private passage-way or other ground near to or adjoining any gate erected, or which shall be erected in pursuance of this act, with an intent to defraud the company and avoid the payment of the toll or duty for passing through any such gate, or if any person or persons shall, with such intent, take off or cause to be taken off, any horse, mare, or gelding, or other cattle, from any sulky, chair, chaise, phaeton, cart, wagon, sleigh, sled, or

other carriage of burden or pleasure, or practice any other
fraudulent means or device, with the intent that the payment
of any such toll or duty may be evaded or lessened, all and
every person or persons, in all and every or any of the ways
or manners offending, shall, for every such offense, respectively forfeit and pay to the president and managers of such
turnpike road or plank road, as the case may be, any sum
not exceeding ten dollars, to be sued for and recovered, with
costs of suit, before any justice of the peace, in like manner
and subject to the same rules and regulations as debts of a
similar amount are by law sued for and recovered.

SEC. 20. The legislature shall have power to alter the rate
of toll fixed by this act; and the managers of any such company may lessen the same whenever they shall believe it
necessary for the well-being of the company or the community
at large.

SEC. 21. The legislature hereby reserves the right to alter,
amend, or repeal the charter and privileges granted by special
act, as aforesaid, whenever in their opinion the same may be
injurious to the citizens of this Commonwealth; in such
manner, however, that no injustice shall be done to the
corporators.

---

## AN ACT TO RESTRAIN CORPORATIONS FROM ISSUING OBLIGATIONS REDEEMABLE OTHERWISE THAN IN GOLD AND SILVER [OR IN CURRENT BANK-NOTES].

*Approved 21st April, 1849.* (*P. L., 1849, page 673.*)

SECTION I. That from and after the passage of this act it
shall not be lawful for any corporation within this Commonwealth, directly or indirectly, either by itself or through any
agent or agents, individual or individuals, to make, issue, or
re-issue, pay out, or circulate, or cause to be issued, re-issued,
put out, or circulated, any certificate, check, order, or due-bill,
or acknowledgment of indebtedness of any description, for
any purpose whatsoever, payable or redeemable in any goods,
property, or effects, or payable or redeemable in anything
except in gold and silver, and that any violation of the provisions of this act shall be held and deemed to be a forfeiture

of the charter of any company so offending, and any privat
citizen may by *quo warranto* proceed, according to law, t
have such forfeiture declared: *Provided*, That this act sha
not be construed to authorize any corporation or individua
not expressly authorized by existing laws, to issue any note
bill, check, or certificate whatever, in the nature or similitud
of a bank-note, and intended for circulation, and that all law
inconsistent with this act be and the same are hereby repealed
*And provided further*, That this section shall not be construe
so as to prevent any corporation from drawing orders in th
ordinary course of business, not intended for circulation o
in payment of interest, and that such orders shall not b
negotiable.

## AN ACT AUTHORIZING INDIVIDUALS TO CONSTRUC' RAILROADS AND PLANK ROADS IN THE COUNTY O] VENANGO, RELATING TO ROAD TAXES, &c.

*Approved 22d March, 1850.* (*P. L., 1850, page 258.*)

SECTION 1. That the second section of an act entitled "A1
act authorizing the paving of the Gray's Ferry road fron
Cedar street to Federal street; providing for the constructio1
of lateral railroads; relating to the appointment of auctioneer.
in the counties of Erie, Mercer, and Bradford; extending th(
Southwark Railroad; and in relation to the collection of poo.
taxes in the city of Pittsburg," passed the fifth day of April
1849, be and the same is hereby extended to Venango county

## AN ACT TO SECURE THE CITIES OF PITTSBURG AN] ALLEGHENY, AND THE NEIGHBORHOOD THEREOF FROM DAMAGE BY GUNPOWDER; TO INCORPORATE AN ASSOCIATION FOR THE ESTABLISHMENT OF A HOUSE OF REFUGE FOR WESTERN PENNSYLVANIA AND RELATIVE TO THE PENNSYLVANIA STATE LUNA· TIC HOSPITAL.

*Approved 22d April, 1850.* (*P. L., 1850, page 539.*)

SECTION 9. That it shall be unlawful for any person to trans·
port gunpowder over any railroad, canal, or slackwater in

this Commonwealth, unless the keg, barrel, box, or other vessel containing the same shall be distinctly and conspicuously marked by having the word "gunpowder" written or printed thereon; and every violation of this section shall subject the person or persons so offending to be prosecuted by indictment in the court of quarter sessions of the proper county, and punished by fine not exceeding five hundred dollars, and imprisonment not exceeding six months, or either of them, at the discretion of the court; and it is hereby made the duty of the canal commissioners to give notice of the provisions of this section along the lines of the public works of this Commonwealth.

---

AN ACT RELATING TO THE BAIL OF EXECUTRIXES; * * TO THE LIMITATION OF ACTIONS AGAINST CORPORATIONS; * * * TO APPEALS FROM AWARDS OF ARBITRATORS BY CORPORATIONS, &c.

*Approved 25th April, 1850. (P. L., 1850, pages 570 and 571.)*

SECTION 7. That the provisions of the act passed the 27th March, 1713, entitled "An act for the limitation of actions," shall not hereafter extend to any suit against any corporation or body politic which may have suspended business, or made any transfer or assignment in trust for creditors, or who may have at the time, and after the accruing of the cause of action, in any manner ceased from or suspended the ordinary business for which said corporation was created.

SEC. 12. That so much of the first section of the act passed on the twentieth day of March, 1845, entitled "An act concerning bail and attachments," as pertains to appeals from the awards of arbitrators, shall from henceforth be construed to extend to all such appeals, whether made by persons natural or artificial.

NOTE.—The act of 1713 provides that actions upon the case other than for slander, actions upon account other than such as concern trade between merchants, &c., actions for trespass, debt, detinue, replevin, and trespass *quare clausum fregit*, shall be brought within six years next after the cause of such action or suit (accrues) and not after. (1 Smith's Laws, page 76.)

66

AN ACT TO INCORPORATE THE FIRST BAPTIST CHURCH
OF LEWISBURG, UNION COUNTY, PENNSYLVANIA
RELATIVE TO RAILROADS AND CANALS IN MIFFLIN
COUNTY, &c.

*Approved 26th April, 1850. (P. L., 1851, page 820.)*

SECTION 10. That in all cases where canals and railroads
may be located through towns and boroughs in Mifflin county
and passing through lanes, streets, or alleys, it shall be lawfu
for the courts of quarter sessions of said county to appoin
viewers to lay out, vacate, or change lanes, streets, or alley
with like effect as if the same had been so laid out by the
original proprietor of such town or borough; and that saic
viewers shall have power to assess damages: *Provided*, Tha
a report of said viewers shall be confirmed by the court o
quarter sessions of said county.

---

A FURTHER SUPPLEMENT TO THE ACT INCORPORATIN(
THE PENNSYLVANIA RAILROAD COMPANY; AND RELA
TIVE TO LATERAL ROADS IN LYKENS VALLEY, II
DAUPHIN COUNTY.

*Approved 26th April, 1850. (P. L., 1850, page 584.)*

SECTION 4. That authority is hereby given to the owner o
owners, lessee or lessees, of coal lands in Lykens, Williams, o
Bear valley, in Dauphin county, to make a lateral railroa(
from any convenient point on the Lykens Valley Railroac
not exceeding in distance one mile from the western terminu
of said Lykens Valley Railroad, to the Wiconisco canal; an
have and use a landing on said canal of such capacity as ma
be necessary for the accommodation and shipment of coal.

SEC. 5. That the said owner or owners, lessee or lessees a
aforesaid, may apply by petition to the court of quarte
sessions of the peace of the county, whose duty it shall be t
appoint three disinterested persons to view the premises, asses
whatever damages, if any, which may have been sustained b
the owner or owners of the ground to be used and occupie

by said lateral railroad and landing; which valuation made by
the viewers shall be reported to the court, shall be conclusive:
*Provided*, That security, to be approved by the said court, shall
be given before the ground shall be broken for the construction of said lateral railroad and landing.

## AN ACT FIXING THE GUAGES OF RAILROADS IN THE COUNTY OF ERIE.

*Approved 11th March, 1851.* (*P. L., 1851, page 155.*)

WHEREAS, The guages or width between the rails of the
several railroad tracks in the State of New York are four feet
eight and one-half inches, or six feet.

AND WHEREAS, By the general railroad law of the State of
Ohio, the guages of the railroads of that State are fixed at four
feet ten inches; therefore,

SECTION 1. That the guage or width between the rails of
any track of any railroad running from the borough of Erie,
in the county of Erie, westwardly to the Ohio State line, or of
any part of any railroad, which shall or may be located between
a line running due south from the town of Erie to the Ohio
river and the Ohio State line, or of any railroad, any part of
which shall or may be used in connecting any railroad leading
eastwardly from the town of Erie, or from any point in the
aforesaid due south line with any railroad leading westwardly
to the Ohio State line, for the construction of which, or either
of which, a company now is or may hereafter be incorporated
by the laws of this Commonwealth, shall be of the width of
four feet and ten inches, and no other.

SEC. 2. That the guage of any railroad running from the
New York State line westwardly shall, as far as the town of
Erie, or as far as the line running due south from the town of
Erie to the Ohio river, be constructed either of the guage of
six feet or of the guage of four feet eight and one-half inches:
*Provided*, That nothing in this act contained shall be so con-
strued as in any way to enlarge the privileges or franchises of

any company now incorporated by the laws of this Common·
wealth, except so far as regards the guage or width betweer
the rails.

(See act 6th February, 1852, fixing guage in other parts o
State.)

(See act 11th April, 1853, allowing guage to be of any widtl
that directors may deem expedient.)

---

AN ACT RELATING TO COUNTY PRISONS, * * * ANI
RELATIVE TO THE SERVICE OF PROCESS ON FOREIGN
INSURANCE COMPANIES AND OTHER CORPORATIONS

*Approved 8th April, 1851. (P. L., 1851, page 354.)*

SECTION 6. That in any case when any insurance compan}
or other corporation shall have an agency, or transact an}
business in any county of this Commonwealth, it shall anc
may be lawful to institute and commence an action agains
such insurance company or other corporation in such county
and the original writ may be served upon the president
cashier, agent, chief, or any other clerk, or upon any director
or agent of such company or corporation within such county
and such service shall be good and valid in law, to all intent
and purposes.

---

AN ACT CONSTRUING THE FIFTH SECTION OF THE AC'
ENTITLED "A FURTHER SUPPLEMENT TO AN ACT T(
INCORPORATE THE PENNSYLVANIA RAILROAD COM
PANY," AND RELATIVE TO THE OBSTRUCTION O]
PRIVATE ROADS BY RAILROAD COMPANIES, &c.

*Approved 12th April, 1851. (P. L., 1851, page 518.)*

SECTION 2. That any chartered railroad company in thi
Commonwealth obstructing or impeding the free use o
passage of any private road or crossing-place, by standin;
burden cars or engines, or placing other obstructions on an·
railroad wherever any private road or crossing-place may b
necessary to enable the occupant or occupants of land o

farms to pass over any railroad with horses, cows, hogs, sheep, carts, wagons, and implements of husbandry, shall for every such offence, after any agent or other person in the employ-ment of any railroad company shall have received at least fifteen minutes' verbal notice to remove burthen cars, engines, or other obstructions from any private road or crossing-place that may pass over any railroad, be liable for a penalty of thirty dollars, which shall be for the use of the person or per-sons aggrieved, and which shall be recovered before any justice of the peace in the same manner that debts not exceeding one hundred dollars are by law recoverable. And in all suits or actions that may be brought against any railroad company for the recovery of said penalty of thirty dollars, the service of legal process on any agent or other person in the employment of any railroad company shall be as good and available in law as if made on the president thereof.

---

## A SUPPLEMENT TO AN ACT ENTITLED AN ACT TO IN-CORPORATE THE LEWISVILLE AND PROSPECTVILLE TURNPIKE ROAD COMPANY, * * * AND RELATIVE TO LATERAL RAILROADS AND COUNTY COMMISSIONERS IN ALLEGHENY COUNTY, &c.

*Approved 12th April, 1851.  (P. L., 1851, page 536.)*

SECTION 3. That it shall and may be lawful for the proprie-tors of lateral railroads, in the county of Allegheny, to charge and receive from all persons using their respective roads such toll as is charged by the railroads throughout this Common-wealth in addition to the tolls they are now empowered to receive.

---

## AN ACT RELATING TO THE COMMENCEMENT OF ACTIONS * * * TO THE PROTECTION OF FENCES, &c.

*Approved 14th April, 1851.  (P. L., 1851, page 615.)*

SECTION 12. That if any person or persons, from and after the passage of this act, shall maliciously or voluntarily break down any post and rail or other fence, put up for the enclosure of lands, and carry away, break, or destroy any post, rail or other material of which such fence was built, within thi: Commonwealth, every person or persons so offending, an( being legally thereof convicted before any justice of the peac or alderman within this Commonwealth, shall, for every sucl offence, forfeit and pay the sum of ten dollars, one half thereo to be paid to the informer, and the other half to the support o the poor of such county, township, borough, or ward wher( the offence has been committed, together with costs of prose cution; and in default of payment, such person or person: shall be imprisoned in the county jail not exceeding thirty day: for the first offence, and sixty days for the second: *Providea* That either of the parties shall have the right of appeal in th( same manner as in civil cases.

(This act has no special reference to railroads, and wa: repealed 23d March, 1865.)

---

AN ACT TO INCORPORATE A COMPANY TO ERECT *Ι BRIDGE OVER THE SCHUYLKILL RIVER AT SPRIN( MILL, * * * TO ACTIONS FOR DAMAGES SUSTAINEI BY INJURIES DONE TO THE PERSON BY NEGLIGENCI OR DEFAULT, &c.

*Approved 15th April, 1851.*   (*P. L., 1851, page 674.*)

SECTION 18. That no action hereafter brought to recove: damages for injuries to the person by negligence or defaul shall abate by reason of the death of the plaintiff; but th( personal representatives of the deceased may be substitutec as plaintiff, and prosecute the suit to final judgment an( satisfaction.

SEC. 19. That whenever death shall be occasioned by unlaw ful violence or negligence, and no suit for damages be brough by the party injured during his or her life, the widow of an) such deceased, or, if there be no widow, the personal repre sentatives, may maintain an action for and recover damage: for the death thus occasioned.

## AN ACT TO INCORPORATE THE SUSQUEHANNA AND ERIE RAILROAD COMPANY.

*Approved 15th April, 1851. (P. L., 1852, page 722.)*

SECTION 7. That it shall not be lawful for any private individual or association of individuals, or any company or companies, to construct a private railroad, connecting with any railroad authorized to be constructed by the laws of this State, with the Ohio and New York State lines, or with any railroad constructed, or to be constructed, in the States of Ohio and New York; and it shall not be lawful for any railroad company authorized by the laws of this State to connect with any such private railroad, and any violation of the provisions of this act shall subject all individuals or associations of individuals violating the same to the jurisdiction of the courts of this State, and to such forfeiture as the legislature may hereafter direct.

---

## ‘AN ACT REGULATING RAILROAD GAUGES, AND SUPPLEMENTARY TO THE ACT INCORPORATING THE CATAWISSA AND TOWANDA RAILROAD COMPANY, WITH AN EXTENSION TO THE NEW YORK AND ERIE RAILROAD AT SOME CONVENIENT POINT ON THE STATE LINE.

*Approved 6th February, 1852. (P. L., 1852, page 35.)*

SECTION 3. That said company shall have the right to locate, build, or construct a railroad of one or more tracks, beginning at some convenient point in the village of Catawissa, in the county of Columbia, thence up Fishing creek, or some of its branches, and through the counties of Sullivan and Bradford to a point at the State line which may give a proper and convenient connection with the New York and Erie Railroad: *Provided*, That the time of commencing the said road be extended to five years from the passing of this act, and the time for completing to ten years from the same time: *And provided further*, That the gauge of the track of said railroad shall be the same as the gauge of the track of the railroads built and owned by the State; and any and every railroad hereafter constructed through any portion of Pennsylvania, from any point eastward of a line running due south across the State from the State line beginning at the east line of Erie county, shall be of the same gauge as the railroads built and owned by the State, and no other; and if any company shall hereafter build or construct a railroad, having a southern or eastern connection with any railroad leading to or towards Philadelphia or Harrisburg, of a different gauge from the gauge of the railroads built and owned by the State, then and in such case all and singular the rights, powers, and privileges conferred on such company by its charter, or by any supplement thereto, shall be adjudged null and void: *Provided*, That nothing contained herein shall be construed to apply to the New York and Erie Railroad, to the Tioga Railroad, to the Lackawanna and Western Railroad already constructed and in operation, nor to the act fixing the gauges of railroads in the county of Erie, passed the eleventh day of March, 1851.

(Repealed 11th April, 1853, as respects gauges.)

---

### AN ACT AUTHORIZING THE PENNSYLVANIA RAILROAD COMPANY TO RUN THEIR CARS OVER CONNECTING AND CONTINUOUS RAILROADS.

*Approved 3d March, 1853.* (*P. L., 1853, page 137.*)

SECTION 1. That the Pennsylvania Railroad Company be and they are hereby authorized to run their cars and locomotives over all connecting and continuous railroads, with the consent of the companies owning the same, and also, their cars over the railroads belonging to this Commonwealth, for the transportation of freight, (passengers, their baggage, and the United States mails,*) with the right of attachment to the motive-power of the State, employed for these respective purposes, upon such terms and conditions as may be agreed upon between the canal commissioners and said Pennsylvania Railroad Company, or in case of failure to agree, then upon terms

---

* Repealed 13th May, 1855.

and conditions that shall not be less favorable to said company than those that may be established from time to time, by the canal commissioners, for the government of individuals doing business on said railroads, except those engaged in the transportation of freight passing the whole distance between Philadelphia and Pittsburg, over the public works: *Provided,* That nothing herein contained shall be so construed as to affect or impair the contract made with Bingham and Dock, for the transportation of passengers and mails over the Philadelphia and Columbia Railroad by said commissioners, which contract is hereby confirmed: *Provided,* That the legislature hereby reserves the right to repeal this act of assembly, in such manner, however, that no injustice shall be done to the parties: *And provided,* That the canal commissioners shall at all times be required to run a sufficient number of engines between Lancaster and Philadelphia to accommodate the local and way freight.

---

## AN ACT REPEALING THE ACTS REGULATING THE GAUGE OF THE TRACK OF RAILROADS.

*Approved 11th April, 1853.   (P. L., 1853, page 366.)*

SECTION 1. That every railroad company heretofore chartered, or which may hereafter be chartered, is hereby authorized to construct or change their gauge or gauges of road to such width as the directors of such railroad company may deem expedient, and all laws inconsistent with this provision be and they are hereby repealed.

---

## AN ACT RELATIVE TO SUITS IN EJECTMENTS.

*Approved 18th April, 1853.   (P. L., 1853, page 467.)*

SECTION 1. That any person wishing to bring ejectment for land claimed adversely to him by any person or corporation not resident or being within the county where such land lies, may bring his action and serve the writ on any person withii the county having charge or superintendence of the land, ii behalf of or as agent of such party claiming adversely *Provided*, That before any trial or judgment shall be had ii such suit, it shall be made to appear to the satisfaction of th« court that the defendant has had notice, in fact, of the suit ii time to appear and defend it, and if the defendant be a corpor ation, this notice may be given to the president or othe chief officer of it.

---

AN ACT TO APPOINT COMMISSIONERS TO RUN ANI MARK THE COUNTY LINES BETWEEN YORK, CUMBER. LAND, AND ADAMS COUNTIES; * * * RELATIVE TC RAILROADS AND PLANK ROADS IN CLARION COUNTY &c.

*Approved 18th April, 1853.* (*P. L., 1853, page 528.*)

SECTION 23. That the provisions of the second section o the act entitled "An act authorizing the paving of Gray'! Ferry road," &c., approved the fifth day of April, A. D. 1849 are hereby extended to the county of Clarion, and that in th« cases mentioned in said section, lateral railroads may be con- structed in said county, not exceeding four miles in length, tc connect with any streams in which logs can be floated in th« time of freshets, instead of plank roads, under and subject tc all the provisions of the act regulating lateral railroads, ap- proved the fifth day of May, Anno Domini eighteen hundrec and thirty-two, and that it may be lawful for any person oi persons owning or using saw-mills on Mill creek, or at th« mouth thereof, to float logs in said creek from his or theii lands to their mills on said creek, or at the mills at the moutl of said creek: *Provided*, This act shall only extend to that parl of said creek in Clarion county from the forks to the mouth thereof.

## AN ACT FOR THE PROTECTION OF MECHANICS AND LABORERS.

*Approved 22d April, 1854.* (*P. L., 1854, page 480.*)

SECTION I. That in all assignments of property, whether real or personal, which shall hereafter be made by any person or persons, or chartered company, to trustees or assignees, on account of inability at the time of the assignment to pay his or their debts, the wages of miners, mechanics, and laborers employed by such person or persons, or chartered company, shall be first preferred and paid by such trustees or assignees, before any other creditor or creditors of the assignor: *Provided,* That any one claim thus preferred shall not exceed one hundred dollars.

## AN ACT TO EXEMPT CERTAIN LOANS AND BONDS FROM TAXATION.

*Approved 1st May, 1854.* (*P. L., 1854, pages 535 and 536.*)

SECTION I. That all certificates of loan now issued, or which may be hereafter issued by the city of Philadelphia, or any of the incorporated districts of the county of Philadelphia, in payment of subscriptions already made, or which may be hereafter made, by the municipal authorities of said city or incorporated districts, to the capital stock of any railroad company, and all bonds or certificates of loans of any railroad company incorporated by this Commonwealth, be and the same shall be liable to taxation for State purposes only.

## AN ACT TO PRESCRIBE THE MANNER OF COLLECTING CERTAIN TAXES.

*Approved 5th May, 1854.* (*P. L., 1854, page 569.*)

SECTION I. That whenever a tax is charged upon the tonnage of any railroad in this Commonwealth, the distance shall be estimated by taking the nearest whole number of miles, rejecting fractions not greater than a half a mile, and adding one to the whole number when the fraction is more than hal: a mile.

SEC. 2. That the tax shall be charged on the whole distance from the place of shipment to the place of delivery, whethei the shipment be made upon a siding or branch belonging tc the company which pays the tax, or upon the main line, subject to the provisions of section one of this act.

---

## AN ACT RELATIVE TO WEIGHMASTERS OF RAILROADS IN SCHUYLKILL COUNTY.

*Approved 5th May, 1854. (P. L., 1854, pages 570 and 571.)*

SECTION I. That from and after the passage of this act, it shall be the duty of the collector or weighmaster on each, and every of the several railroads within the county of Schuylkill, to weigh separately, each and every consignment of coal passing over said railroads, and keep a correct record of such consignments in a book, or books to be kept for that purpose, and on application, shall furnish monthly to each, and all the owners, (or their agents,) of coal lands lying in the county of Schuylkill, a certified copy of the record of the weights of each kind of coal, and each and every separate consignment of coal passed over the scale of each of said railroads, respectively mined from lands of said owners, and for each and every certificate so furnished, the said collectors or weighmasters shall be allowed to charge the sum of twelve and a half cents, and any collector or weighmaster refusing to furnish such certificate on application as aforesaid, shall be subject to a fine or penalty of fifty dollars for each, and every such refusal, to be recovered as sums of like amount are now recoverable by law: *Provided,* That nothing herein contained shall alter, or change the authority of any of the said railroad companies to charge the rates now allowed to be charged for weighing coal.

AN ACT SUPPLEMENTAL TO AN ACT ENTITLED "AN ACT TO INCORPORATE THE CLEVELAND AND PITTSBURG RAILROAD COMPANY."

*Approved 2d March, 1855. (P. L., 1855, page 63.)*

SECTION 1. That the Cleveland and Pittsburg Railroad Company be and it is hereby authorized to sell any bonds held by it in payments for subscriptions made to the capital stock of said company, by the counties of Beaver and Allegheny, at such rates below par as may be agreed upon between said company and the parties purchasing the same: *Provided*, That no sale shall be consummated until the commissioners of the county which issued the bonds shall have by resolution, determined the lowest price at which said railroad company may sell the same, said resolution to be recorded in the minutes of their proceedings; and so much of any act or acts of assembly as is hereby altered or supplied, be and the same is hereby repealed.

---

AN ACT RELATING TO THE SUBSCRIPTIONS OF ALLEGHENY COUNTY TO CERTAIN RAILROAD COMPANIES.

*Approved 27th March, 1855. (P. L., 1855, page 129.)*

SECTION 1. That the provisions of an act, entitled " An act supplemental to an act, entitled ' An act to incorporate the Cleveland and Pittsburg Railroad Company,' " approved the second day of March, 1855, be and the same are hereby extended to all railroad companies, to the capital stock of which companies subscription has been made by the county of Allegheny, on special contract or agreement with the county commissioners.

SUPPLEMENT TO AN ACT RELATING TO THE COM·
MENCEMENT OF ACTIONS, APPROVED THE THIR·
TEENTH DAY OF JUNE, 1836.

*Approved 12th April, 1855.* (*P. L., 1855, page 213.*)

SECTION 1. That no person or company engaged in the business of forwarding or transporting goods, wares, and merchandise shall be made liable in any proceedings in attachments as garnishee or otherwise, when such goods, wares, or merchandise are in transitu, and at the time of service of process beyond the limits of this Commonwealth, without default, collusion, or fraud on the part of such person or company.

---

AN ACT RELATIVE TO THE ERECTION OF BRIDGES
OVER CANALS AND RAILROADS.

*Approved 12th April, 1855.* (*P. L., 1855, page 220.*)

SECTION 1. That the provisions of the laws of this Commonwealth relative to the erection of bridges over rivers, creeks, or rivulets, be and the same are hereby extended to the erection of bridges over canals and railroads: *Provided,* That bridges erected under the provisions of this act shall not obstruct any canal or railroad over which such bridge may be erected: *And provided further,* That nothing in this act shall release railroad, or other companies, or the Commonwealth, from the requirements of existing laws.

---

A SUPPLEMENT TO THE ACT CONSOLIDATING THE CITY
OF PHILADELPHIA.

*Approved 21st April, 1855.* (*P. L., 1855, pages 264–66.*)

SECTION 10. That hereafter no railroad company, whose road does or shall terminate within the city of Philadelphia, shall have the right or power to locate and construct that part of said road which shall extend within the limits of said city, without first submitting the plans and surveys thereof, exhibiting the grades and routes, to the board of survey of said city, who shall have the power to conform the same as far as may be practicable, to the general plan and regulations of said city, as adopted at that time ; and all charters authorizing the construction of any railroad within said city, shall be taken to be subject to the above restriction : *Provided*, That this shall not be construed to apply to any railroad already graded or laid with rails in said city, unless the route or grade thereof shall be altered.

---

## AN ACT RELATING TO DAMAGES FOR INJURIES PRODUCING DEATH.

*Approved 26th April, 1855. (P. L., 1855, page 309.)*

SECTION I. That the persons entitled to recover damages for any injury causing death shall be the husband, widow, children, or parents of the deceased, and no other relative; and the sum recovered shall go to them in the proportion they would take his or her personal estate in case of intestacy, and that without liability to creditors.

SEC. 2. That the declaration shall state who are the parties entitled in such action; the action shall be brought within one year after the death, and not thereafter.

---

## AN ACT RELATING TO CORPORATIONS, AND TO ESTATES HELD FOR CORPORATE, RELIGIOUS, AND CHARITABLE USES.

*Approved 26th April, 1855. (P. L., 1855, pages 328 and 329.)*

SECTION I. That it shall not be lawful for any councilman, burgess, trustee, manager, or director of any corporation, municipality, or public institution to be at the same time a

treasurer, secretary, or other officer, subordinate to the presi
dent and directors, who shall receive a salary therefrom, or b
the surety of such officer; nor shall any member of an
corporation or public institution, or any officer or agent there
of, be in anywise interested in any contract for the sale o
furnishing of any supplies or materials to be furnished to o
for the use of any corporation, municipality, or public institu
tion of which he shall be a member or officer, or for whicl
he shall be an agent, nor directly nor indirectly intereste
therein, nor receive any reward or gratuity from any perso
interested in such contract or sale; and any person violatin
these provisions, or either of them, shall forfeit his member
ship in such corporation, municipality, or institution, and hi
office or appointment thereunder, and shall be held guilty o
a misdemeanor, and on conviction thereof, shall forfeit an
sum not less than three times any advantage he may hav
derived by such offence, if any, and if no such advantag
have been received, then any sum in the discretion of th
court of quarter sessions of the proper county, not exceeding
five hundred dollars for each offence: *Provided*, That privat
corporations heretofore incorporated, with any right or privilege in conflict with this section, shall not be affected thereby
until such corporation shall, by resolution, agree to adopt
the provisions hereof, which it is hereby authorized to do.

SEC. 2. That any person who shall contract for the sale or
sell any supplies or materials as aforesaid, and shall cause to
be interested in any such contract or sale any member,
officer, or agent of any corporation, municipality, or institution, or give or offer any such person any reward or gratuity,
to influence him or them in the discharge of their official
duties, shall not be capable of recovering anything upon any
contract or sale, in relation to which he may have so practiced
or attempted to practice corruptly, but the same shall be void;
and such party shall be liable to conviction for a misdemeanor
in the court of quarter sessions of the proper county, and
shall be fined three times the amount so given or offered
corruptly, if ascertained, and if not ascertained, any sum
not exceeding five hundred dollars, in the discretion of
said court.

## AN ACT EXTENDING THE RIGHT OF TRIAL BY JURY TO CERTAIN CASES.

*Approved 27th April, 1855. (P. L., 1855, page 365.)*

SECTION 1. That in all cases that may hereafter arise under the act of assembly regulating railroad companies, approved the nineteenth day of February, Anno Domini one thousand eight hundred and forty-nine, any party or parties who may be aggrieved by the report or award of viewers appointed under said act, may at any time, within thirty days after the confirmation of such report, appeal from the same to the court of common pleas by which said viewers were appointed.

---

## AN ACT RELATING TO CORPORATIONS.

*Approved 3d May, 1855. (P. L., 1855, pages 423 and 424.)*

SECTION 1. That every charter of incorporation granted or to be granted shall be deemed and taken to be subject to the power of the legislature, unless expressly waived therein, to alter, revoke, or annul the same, whenever in their opinion it may be injurious to the citizens of the Commonwealth; in such manner, however, that no injustice shall be done to the corporators, and as fully as if the reservation of said power had been therein expressed.

---

## AN ACT TO PROVIDE FOR THE DESTRUCTION OF CANADA THISTLES AND OTHER NOXIOUS WEEDS, AND THE MAINTAINING OF DITCHES ON THE BANKS OF RAILROADS IN THE COUNTY OF ERIE.

*Approved 7th May, 1855. (P. L., 1855, pages 476 and 477.)*

SECTION 1. That it shall be the duty of the several railroad corporations owning or working railroads within the county of Erie, wherever water accumulates along the same to the injury of the adjoining land, to excavate and maintain, on both sides thereof, ditches, of sufficient width and depth and of suitable grade to drain off the water in such manner as to protect the adjoining land from wash or soakage ; and it shall further be the duty of the several railroad companies aforesaid to cause all Canada thistles and other noxious weeds growing on any lands owned or occupied by such corporation to be cut down twice in each and every year,—once between the fifteenth day of June and first day of July, and once between the fifteenth day of August and the first day of September.

SEC. 2. That if the said corporations, or any or either of them, shall neglect to make and maintain good and sufficient drains or ditches to carry off the water, so as to prevent wash or soakage on the adjacent land, or shall neglect to cause to be cut down all Canada thistles and other noxious weeds at the times mentioned in this act, it shall be lawful for any person to cut the same between the first and fifteenth days of July and between the first and fifteenth days of September and to make, open, and repair said drains and ditches, at the expense of the corporation on whose lands said drains and ditches are to be made and on which said Canada thistles or other noxious weeds shall be so cut, at the rate of one dollar per day for the time so occupied in doing the same, to be recovered as debts of like amount are recoverable, in any court of justice within the county of Erie.

---

## AN ACT DECLARATORY OF THE CONSTRUCTION OF THE ELEVENTH SECTION OF AN ACT PASSED ON THE TWENTY-SIXTH DAY OF JULY, ANNO DOMINI ONE THOUSAND EIGHT HUNDRED AND FORTY-TWO.

*Approved 25th February, 1856.* (*P. L., 1856, page 61.*)

SECTION 1. That it is hereby declared to be the true intent and meaning of the eleventh section of an act to incorporate the Liberty Fire Company, of Holmesburg, in the county of Philadelphia, approved the twenty-sixth day of July, Anno

Domini one thousand eight hundred and forty-two, and its true and legal effect shall be, that in all cases where any railroad or canal company, authorized by existing laws to issue bonds, certificates of loan, or evidences of indebtedness secured by mortgage, may have issued or shall hereafter issue any such bonds, certificates of loan, or evidences of indebtedness, executed by such company, and has disposed of or may hereafter dispose of the same at less than their par value, such transactions shall not be deemed usurious or in violation of any law of this Commonwealth prohibiting the taking of more than six per cent. interest.

---

## A SUPPLEMENT TO AN ACT ENTITLED "AN ACT REGULATING RAILROAD COMPANIES," APPROVED THE NINETEENTH DAY OF FEBRUARY, ANNO DOMINI ONE THOUSAND EIGHT HUNDRED AND FORTY-NINE.

*Approved 9th April, 1856.  (P. L., 1856, pages 288 and 289.)*

WHEREAS, Some doubts and difficulties have arisen in regard to the intention and proper construction of the first section of a certain act, approved the twenty-seventh day of April, Anno Domini one thousand eight hundred and fifty-five, entitled "An act extending the right of trial by jury to certain cases;" now, for the removal of said doubts and difficulties and for certainty in the premises—

SECTION 1. *Be it enacted, &c.*, That the true intent and meaning of the said act was, that it should apply to and embrace cases pending at the time of the passage of the said act.

SEC. 2. That hereafter in all cases where the parties cannot agree upon the amount of damages claimed, or by reason of the absence or legal incapacity of such owner or owners, no such agreement can be made, either for lands, water, water-rights, or materials, the company shall tender a bond, with at least two sufficient sureties, to the party claiming or entitled to any damages, or to the attorney or agent of any person absent, or to the guardian or committee of any one under legal incapacity, the condition of which shall be, that the company will pay or cause to be paid such amount of damages as the party shall be entitled to receive, after the same shall have been agreed upon by the parties, or assessed in the manner provided for by this and the act to which it is a supplement *Provided*, That in case the party or parties claiming damages refuse or do not accept the bond as tendered, the said company shall then give the party a written notice of the time when the same will be presented for filing in court; and thereafter the said company may present said bond to the court of common pleas of the county where the lands, water or materials are, and if the bond and sureties are approved the bond shall be filed in said court for the benefit of those interested; and recovery may be had thereon for the amoun of damages assessed, if the same be not paid or cannot be made by execution on the judgment in the issue formed to try the question.

SEC. 3. That the viewers provided for in the eleventl section of the act to which this is a supplement, may be appointed before or after the entry for constructing said roa or taking materials therefor, and upon the report of sai viewers, or any four of them, being filed in said court, eithe party, within thirty days thereafter, may file his, her, or thei appeal from said report to the said court; after such appea either party may put the cause at issue in the form directe by said court, and the same shall then be tried by said cour and a jury; and after final judgment, either party may have writ of error thereto from the supreme court, in the manne prescribed in other cases. The said court shall have powe to order what notices shall be given connected with any pa of the proceedings, and may make all such orders connecte with the same as may be deemed requisite. If any exception be filed with any appeal to the proceedings, they shall b speedily disposed of; and if allowed, a new view shall b ordered; and if disallowed, the appeal shall proceed as befo provided.

## SUPPLEMENT TO THE ACTS RELATING TO INCORPORATIONS BY THE COURTS OF COMMON PLEAS.

*Approved 9th April, 1856. (P. L., 1856, page 293.)*

SECTION I. That it shall be lawful for any court of common pleas of the proper county to hear the petition of any corporation under the seal thereof, by and with the consent of a majority of a meeting of the corporators, duly convened, praying for permission to surrender any power contained in its charter, or for the dissolution of such corporation; and if such court shall be satisfied that the prayer of such petition may be granted without prejudice to the public welfare or the interests of the corporators, the court may enter a decree in accordance with the prayer of the petition, whereupon such power shall cease or such corporation be dissolved : *Provided*, That the surrender of any such power shall not in anywise remove any limitation or restriction in such charter, and that the accounts of the managers, directors, or trustees of any dissolved company shall be settled in such court and be approved thereby, and dividends of the effects shall be made among any corporators entitled thereto, as in the case of the accounts of assignees and trustees : *Provided further*, That no property devoted to religious, literary, or charitable uses shall be diverted from the objects for which they were given or granted : *Provided*, That the decree of said court shall not go into effect until a certified copy thereof be filed and recorded in the office of the secretary of the Commonwealth.

(By the title of this act it appears to apply only to charters granted by courts of common pleas.)

---

## AN ACT RELATING TO THE SERVICE OF PROCESS IN CERTAIN CASES.

*Approved 17th March (April), 1856. (P. L., 1856, page 388.)*

SECTION I. That hereafter when any action is commenced by any person against any corporation in any county in which the property of said corporation was wholly or in part situated, it shall be lawful, if the president, treasurer, secretary, or chief clerk do not reside or cannot be found in such county, for the sheriff or officer to whom any process may be directed to serve the same on any manager or director in such county, and the service so made shall be deemed sufficient; and in case no director or manager can be found in such county, it shall be lawful for the sheriff or other officer to whom such process is directed to go into any county to serve the process aforesaid.

---

## AN ACT TO PROVIDE FOR THE ORDINARY EXPENSES OF GOVERNMENT, THE REPAIRS OF THE PUBLIC CANALS AND RAILROADS, AND OTHER GENERAL AND SPECIAL APPROPRIATIONS.

*Approved 13th May, 1856.* (*P. L., 1856, page 560.*)

SECTION 41. That so much of the act entitled "An act authorizing the Pennsylvania Railroad Company to run their cars over connecting and continuous railroads," approved the third day of March, 1853, as relates to carrying passengers and baggage and mails on the Philadelphia and Columbia railroad, be and the same is hereby repealed; and the canal commissioners are hereby authorized to contract with responsible persons, or companies incorporated by any law of this commonwealth, for carrying passengers, their baggage, and United States mails, on the Philadelphia and Columbia railroad, for a period not exceeding five years from and after the expiration of the contract now existing between the canal commissioners and Bingham & Dock, on such terms and conditions as will best promote the interest of the Commonwealth: *Provided*, That from and after the first day of May next it shall not be lawful for the city of Philadelphia to charge and collect tolls on the city railroad for any greater distance than that actually used, including the bridge over the Schuylkill river, at Market street.

A SUPPLEMENT TO AN ACT RELATING TO DAMAGES
FOR INJURIES PRODUCING DEATH.

*Approved 10th December, 1856.* (*P. L., 1857, page 798.*)

SECTION 1. That the act, approved the twenty-sixth day of April, 1855, entitled "An act relating to damages for injuries producing death," shall not be construed retrospectively, either as to rights of actions accrued or actions pending, but that the limitation of one year therein named shall be restricted to cases accruing from and after the passage of said act.

AN ACT RELATIVE TO ASSIGNEES AND TRUSTEES OF
RAILROAD COMPANIES.

*Approved 16th May, 1857.* (*P. L., 1857, page 538.*)

SECTION 1. That hereafter no assignees or trustees who, in the discharge of the duties of their trust, have entered or shall enter into the possession and management of any railroad under any deed of assignment or mortgage, shall be personally responsible for any damage which may occur to any passenger or other person by collision, force, or violence occurring in the operation of the railroad and locomotives so in their management, without any default or misconduct of such assignees or trustees; and if any case of damages shall occur by reason aforesaid, for which the railroad company if managing the road would be liable, the damage may be recovered against the assigning or mortgaging company, and execution therefor shall be levied of the property and effects held in trust by such assignees or trustees, or of any trust funds in their hands, by execution or attachment of execution, and be paid as part of the expenses of administering the trust, in preference to the creditors of the company, and the assignees and trustees shall accordingly have credit therefor in their accounts; and it shall be lawful for such assignees or trustees to make settlement of such claims for damages by compromise, approved by any court having jurisdiction of their accounts.

A SUPPLEMENT TO THE ACT REGULATING RAILROADS

*Approved 20th May, 1857.  (P. L., 1857, page 629.)*

SECTION I. That no lateral or private railroad leading from
any ore mine, coal mine, or limestone or other quarry, now
having the right to cross, at grade, the track of any railroad
authorized to be built by any special charter granted by this
Commonwealth, shall be permitted to cross such track of such
chartered railroad at more than two crossings, or with more
than a double track; and the proprietors of any such lateral
or private railroad leading from any such mine, opening, or
tunnel, shall, at the point of crossing such chartered railroad
be confined to a double track; and the company owning such
chartered railroad shall have the right, in any case, to enforce
compliance with the provisions of this section, by refusing to
permit more than a double crossing, as aforesaid.

---

AN ACT FOR THE BETTER SECURITY OF LABORERS
MECHANICS, AND OTHERS, IN CERTAIN CORPORATIONS.

*Approved 13th October, 1857.  (P. L., 1858, pages 615 and 616.)*

SECTION I. That for the purpose of providing additional
security for the payment of miners, laborers, operatives, and
mechanics for services rendered or which may be hereafter
rendered, supplies and materials furnished or hereafter to be
furnished, to any coal, iron, canal, navigation, railroad, or
turnpike company, incorporated in whole or in part by the
laws of this Commonwealth, it shall be lawful and competent
for any such company to execute a lien or liens, or instrument
of writing sufficient thereto, with inventory attached, and
attested by the common seal of said company, if said company
have such common seal, and if such company have no common
seal, then said instrument of writing to be signed by the
president of the board of directors or managers, attested by
the secretary, to a trustee or trustees, upon any or all their
wagons, teams, horses, mules, cars, carts, boats, equipments,
engines, tools, and machinery used in conducting the business
of any such company, to be held by said trustee or trustees

as a lien for the sole purpose or purposes aforesaid, until said debts herein contemplated are fully discharged, by the sale thereof or otherwise: *Provided*, That the said instrument or instruments of writing be first acknowledged as other deeds are and recorded in the office for recording deeds, in the respective counties wherein said companies transact business, within thirty days from the execution thereof: *And provided further,* That this act shall continue in force until the first day of February, 1859, and no longer, unless extended by a subsequent legislature.

(This act does not appear to have been extended.)

---

## AN ACT RELATIVE TO BONDS ISSUED BY THE COUNTY OF ALLEGHENY FOR STOCK IN RAILROAD COMPANIES.

*Approved 13th April, 1858. (P. L., 1858, pages 252 and 253.)*

SECTION I. That the commissioners of the county of Allegheny be and they are hereby authorized to exchange with any one or more holders or owners or trustees, or guardians of any holder or owner of bonds of said county, issued in payment for stock in any railroad company, any amount of said stock now owned by said county, for an equal amount of the said bonds, each at their par value: *Provided*, That no stock shall be exchanged except for bonds issued in payment for stock in the same company; and within one month after effecting any such exchange, said commissioners shall publicly cancel any bonds received for stock, in the presence of one or more judges of the court of common pleas, who shall sign a certificate of such cancellation upon the minutes of the board.

---

## A FURTHER SUPPLEMENT TO THE ACT ENTITLED "AN ACT REGULATING LATERAL RAILROADS," PASSED MAY 5th, 1832.

*Approved 20th April, 1858. (P. L., 1858, page 361.)*

SECTION I. That hereafter, in all cases where a petition has been presented for the appointment of viewers, under the provisions of the said act and its supplements, it shall be the duty

of the viewers so appointed to report in writing whether th
road asked for is necessary for public or private use, as we
as the damages which will be sustained by the owner (
owners of intervening lands; and when, in the opinion of th
court, the road is necessary for public or private use, it sha
be lawful for the petitioner or petitioners, upon giving bon(
with one or more sureties, to be filed with the petition, and t
be approved by the court to which such petition shall hav
been presented, conditioned for the payment of such damag(
as shall be assessed under the provisions of the acts to whic
this is a supplement, to proceed in the opening, constructin(
completing, and using the said railroad, with one or mor
tracks, as prayed for in said petition.

---

### A FURTHER SUPPLEMENT TO THE ACT INCORPORATIN·
### THE CITY OF PHILADELPHIA.

*Approved 21st April, 1858. (P. L., 1858 page 385.)*

SECTION I. That the offices, depots, car-houses, and othe
real property of railroad corporations situated in said city, th
superstructure of the road and water stations only except(
are and hereafter shall be subject to taxation by ordinances fo
city purposes.

---

### A SUPPLEMENT TO THE ACT OF 16th JUNE, 1836, ENTITLE)
### "AN ACT RELATING TO EXECUTIONS."

*Approved 22d April, 1858. (P. L., 1858, page 458.)*

SECTION I. That so much of the act to which this is a sup
plement as relates to the appointment of sequestrators in case
where judgments have been obtained against corporation:
executions issued thereon and returned unsatisfied, is hereb:
declared not to apply to any unfinished railroad: *Provide(*
That nothing herein contained shall be so construed as t(
prevent a sequestrator from taking custody of the receipts an(
revenues of any portion of any such road that may be so fa
completed as to be in running order.

## AN ACT TO ENABLE THE CITY OF PITTSBURG TO RAISE ADDITIONAL REVENUE.

*Approved 4th January, 1859. (P. L., 1859, page 828.)*

SECTION 3. That all real estate situated in said city, owned or possessed by any railroad company, shall be and is hereby made subject to taxation for city purposes, the same as other real estate in said city.

---

## A SUPPLEMENT TO AN ACT IN REFERENCE TO RUNNING OF LOCOMOTIVE-ENGINES AND CARS ON CONNECTING RAILROADS, APPROVED 13th MARCH, 1847.

*Approved 29th March, 1859. (P. L., 1859, page 290.)*

SECTION 1. That the act passed on the 13th day of March, Anno Domini one thousand eight hundred and forty-seven, entitled "An act in reference to running of locomotive-engines and cars on connecting railroads," shall be so construed as to authorize companies owning any connecting railroads in the State of Pennsylvania to enter into any leases and contracts with each other in respect to the use, management, and working of their several railroads: *Provided*, That the company so contracting for or leasing any such railroad may have the right to fix the tolls thereon, but not at a higher rate than is authorized by the charter of either of the said railroad companies.

---

## AN ACT TO CONSOLIDATE, REVISE, AND AMEND THE PENAL LAWS OF THIS COMMONWEALTH.

*Approved 31st March, 1860. (P. L., 1860, pages 391, 412, 416, and 417.)*

SECTION 29. If any person shall be maimed, or otherwise injured in person, or injured in property, through or by reason of the wanton and furious driving or racing, or by reason of the gross negligence or willful misconduct of the driver of any public stage, mail coach, coachee, carriage, or car employed

in the conveyance of passengers; or through or by reason
the gross negligence or willful misconduct of any engineer
conductor of any locomotive-engine or train of railroad ca
or carriages; or any captain or other officer of any steambc
employed in the conveyance of passengers, or of goods, wari
merchandise, or produce of any description, such drivi
engineer, conductor, captain, or officer, shall, on convicti
thereof, be sentenced to pay a fine not exceeding five hundr
dollars and undergo an imprisonment, by separate or solita
confinement, or by simple imprisonment, not exceeding fi
years: *Provided,* That the provisions of this act shall not i
terfere with the civil remedies against the proprietors ar
others to which the injured party may by law be now entitle

SEC. 126. If any person, engaged in carrying or transportii
coal, iron, lumber, or other articles of merchandise or proper
whatsoever within this commonwealth, shall fraudulently si
or dispose of or pledge the same, or any part thereof, witho
the consent of the owner thereof, such offense shall be deemi
a misdemeanor, and the offender shall, on conviction, be se
tenced to pay a fine not exceeding five hundred dollars, ar
to undergo an imprisonment not exceeding one year; or
any person shall knowingly buy and receive the said me
chandise, knowing the same to have been sold, disposed r
or pledged fraudulently, he shall, on conviction, be sentenci
to the like punishment.

SEC. 142. If any person shall willfully and maliciously pi
place, cast, or throw upon or across any railroad any woo
stone, or other matter or thing; or shall willfully and ma
ciously take up, remove, or displace any rail, sleeper, or oth
matter or thing belonging to any railroad; or shall willful
and maliciously turn, move, or divert any switch or oth
machinery belonging to any railroad; or shall willfully ar
maliciously make or show, hide or remove any signal or lig
upon or near any railroad; or shall willfully and malicious
do, or cause to be done, any other matter or thing, with inter
in any of the cases aforesaid, to obstruct, upset, overthroi
injure, or destroy any tender, carriage, car, or truck used r
such railroad, or to endanger the safety of any person trave
ing or being upon such railroad, every such offender shall I

guilty of felony, and, being thereof convicted, shall be sentenced to pay a fine not exceeding ten thousand dollars, and to undergo an imprisonment, by separate or solitary confinement, at labor, not exceeding ten years.

SEC. 143. If any person shall willfully and maliciously cast, throw, or cause to fall or strike against, into, or upon any engine, tender, carriage, car, or truck used upon any railroad, any wood or stone or other matter or thing, with intent to endanger the safety of any person being in or upon such engine, tender, carriage, car, or truck, every such offender shall be guilty of misdemeanor, and being thereof convicted shall be sentenced to pay a fine not exceeding one thousand dollars, and to undergo an imprisonment not exceeding three years.

SEC. 147. If any person shall unlawfully and maliciously break, injure, or otherwise destroy or damage any part of any locomotive or stationary engine, inclined plane, engine-house, station, or depot, bridge, culvert, trestle work, or other building or structure belonging to any railroad, or any other part of such railroad; or shall wantonly and maliciously derange or displace the fixtures or machinery of any locomotive or stationary engine used or employed on any railroad; or shall willfully and maliciously destroy or injure any fence or wall, cross-road passing over or under such railroad; or shall unlawfully and maliciously break, injure, or otherwise destroy or damage any of the posts, wires, or other materials or fixtures employed in the construction and use in any line of an electrical telegraph, or shall willfully and maliciously interfere with such structure so erected, or in any way attempt to lead from its uses or make use of the electrical current, or any portion thereof, properly belonging to and in use, or in readiness to be made use of, for the purpose of communicating telegraphically from one station of a telegraph company to another established station of the same, or a connecting telegraph line; or shall unlawfully and maliciously break, injure, or otherwise destroy or damage any bridge, river, or meadow bank or mill-dam; or willfully and maliciously take down, injure, remove, or in any manner damage or destroy any flag, flag-staff, beacon, buoy, or other way or water marks which now are or hereafter may be put, erected, or placed, by lav authority, near or in any streams that are or may be decla public highways; or shall unlawfully and maliciously ( break, or otherwise destroy any lead, tin, copper, or iron sp affixed to any house or other building, public or private; shall unlawfully and maliciously daub, paint, or othern deface any dwelling-house, such offender shall be guilty o misdemeanor, and, upon conviction, be sentenced to pay a 1 not exceeding five hundred dollars, and undergo an impris ment not exceeding twelve months, or both, or either, at discretion of the court.

---

## A SUPPLEMENT TO AN ACT ENTITLED "AN ACT REI TIVE TO BONDS ISSUED BY THE COUNTY OF ALI GHENY, FOR STOCK IN RAILROAD COMPANIES," A PROVED THE THIRTIETH DAY OF APRIL, ANNO DOMI ONE THOUSAND EIGHT HUNDRED AND FIFTY-EIGHT

*Approved 2d April, 1860. (P. L., 1860, page 589.)*

SECTION I. That it shall and may be lawful for any executc administrators, guardians, and trustees holding bonds of 1 said county of Allegheny, such as are mentioned in the a to which this is a supplement, to exchange the same for sto in the several and respective railroad companies, in the ma ner mentioned in the said act, and to hold or dispose of t said stock so taken in exchange, without responsibility on th part for any loss which may be occasioned by any depreciati in the value of the said stock or the non-payment of any di dend by the said companies.

---

## AN ACT TO ENABLE CITIZENS TO HOLD TITLE WHIC HAD BEEN HELD BY ALIENS AND CORPORATIONS.

*Approved 9th January, 1861. (P. L., 1861, pages 2 and 3.)*

SECTION I. That whensoever any alien, or any foreign cc poration, or corporations of another State, or of this Stai shall have held title to real estate within this State, which 1 or they were not by the laws of this Commonwealth authorized to hold, and shall have heretofore conveyed such title to any citizen of the United States, before any inquisition shall have been taken against the real estate so held to escheat the same, such citizen shall hold, and may convey such title and real estate indefeasibly, as to any right of escheat in this Commonwealth, by reason of such real estate having been held by an alien, or corporation not authorized to hold the same, or to the extent in which it had been held.

---

## AN ACT CONCERNING THE SALE OF RAILROADS, CANALS, TURNPIKES, BRIDGES, AND PLANK ROADS.

*Approved 8th April, 1861.* (*P. L., 1861, pages 259 and 260.*)

SECTION I. That ·whenever any railroad, canal, turnpike, bridge, or plank road of any corporation created by or under any law of this State, shall be sold and conveyed under and by virtue of any process or decree of any court of this State, or of the circuit court of the United States, the person or persons for, or on whose account such railroad, canal, turnpike, or plank road may be purchased, shall be, and they are hereby constituted a body politic and corporate, and shall be vested with all the right, title, interest, property, possession, claim, and demand in law and equity, of, in, and to such railroad, canal, turnpike, bridge, or plank road, with its appurtenances, and with all the rights, powers, immunities, privileges, and franchises of the corporation as whose the same may have been so sold, and which may have been granted to or conferred thereupon by any act or acts of assembly whatsoever, in force at the time of such sale and conveyance, and subject to all the restrictions imposed upon such corporation by any such act or acts, except so far as the same are modified hereby; and the person for or on whose account any such railroad, canal, turnpike, bridge, or plank road may have been purchased, shall meet within thirty days after the conveyance thereof shall be delivered,— public notice of the time and place of such meeting having been given at least once a week for two weeks, in at least one newspaper published in the city or county in which such sale may

have been held,—and organize said new corporation, by electin
a president and board of six directors, (to continue in offic
until the first Monday of May succeeding such meeting, whe:
and annually thereafter, on the said day, a like election for
president and six directors shall be held, to serve for one yeaɪ
and shall adopt a corporate name and common seal, determir
the amount of capital stock thereof, and shall have power an
authority to make and issue certificates therefor to the pu:
chaser or purchasers aforesaid, to the amount of their respectiv
interests therein, in shares of fifty dollars each, and may theɪ
or at any time thereafter, create and issue preferred stock t
such an amount and on such terms as they may deem neceꞅ
sary, and from time to time to issue bonds, at a rate of intereꞅ
not exceeding seven per cent., to any amount not exceedin
their capital stock, and to secure the same by one or mor
mortgages upon the real and personal property and corporat
rights and franchises, or either or any part or parts thereof.

Sᴇᴄ. 2. That it shall be the duty of such new corporatioɪ
within one calender month after its organization, to make
certificate thereof, under its common seal, attested by the sig
nature of its president, specifying the date of such organizatioɪ
the name so adopted, the amount of capital stock, and th·
names of its president and directors, and transmit the saiꞇ
certificate to the secretary of State at Harrisburg, to be fileꞇ
in his office, and there remain of record; and a certified cop⁊
of such certificate so filed shall be evidence of the corporat·
existence of said new corporation.

---

### AN ACT SUPPLEMENTARY TO AN ACT, PASSED 14th APRIL 1834, ENTITLED "AN ACT RELATIVE TO SUITS BROUGH⁊ BY AND AGAINST CANAL AND RAILROAD COMPANIES.'

*Approved 17th April, 1861.* (*P. L., 1861, page 385.*)

Sᴇᴄᴛɪᴏɴ 1. That the act to which this is a supplement shaɪ
be and hereby is extended to all suits, actions, and proceeding:
instituted against any canal or railroad company, as well foɪ
the assessment of damages occasioned by construction of sucɪ
canals or railroads as for any other cause.

## AN ACT RELATING TO CERTAIN CORPORATIONS.

*Approved 23d April, 1861. (P. L., 1861, pages 410 and 411.)*

SECTION 1. That it shall and may be lawful for any railroad company created by and existing under the laws of this Commonwealth, from time to time to purchase and hold the stock and bonds, or either, of any other railroad company or companies chartered by or of which the road or roads is or are authorized to extend into this Commonwealth; and it shall be lawful for any railroad companies to enter into contracts for the use or lease of any other railroads, upon such terms as may be agreed upon with the company or companies owning the same, and to run, use, and operate such road or roads in accordance with such contract or lease: *Provided,* That the roads of the companies so contracting or leasing shall be directly, or by means of intervening railroads, connected with each other.

---

## AN ACT SUPPLEMENTARY TO AN ACT TO CONSOLIDATE, REVISE, AND AMEND THE PENAL LAWS OF THIS COMMONWEALTH, PASSED THE THIRTY-FIRST DAY OF MARCH, ANNO DOMINI ONE THOUSAND EIGHT HUNDRED AND SIXTY.

*Approved 1st May, 1861. (P. L., 1861, page 465.)*

SECTION 1. That whenever any person in the employ of any railroad company, whether such company is incorporated by this or any other State, shall fraudulently neglect to cancel or return to the proper officer, company, or agent, any coupon or other railroad ticket, with the intent to permit the same to be used in fraud or injury of any such company; or if any person shall steal or embezzle any such coupon or other railroad ticket, or shall fraudulently stamp or print or sign any such ticket, or shall fraudulently sell or put in circulation any such ticket, any person so offending, shall, upon conviction thereof, be sentenced to pay a fine not exceeding one thousand dollars, and to undergo an imprisonment, by separate or solitary confinement, at labor, not exceeding five years.

## A FURTHER SUPPLEMENT TO AN ACT IN REFERENCE TO RUNNING LOCOMOTIVE-ENGINES AND CARS ON CONNECTING RAILROADS, APPROVED 13th MARCH, 1847

*Approved 1st May, 1861. (P. L., 1861, page 485.)*

SECTION 1. That where any railroad company, incorporated under the provisions of the act of February 19th, 1849, entitled "An act regulating railroad companies," shall have leased their road to another company owning a connecting railroad in this State, as authorized by the supplement of March 29th 1859, to the act to which this is a further supplement, and when the terms of such lease shall specify that the road is to be kept in repair by the lessees, the said lessees shall enjoy the same rights and privileges, in regard to the repairs and maintenance of said road, as are conferred upon the company owning the same, by the tenth and eleventh sections of the said act of February 19th, 1849; and the said lessees shall also be entitled to the benefit of the penalties provided in the fifteenth section of said act, and may sue for and recover the same for their own use and advantage.

---

## AN ACT RELATING TO RAILROAD COMPANIES.

*Approved 16th May, 1861. (P. L., 1861, pages 702 to 704.)*

SECTION 1. That it shall be lawful for any railroad company chartered by this Commonwealth to merge its corporate rights powers, and privileges into any other railroad company, so chartered, connecting therewith, so that by virtue of this act such companies may be consolidated, and so that all the property, rights, franchises, and privileges then by law vested in such company so merged, may be transferred to and vested in the company into which such merger shall be made.

SEC. 2. That such consolidation and merger shall be made under the following conditions and restrictions, to wit:—

I. The directors or managers of each corporation may enter into a joint agreement, under the corporate seal of each company, for the consolidation of the said companies and of such merger, prescribing the terms and conditions thereof, and the manner of converting the capital stock of the said company so to be merged into the stock of the company into which such merger shall be made, and all other such provisions as they shall deem necessary to perfect the said consolidation and merger.

II. Said agreement shall be submitted to the stockholders of each of such companies, at a meeting thereof, called separately; of the time, place, and object of which meeting due notice shall be given by publication once a week for two successive weeks, before said meeting, in one newspaper published in each of the counties through or into which the railroads of said companies respectively shall or may be authorized to extend; and at said meeting the said agreement shall be considered, and a vote by ballot, in person or by proxy taken for the adoption or rejection of the same, each share entitling the holder thereof to one vote; and if a majority of all the votes cast at each of such meetings shall be in favor of said agreement, consolidation, and merger, then that fact shall be certified by the secretary of such company, and said certificate, together with a copy of the agreement, shall be filed in the office of the secretary of the Commonwealth; whereupon, the said agreement shall be deemed and taken to be the act of consolidation of said companies.

SEC. 3. That upon the filing of the said certificate and copy of agreement in the office of the secretary of the Commonwealth, the said merger shall be deemed to have taken place, and the said companies to be one corporation, possessing all the rights, privileges, and franchises theretofore vested in either of them; and all the property, real, personal, and mixed, and debts due, and rights of action, shall be deemed and taken to be transferred to and vested in the company into which such merger may have been made, without further act or deed; and all property, all rights of way, and all other interests shall be as effectually the property of such company or corporation into which such merger may have been made, as they were of either of the former corporations, parties to said agreement: *Provided*, That all rights of creditors, and all liens upon the property of either of said corporations, shall continue unimpaired, and the respective corporations may be deemed to

be in existence to preserve the same; and all debts, dutie:
and liabilities of either of said companies shall thenceforth
attach to the consolidated company, and may be enforce
against it to the same extent and by the same process as
said debts, duties, and liabilities had been contracted by it
*And provided further*, That in case of any differences or incon
sistencies of any nature, between the acts regulating sai
companies respectively, then the said consolidated compan
shall in all respects be regulated by the laws then governing an
applicable to that company into which such merger may hav
been made: *And provided further*, That a certified copy of th
said certificate and copy of agreement so to be filed in th
office of the secretary of the Commonwealth, shall be evidenc
of the lawful holding and action of such meeting and of th
consolidation of such companies and of the said merger: *An
provided further*, That if any stockholder or stockholders c
any railroad companies shall be dissatisfied with or object t
any such consolidation, then it shall and may be lawful fo
any such stockholder or stockholders, within thirty days afte
the execution of said agreement for consolidation, to appl
by petition to the court of common pleas of the county i
which the chief office of the said companies may respectivel
be held, to appoint three disinterested persons to estimat
and appraise the damage, if any, done to such stockholde
or stockholders by said proposed consolidation, and whos
award, or that of a majority of them, when confirmed b
the said court, shall be final and conclusive; and the person
so appointed shall also appraise the share or shares of sai
stockholders in the said company at the full market valu
thereof, without regard to any depreciation in consequenc
of the said proposed consolidation; and the said company ma}
at its election, either pay to the said holder the amount (
damages so found, or the value of the stock so ascertaine(
and upon payment of the value of the stock, as aforesaid, th
said stockholders shall transfer the stock so held by then
to said company, to be disposed of by the directors of sai
company, or retained by them for the benefit of the remainin
stockholders.

(Supplied but not repealed by act of 24th March, 1865.)

AN ACT TO ENCOURAGE THE DEVELOPMENT OF COAL
AND MINERAL LANDS IN THE COUNTIES OF HUNTING-
DON, CAMBRIA, AND BEDFORD.

*Approved 21st March, 1862.* (*P. L., 1862, pages 149 and 150.*)

SECTION 1. That in all cases where the owner or owners of
coal or mineral lands, situated in either of the counties of
Bedford, Cambria, or Huntingdon, has or have obtained, or
may hereafter obtain, the right to construct a lateral railroad,
under the act of assembly of 5th May, one thousand eight
hundred and thirty-two, relating to lateral railroads, and the
several supplements thereto, or may desire to construct such
lateral railroad from the line of the established railroad of any
incorporated company over his, her, or their own lands, it
shall and may be lawful for any incorporated company in this
Commonwealth to aid such owner or owners, whether an
individual, an association of individuals, or another incorporated company, by furnishing money, labor, and materials, or
either or all of them, for the construction of such lateral
railway, sidings, *et cetera*, not exceeding three miles in length.

SEC. 2. That it shall be lawful for any incorporated company
in this Commonwealth, which shall agree to aid any individual
or association of individuals, or other incorporated company,
in pursuance of the first section of this act, to take a mortgage
upon such lateral railroad, its sidings, turnouts, and appurtenances, and upon the real estate intended to be developed
thereby, or upon either or all of them, to secure all advances
of money, labor, and materials intended to be made, within
twelve months from the date of such mortgage, setting out
clearly in such mortgage the purpose and intent for which it
is given; and such mortgage shall be prior in lien to any
incumbrance that may be entered between the recording of
such mortgage and the expiration of twelve months from the
date of the mortgage.

SEC. 3. That within one month after the completion of
such lateral railroad, or at the expiration of twelve months
from the date of the mortgage, if such lateral railroad be not
then completed, it shall be the duty of the president of the
company mortgagee to have recorded in the office of the

recorder of deeds, and to file in the office of the prothonotary
of the court of common pleas of the proper county, statements
verified by his oath or affirmation, setting forth the advances
actually made, and the dates when made, of money, labor, or
materials, or either or all of them, intended to be secured by said
mortgage, which statements shall be indexed by the recorder
among mortgages, and by the prothonotary on the judgment
docket; and at any time after such statements shall be so recorded and filed, it shall be the right either of the mortgagee or
mortgagees, or any lien creditor of the mortgagor or mort-
gagors, upon application to the court of common pleas or any
judge thereof in vacation, with notice to the mortgagee, when
application is made by the mortgagor, and to the mortgagee and
mortgagor, when application is made by lien creditor, upon
cause shown, to have issued, by order of said judge or court,
a *scire facias*, upon such mortgage, to determine the amount
actually advanced by such mortgagee, whether the same be
then due and payable or not, which amount so ascertained shall
stand as the amount of incumbrance by virtue of said mortgage, upon the railroad or lands described therein, and may
be collected by due process of law, at such time or times as
the same may be due and payable by the terms and conditions
of said mortgage: *Provided*, That unless the statements
hereinbefore provided for be recorded and filed as hereinbefore directed, such mortgage shall lose its lien as against all
lien creditors or *bona fide* purchasers subsequent to the date of
such mortgage.

---

## AN ACT TO PROVIDE FOR THE DESTRUCTION AND TO PREVENT THE SPREAD OF CANADA THISTLES.

*Approved 22d March, 1862. (P. L., 1862, page 164.)*

SECTION 1. That from and after the passage of this act, it
shall be the duty of every person or persons, and of every
corporation holding lands in this Commonwealth, either by
lease or otherwise, on which any Canada thistles, or weed
commonly known as Canada thistle, may be growing, to cut
the same, so as to prevent such weeds or thistles from going

to seed, and the seed of the same from ripening; and any person or persons, or corporation as aforesaid, who shall or may have land as aforesaid, in the said counties, and who shall neglect or refuse to comply with the provisions of this act, shall forfeit and pay a fine of fifteen dollars, one-half to the county treasurer, and the other half to the use of the person suing for the same, who shall be a competent witness to prove the facts, to be recovered as other debts of the like amount, before any justice of the peace, or in any court of record in said county.

SEC. 2. That if any person or persons or corporation so holding land as aforesaid, on which Canada thistles, or the weeds commonly known as such, shall be growing and likely to ripen seed thereon, shall neglect or refuse to cut and destroy the same, so as to prevent the seed thereof from ripening, it shall and may be lawful for any person or persons who may consider themselves aggrieved, or about to be injured by such neglect or refusal, to give five days' notice in writing to such person or persons or corporation, to cut and destroy such weeds or thistles; and on their neglect or refusal to cut and destroy the same at the end of five days, it shall and may be lawful for any person or persons so aggrieved, or believing themselves about to be injured thereby, to enter upon or hire other persons to enter upon such premises, and cut down and destroy such Canada thistles; and the person or persons so employed shall be entitled to recover from such person or persons or corporation owning or holding such land, compensation at the rate of two dollars per day, to be sued for and recovered as debts of like amount, before any justice or court in said counties.

---

## A SUPPLEMENT TO A RESOLUTION TO PROTECT LABORERS AND CONTRACTORS. APPROVED JANUARY 21st, ANNO DOMINI 1843.

*Approved 4th April, 1862.* (*P. L., 1862, pages 235 and 236.*)

WHEREAS, It frequently happens that incorporated companies, by assignment, conveyance, mortgage, or other transfer, divest themselves of their real and personal estate, in contravention of the provisions of the resolution of January 21st, 1843 therefore,

SECTION 1. *Be it enacted*, That whenever any incorporated company, subject to the provisions of the above resolution shall divest themselves of their real or personal estate, contrary to the provisions of said resolution, it shall and may be lawful for any contractor, laborer, or workman employed in the construction or repair of the improvements of said company, having obtained judgment against the said company, to issue a *scire facias* upon said judgment, with notice to any person or to any incorporated company claiming to hold or own said real or personal estate, to be served in the same manner as a summons upon the defendant, if it can be found in the county, and upon the person or persons or incorporated company claiming to hold or own such real estate; and if the defendant cannot be found, then upon the return of one *nihil* and service as aforesaid, on the person or persons or company claiming to hold or own as aforesaid, the case to proceed as in other cases of *scire facias* on judgment against *terre tenants*.

---

## AN ACT FOR THE MORE EFFICIENT COLLECTION OF DEBTS DUE THE COMMONWEALTH.

*Approved 7th April, 1862.   (P. L., 1862, pages 304 and 305.)*

SECTION 1. That the several provisions of the twelfth section of the act of 16th April, 1845, entitled " An act to increase the revenues and diminish the legislative expenses of the Commonwealth," and of the fourth section of the act of the 21st April, 1846, entitled " A supplement to the law relating to defaulting public officers," are hereby extended to all suits by the Commonwealth against counties, corporations, and persons whatsoever ; and the said fourth section of the said act of the 21st April, 1846, shall be so construed as to require that the affidavit of defence shall set forth specifically the nature and character of the defence: *Provided*, That a county shall not be required to file an affidavit of defence.

AN ACT SUPPLEMENTARY TO AN ACT ENTITLED "AN ACT CONCERNING THE SALE OF RAILROADS, CANALS, BRIDGES, AND PLANK ROADS." APPROVED APRIL, A. D. 1861.

*Approved 11th April, 1862. (P. L., 1862, pages 450 and 451.)*

SECTION I. That in all cases in which any railroad, canal, bridge, or plank road may be sold in the manner contemplated by the act to which this is a supplement, and a debt or debts may be due to the Commonwealth from the company, as whose property such railroad, canal, bridge, or plank road may have been sold, the purchaser or purchasers of such roads, canal, or bridge shall not be entitled to the benefits and privileges conferred by said act, or any of them, until he or they shall have paid such debt or debts to the Commonwealth, or until the payment of the same, with interest, shall be secured by bond or bonds and first mortgage upon all the real and personal property, corporate rights and franchises, which shall pass to the said purchaser or purchasers by such sale.

---

AN ACT SUPPLEMENTARY TO AN ACT ENTITLED "AN ACT TO REQUIRE CORPORATIONS TO GIVE BAIL IN CERTAIN CASES, AND RELATIVE TO THE COMMENCEMENT OF SUITS AGAINST FOREIGN CORPORATIONS, &c., &c." APPROVED 15th MARCH, 1847.

*Approved 11th April, 1862. (P. L., 1862, pages 449 and 450.)*

SECTION I. That in all cases where any company has been incorporated by this Commonwealth, and the principal office for the transaction of business thereof shall be located out of this State, and where none of the officers upon whom process can be served, under the existing laws of the Commonwealth, reside in the State, it shall be lawful to sue said company, in any county in this State where the said company, at any time, transacted the business thereof, or where the works or real estate of such company were located; and such legal process may be served on such company, by publication of a copy of

the process in such newspaper as the court may direct, for s
weeks previous to the return day; and for every purpose
legal proceeding, such company shall be taken, both in la
and equity, to be located in this State, and shall be liable
writs of *quo warranto, mandamus*, attachment, and executio
and service of such process, by publication as aforesaid, sha
be, to all intents and purposes, as effective as if served up(
the president of such company, or other officer of the sam
and he or they resident of the proper county of this State, ai
as if the company's office were within the State; and ai
property, of any description, of such company, within the Stat
shall be liable to attachment and execution ; and any su(
property, which would be liable to attachment or executio
if the said office were located in this State, shall be taken
be in this State for such purpose, and shall be liable to lev
and sale, in the same manner as if the officers of said compai
resided in the county in this State in which the same is liab
to be sued by the provisions of this act.

---

## AN ACT GRANTING TO THE SUPREME COURT JURISDI TION OF A COURT OF CHANCERY IN ALL CASES C MORTGAGES, ET CETERA.

*Approved 11th April, 1862.* (*P. L., 1862, page 477.*)

SECTION I. That the Supreme Court of this Commonweal
shall have and exercise all the powers and jurisdiction of
court of chancery in all cases of mortgages given by corpor
tions.

---

## AN ACT TO PROTECT THE WAGES OF LABOR IN CEI TAIN COUNTIES OF THIS COMMONWEALTH.

*Approved 11th April, 1862.* (*P. L., 1862, pages 479, 480, and 481.*)

SECTION I. That in all assignments of property, whether re
or personal, which may hereafter be made by any person (
persons, firm, company, or association, whether chartered (

not, to trustees or assignees, on account of inability or pre-
tended inability, at the time of such assignment, to pay his,
her, their, or its debts, the wages and salaries of persons
employed by such person or persons, firm, company, or
association, shall be preferred and paid, by such assignees
or trustees, before any other creditors of such assignor or
assignors.

SEC. 2. That in case of the death of any person, resident
within this Commonwealth, the wages or salaries of any
person employed by him shall be first paid out of his estate,
before any other debts, except necessary funeral expenses, and
medicine and attendance furnished in the last sickness; and
in case of the dissolution of any firm, company, or association,
as aforesaid, or of the private sale or transfer, or determination
whatsoever, of the business of such firm, company, or association, the wages and salaries of persons employed by them
shall be a lien upon their property, and shall be first paid out
of the estate, effects, and assets of such firm or company.

SEC. 3. That in all cases of executions, landlords' warrants,
*venditioni exponas, levari facias*, and writs of a like nature,
hereafter to be issued, for the sale of real or personal property,
against any person or persons, firm, company, or association,
as aforesaid, it shall be the duty of the sheriff, or other officer
executing such writ, to give to the persons employed by the
defendant in said writ notice of the issuing thereof, by ten
written or printed handbills, put up in public places in the
neighborhood of the property to be sold, at least ten days
before the proposed sale, requiring them to make known to
him, before the sale of said property, the kind and amount of
their respective claims against such defendant; and such
claims, when so made known, shall be first paid out of the
proceeds of such sale, by the officer or court making distribution ; such claims being subject, however, to all legal objec-
tions which may be made as to the amount or existence
thereof.

SEC. 4. The claims for wages, or on account of salaries,
mentioned in the foregoing sections, shall be a lien on the
real estate of the person, firm, company, or association liable
to pay the same, prior and superior to all other liens upon

said real estate, except the lien of judgments and mortgag
given for the purchase-money of the property on which the
are liens, and the liens of judgments and mortgages enter
prior to the commencement of the work for which such wag
are due, and the liens of mechanics and material-men, fili
under the act of 16th June, 1836, and its supplements, ar
except as may be in the foregoing sections excepted: *Provide*
That the persons who may be entitled to demand the clain
intended to be preferred by the provisions of this act shall,
every case, first exhaust the proceeds of the personalty,
there be such, before resorting to the realty, and that no or
claim so preferred, or hereby made a lien, shall exceed tl
sum of one hundred dollars: *Provided further*, That the lie
provided for shall not continue beyond the period of si
months from the end of the time during which the work (
service was rendered, unless judgment for the amount di
shall, before that time, have been received, and a transcrij
thereof filed and docketed in the office of the prothonotary ·
the court of common pleas of the proper county.

SEC. 5. The provisions of the foregoing sections shall onl
apply to cases for the recovery of wages of labor done an
performed, within six months immediately preceding th
assignment, death, or levy by execution mentioned therein.

SEC. 6. In all cases in appeals, by defendants, from th
judgment of justices of the peace or award of arbitràtor
obtained in any suit brought or to be brought, for th
recovery of wages or salaries, by any miner, mechanic, la
borer, or clerk, against any person or persons or chartere
company, engaged in the mining of coal or manufacture (
iron, either as owner of the soil or having a lease of coa
mine or mines, furnace or rolling-mill, the said defendan
or his agent or attorney, shall, before any such appeal b
granted, declare, on oath or affirmation, in writing, that th
appeal is not for the purpose of delay, but that the judgmer
to be appealed from is unjust, and for more money than :
justly due.

SEC. 7. The provisions of this act shall extend only to th
counties of Schuylkill, Bedford, and Blair.

## AN ACT AUTHORIZING RAILROAD COMPANIES TO RE-LOCATE THEIR ROADS IN CERTAIN CASES.

*Approved 11th April, 1862.  (P. L., 1862, pages 497 and 498.)*

SECTION I. That whenever any portion or portions of any railroad, which has been or may hereafter be constructed by any railroad company, under the authority of this Commonwealth, shall be found to pass over or in proximity to any workable vein or veins of iron-ore, coal, or other mineral, so as to interfere with the ordinary method of mining the same, or with the safety of said road, then, and in every such case, it shall be lawful for such railroad company to relocate the said road, in such manner as·they may deem best; said relocation shall not exceed five hundred yards from their old location, so as to avoid the interference aforesaid; and for this purpose every such company shall have all the powers and authorities conferred, and be subject to all the liabilities imposed, by its charter of incorporation, as existing at the time such relocation is made: *Provided*, That all rights of such company, over the location so abandoned by them, shall cease from and after the relocation and occupation of the new route selected.

---

## AN ACT TO PREVENT ACTIONS AT LAW OR PROCEEDINGS IN EQUITY IN CERTAIN CASES.

*Approved 11th April, 1863.  (P. L., 1863, page 334.)*

SECTION I. That if it shall appear in any proceeding at law or equity, heretofore instituted and now pending, or hereafter instituted in any of the courts of this Commonwealth, by or in the name of any sequestrator, county, city, or borough, to recover or compel payment of any subscription or subscriptions, or part or parts thereof, made by any person or persons to the capital stock of any railroad company incorporated by the general assembly of this Commonwealth, subject to the provisions of the act entitled "An act regulating railroad companies," approved the nineteenth day of February, 1849, that before such proceeding was instituted the act incorporating such railroad company had been repealed, or the charter thereof revoked by an act of the general assembly of this Commor wealth, no judgment or decree shall be entered or mad against the person or persons aforesaid, but he or they sha have judgment, or an order for his or their reasonable an proper costs.

---

## AN ACT TO ENCOURAGE THE EXTENSION OF LATERA RAILROADS.

*Approved 22d April, 1863.* (*P. L., 1863, pages 532 and 533.*)

SECTION 1. That any railroad company heretofore or here after authorized to build any branch, lateral, or diverging lin of railroad, or extension of such railroad, may, to encourag the construction thereof, specially mortgage any such brancl lateral, or diverging line, the road-bed and other real estate ac quired, or to be acquired therefor, the income thereof and th franchise, so far as they are specially applicable thereto, an may issue plain or coupon bonds secured by such mortgag and may negotiate them on such terms, as to rate of interes and price and place of payment, as they may deem advisable *Provided*, That such mortgage shall not exceed fifteen thou sand dollars for each mile of road it covers, and that no bon for a less amount than one hundred dollars shall be issue under this act: *And provided further*, That every such mort gage shall be recorded in the county or counties in or througl which such branch, diverging, or lateral line is or shall b constructed: *And provided*, Such mortgage shall not operat against the lien of laborers and material-men, on work an labor done, and materials furnished in the construction o said road.

---

## AN ACT TO REGULATE RAILROAD GAUGES.

*Approved 22d April, 1863.* (*P. L., 1863, page 534.*)

SECTION 1. That the gauge of all railroads heretofore o hereafter authorized to connect with the Philadelphia and Eric Railroad, and on which the track is not now wholly or partl laid, shall conform to and be the same as the gauge of th said Philadelphia and Erie Railroad.

AN ACT AUTHORIZING NOTARIES PUBLIC IN THIS STATE, AND IN ANY STATE OR TERRITORY IN THE UNITED STATES, TO TAKE ACKNOWLEDGMENTS OF DEEDS AND LETTERS OF ATTORNEY, AND TO CONFIRM ACKNOWLEDGMENTS HERETOFORE MADE.

*Approved 22d April, 1863. (P. L., 1863, page 549.)*

SECTION 3. That where any deed of conveyance, mortgage, or other instrument of writing has been heretofore executed or acknowledged, or both, by any corporation, under any power sufficiently authorizing the same, and shall have been informally executed or acknowledged by any officer *de facto* of such corporation, or shall have been executed or acknowledged by the officers of such corporation, in the manner prescribed by law for the acknowledgment of deeds and mortgages by individuals, such deed, mortgage, or instrument shall be taken to be of the same validity and effect as if executed and acknowledged in the manner prescribed by law for the execution and acknowledgment of deeds, mortgages, and other instruments by corporations : *Provided*, That no case heretofore judicially decided shall be affected by this act.

---

AN ACT TO PREVENT FRAUDS UPON TRAVELERS.

*Approved 6th May, 1863. (P. L., 1863, pages 582 and 583.)*

WHEREAS, Numerous frauds have been practiced upon un-suspecting travelers, by means of the sale, by unauthorized persons, of railway and other tickets; and also upon railroads and other corporations, by the fraudulent use of tickets, in violation of the contract of their purchase; now, therefore, with the view of preventing and punishing such frauds—

SECTION 1. That it shall be the duty of the owner or owners of any railroad, steamboat, or other conveyance for the transportation of passengers, to provide each agent who may be authorized to sell tickets, or other certificates entitling the holder to travel upon any railroad, steamboat, or other public conveyance, with a certificate, setting forth the authority of such agent to make such sales; which certificate shall be duly attested by the corporate seal, if such there be, of the owner of such railroad, steamboat, or other public conveyance, and also by the signatures of the owner or officer whose name signed upon the tickets or coupons which such agents may se

SEC. 2. That it shall not be lawful for any person, not po sessed of such authority so evidenced, to sell, barter, or tran fer, for any consideration whatever, the whole or any part any ticket or tickets, passes, or other evidences of the holder title to travel on any railroad, steamboat, or other public co veyance, whether the same be situated, operated, or owne within or without the limits of this Commonwealth.

SEC. 3. That any person or persons violating the provisio of the second section of this act shall be deemed guilty misdemeanor, and shall be liable to be punished, by a fine n exceeding five hundred dollars, and by imprisonment not e: ceeding one year, or either or both, in the discretion of th court in which such person or persons shall be convicted.

SEC. 4. That it shall be the duty of every agent who sha be authorized to sell tickets or parts of tickets, or other ev dences of the holder's title to travel, to exhibit to any perso desiring to purchase a ticket, or to any officer of the law wh may request him, the certificate of his authority thus to sel and to keep said certificate posted in a conspicuous place i his office, for the information of travelers.

SEC. 5. That it shall be the duty of the owner or owners ( railroad, steamboat, and other public conveyances, to provid for the redemption of the whole or any parts or coupons ( any ticket or tickets, as they may have sold, as the purchase for any reason, has not used and does not desire to use, at rate which shall be equal to the difference between the pric paid for the whole ticket and the cost of a ticket between th points for which the proportion of said ticket was actuall used; and the sale, by any person, of the unused portion ( any ticket, otherwise than by the presentation of the same fo redemption, as provided for in this section, shall be deemed t be a violation of the provisions of this act, and shall be pun ished as is hereinbefore provided: *Provided*, That this act sha not prohibit any person who has purchased a ticket from an' agent, authorized by this act, with the *bona fide* intention o traveling upon the same, from selling any part of the same t any other person, if such person travels upon the same.

## AN ACT RELATING TO THE LIENS OF COMMON CARRIERS AND OTHERS.

*Approved 14th December, 1863. (P. L., 1864, pages 1127 and 1128.)*

SECTION 1. That in all cases in which commission merchants, factors, and all common carriers, or other persons shall have a lien under existing laws upon any goods, wares, merchandise, or other property, for or on account of the costs or expenses of carriage, storage, or labor bestowed on such goods, wares, merchandise, or other property, if the owner or consignee of the same shall fail or neglect or refuse to pay the amount of charges upon any such property, goods, wares, or merchandise, within sixty days after demand thereof, made personally upon such owner or consignee, then and in such case it shall and may be lawful for any such commission merchant, factor, common carrier, or other person having such lien, as aforesaid, after the expiration of said period of sixty days, to expose such goods, wares, merchandise, or other property to sale at public auction, and to sell the same, or so much thereof as shall be sufficient to discharge said lien, together with costs of sale and advertising: *Provided*, That notice of such sale, together with the name of the person or persons to whom such goods shall have been consigned, shall have been first published for three successive weeks in a newspaper published in the county, and by six written or printed handbills, put up in the most public and conspicuous places in the vicinity of the depot where the said goods may be.

SEC. 2. That upon the application of any of the persons or corporations having a lien upon goods, wares, merchandise, or other property, as mentioned in the first section of this act, verified by affidavit, to any of the judges of the courts of common pleas of this Commonwealth, setting forth that the places of residence of the owner and consignee of any such goods, wares, merchandise, or other property are unknown, or that such goods, wares, merchandise, or other property are of such perishable nature, or so damaged, or showing any other cause that shall render it impracticable to give the notice as

provided for in the first section of this act, then and in suc
case it shall and may be lawful for a judge of the city c
county in which the goods may be to make an order, to be b
him signed, authorizing the sale of such goods, wares, merchar
dise, or other property, upon such terms as to notice as th
nature of the case may admit of and to such judge shall seer
meet : *Provided*, That in cases of perishable property, th
affidavit and proceedings required by this section may be ha
before a justice of the peace.

SEC. 3. That the residue of moneys arising from any suc
sales, either under the first or second sections of this act, aft
deducting the amount of the lien, as aforesaid, together wit
costs of advertising and sales, shall be held subject to th
order of the owner or owners of such property.

SEC. 4. That an act of the general assembly, entitled "A
act in reference to liens of common carriers and others
approved the sixteenth day of March, Anno Domini or
thousand eight hundred and fifty-eight, be and the same
hereby repealed.

---

## AN ACT IN RELATION TO FEEDING STOCK WHIL
## AWAITING TRANSPORTATION ON RAILROADS.

*Approved 16th of December, 1863. (P. L., 1864, pages 1124 and 1125.)*

SECTION I. That it shall be lawful for drovers, owners,
shippers of horses, cattle, sheep, hogs, and other anima
upon the several railroads of this Commonwealth, and they
either of them, by themselves or their agents, shall have th
right at all seasonable hours to enter any of the stock
cattle yards of any of said companies, used in connection wi
said railroads, for the purpose of feeding and taking care
said animals while in said yards waiting transportation ; ar
when the cars have been designated by railroad companies
their agents to receive any of said animals for transportati
on said roads, it shall be lawful, and the said drovers, owne
or shippers of said animals, or their agents, shall have t
right to provide suitable and customary bedding for the ki

of animals to be transported, and place same in said cars before said animals are put into the same for transportation: *And provided*, That said bedding shall be of the usual and customary kind used for that purpose, and shall not increase the risk or hazard of said companies in the said transportation.

---

## AN ACT RELATING TO RAILROAD AND CANAL COMPANIES.

*Approved 11th April, 1864. (P. L., 1864, pages 393 and 394.)*

SECTION 1. That it shall and may be lawful for any canal company incorporated by this Commonwealth, to enter into any contract or contracts with any other canal or railroad company with reference to the traffic to be carried on their respective works, the proportion thereof, the rates to be paid therefor, and for paying a proportion of the expenses of operating any railroads, transporting freight, using either of the improvements; and all contracts heretofore made with respect to the matters aforesaid are validated and confirmed: *Provided, however*, That nothing herein contained shall authorize either of the parties to said contract to make higher or greater charges than are now allowed by law, nor to affect in any way the right of companies, individuals, and the public to use the respective works and to pursue, without interference, their lawful employments on the same respectively, under existing laws.

---

## A SUPPLEMENT TO THE ACT CONCERNING THE SALE OF RAILROADS, CANALS, TURNPIKES, BRIDGES, AND PLANK ROADS, APPROVED THE EIGHTH DAY OF APRIL, A. D. 1861.

*Approved 18th April, 1864. (P. L., 1864, page 452.)*

SECTION 1. That whenever any railroad, canal, turnpike, bridge, or plank road of any corporation created by or under any law of this State, shall be sold and conveyed by an assignee or trustee of the property of such corporation as

such, constituted for the use or benefit of all the creditor
thereof, such sale and conveyance shall confer the same privi
leges and impose the same duties and restrictions upon th(
person or persons for or on whose account the same may b(
purchased, and otherwise operate in all respects as is provide(
in the said act to which this is a supplement in regard to an;
sale or conveyance under or by virtue of any process or decre(
of any court.

---

## AN ACT RELATIVE TO RAILROADS USING STEAM IN THI CITY OF PHILADELPHIA.

*Approved 23d April, 1864.* (*P. L., 1864, page 550.*)

WHEREAS, The public safety and convenience require tha
the railroads using steam should, whenever it is reasonabl;
convenient, pass over or under the public highways; therefore
SECTION 1. That the tenth section of the act, approved th
twenty-first day of April, Anno Domini one thousand eigh
hundred and fifty-five, entitled " A supplement to the act con
solidating the city of Philadelphia," shall not apply to an;
railroad chartered, or which may hereafter be charterec
authorized by law to use steam as a motive-power, and shal
only apply to passenger railways using public streets laid ou
according to law.

---

## A SUPPLEMENT TO AN ACT ENTITLED "AN ACT RE LATING TO RAILROAD COMPANIES," PASSED MA' 16th, 1861.

*Approved 27th April, 1864.* (*P. L., 1864, pages 617 and 618.*)

SECTION 1. That whenever any merger or consolidatio
shall take place between two or more railroad companie
under and by virtue of the act of assembly to which this is
supplement, the company into which such merger shall tak
place shall have power and authority to make such increas
in its capital stock and shares as may be expedient in carryin

such merger or consolidation into effect: *Provided, however,*
That such increase shall not be more than the amount of the
capital stock and shares of the company or companies so
merged and consolidated.

---

## AN ACT TO PROVIDE ADDITIONAL REVENUE FOR THE USE OF THE COMMONWEALTH.

*Approved 25th of August, 1864.* (*P. L., 1864, pages 988 and 989.*)

SECTION 1. That the president, treasurer, cashier, or other
financial officer of every railroad company, steamboat company, canal company, and slack-water navigation company,
and all other companies now or hereafter doing business
within this State, and upon whose works freight may be
transported, whether by such company or by individuals, and
whether such company shall receive compensation for transportation, for transportation and toll, or shall receive tolls
only, except turnpike companies, plank road companies, and
bridge companies, shall, within thirty days after the first days
of January, April, July, and October of every year, make
return in writing to the auditor-general, under oath or affirmation, stating fully and particularly the number of tons of freight
carried over, through, or upon the works of said company for
the three months immediately preceding each of the above-
mentioned days; and each of said companies, except as aforesaid, shall, at the time of making such return, pay to the State
treasurer for the use of the Commonwealth, on each two
thousand pounds of freight so carried, tax at the following
rates, viz.:—*First*, on the product of mines, quarries, and clay
beds, in the condition in which said products may be taken
therefrom, two cents; *second*, on hewn timber, animal food,
including live stock, also on the product of the forest, vegetable and other agricultural products, the value of which has
not been increased by labor, three cents; *third*, on all other
articles, five cents. Where the same freight shall be carried
over and upon different but continuous lines, said freight shall
be chargeable with tax as if it had been carried but upon one
line, and the whole tax shall be paid by such one of said

companies as the State treasurer may select and notify thereo
Corporations whose lines of improvement are used by othei
for the transportation of freight, and whose only earning
arise from tolls charged for such use, are authorized to ad
the tax hereby imposed to said tolls, and collect the sam
therewith, but in no case shall tax be twice charged on th
same freight carried on or over the same line of improvi
ments: *Provided*, That every company now or hereafter inco:
porated by this Commonwealth, whose line extends into an
other State, and every corporation, company, or individual (
any other State, holding and enjoying any franchises, propert;
or privileges whatever in this State, by virtue of the law
thereof, shall make returns of freight and pay for the freig]
carried over, through, and upon that portion of their lin(
within this State as if the whole of their respective lines wei
in this State.

(Supplied but not repealed in direct terms by act of May I'
1868.)

---

## AN ACT EMPOWERING RAILROAD COMPANIES TO EMPLO
## POLICE FORCE.

*Approved 27th February, 1865. (P. L., 1865, pages 225 and 226.)*

SECTION I. That any corporation owning or using a railroa
in this State may apply to the governor to commission suc
persons as the said corporation may designate to act ;
policemen for said corporation.

SEC. 2. The governor, upon such application, may appoi:
such persons, or so many of them as he may deem proper, '
be such policemen, and shall issue to such person or perso1
so appointed a commission to act as such policemen.

SEC. 3. Every policeman so appointed shall, before enterir
upon the duties of his office, take and subscribe the oa
required by the eighth article of the Constitution, before tl
recorder of any county through which the railroad for whi(
such policeman is appointed shall be located; which oat
after being duly recorded by such recorder, shall be filed

the office of the secretary of State, and a certified copy of such oath, made by the recorder of the proper county, shall be recorded with the commission in every county through or into which the railroad for which such policeman is appointed may run, and in which it is intended the said policeman shall act; and such policemen so appointed shall severally possess and exercise all the powers of policemen of the city of Philadelphia, in the several counties in which they shall be so authorized to act as aforesaid; and the keepers of jails or lock-ups or station-houses, in any of said counties, are required to receive all persons arrested by such policemen for the commission of any offense against the laws of this Commonwealth upon or along said railroads or the premises of any such corporation, to be dealt with according to law.

SEC. 4. Such railroad police shall, when on duty, severally wear a metallic shield, with the words "railway police" and the name of the corporation for which appointed inscribed thereon, and said shield shall always be worn in plain view, except when employed as detectives.

SEC. 5. The compensation of such police shall be paid by the companies for which the policemen are respectively appointed, as may be agreed upon between them.

SEC. 6. Whenever any corporation shall no longer require the services of any policeman so appointed as aforesaid, they may file a notice to that effect, under their corporate seal, attested by their secretary, in the several offices where the commission of such policeman has been recorded, which shall be noted by the several recorders upon the margin of the record where such commission is recorded, and thereupon the power of such policeman shall cease and be determined.

---

## AN ACT TO PROMOTE THE SAFETY OF TRAVELERS ON RAILROADS, AND TO PUNISH NEGLIGENT AND CARELESS EMPLOYEES THEREOF.

*Approved 22d March, 1865. (P. L., 1865, pages 30 and 31.)*

SECTION 1. From and after the passage of this act, if any person or persons in the service or employ of a railroad or

other transportation company doing business in this Stat
shall refuse or neglect to obey any rule or regulation of sucl
company, or, by reason of negligence or willful misconducl
shall fail to observe any precaution or rule which it was hi
duty to obey and observe, and injury or death to any persoı
or persons shall thereby result, such person or persons s‹
offending shall be deemed guilty of a misdemeanor, and o;
conviction thereof shall be sentenced to pay a fine not exceed
ing five thousand dollars and to undergo an imprisonment i;
the county jail, or in the State penitentiary, not exceeding fiv
years : *Provided,* That nothing in this act shall be construe‹
to be a bar to a trial and conviction for any other or highe
offense, or to relieve such person or persons from liability i;
a civil action for such damages as may have been sustained.

Sec. 2. It shall be the duty of the prosecuting attorney c
the city or county where any such injuries may have happenec
as soon as he shall have notice of the same, to take immediat
action and legal measures for the apprehension and arrest c
the person or persons who may be charged with causing th
injuries as aforesaid, and to direct *subpœnas* to issue from anː
justice of the peace to witnesses, to appear and testify on th
part of the Commonwealth touching such offenses charged a
aforesaid, and to prosecute the offenders as in other cases c
misdemeanor : *And provided further,* That no conviction c
the employees shall relieve the company from any liability fo
any such injuries or death.

---

## AN ACT TO AUTHORIZE RAILROAD COMPANIES WHOSl LINES REACH NAVIGABLE STREAMS TO ERECT DOCKS PIERS, OR WHARVES THEREIN, AND TO TAKE PRIVATl PROPERTY FOR SUCH PUBLIC USE, ON COMPENSATION AND RATIFYING THE PURCHASE OF THE SAME.

*Approved 23d March, 1865.  (P. L., 1865, page 33.)*

Section 1. That it may be lawful for any railroad compan·
chartered by this Commonwealth, the line of whose roa‹
crosses or reaches any navigable streams, to erect in sucl

stream such docks, wharves, and piers as may by them be deemed needful for the accommodation of the public and the . business thereof; and for such purpose such companies may, from time to time, purchase or take and hold any lands, wharves, docks, or piers, giving security and making compensation to the owners thereof in the manner provided by the act entitled "An act regulating railroad companies," approved the nineteenth day of February, Anno Domini one thousand eight hundred and forty-nine, and all supplements thereto : *Provided always*, That the navigation of such rivers or streams shall not be impeded by the construction of such docks, piers, or wharves, and that the same shall not be constructed in the rivers Delaware or Schuylkill, at the city of Philadelphia without the license and authority of the board of wardens of the said city of Philadelphia, and in the way and manner now authorized by law ; and all purchases heretofore made by any railroad company for such purpose or purposes be and the same are hereby ratified and confirmed.

## A FURTHER SUPPLEMENT TO "AN ACT RELATING TO RAILROAD COMPANIES," PASSED MAY 16th, 1861.

*Approved 23d March, 1865.* (*P. L., 1865, pages 41 and 42.*)

SECTION 1. That in all cases of merger or consolidation of two or more railroad companies, under and by virtue of the act of assembly to which this is a further supplement, the company into which such merger shall heretofore have been or may be hereafter made, shall have the power and authority to issue bonds, with coupons for interest thereto attached, and to create a mortgage of all its property, real and personal, and also of all its rights, privileges, and franchises, to trustees, to secure the payment of the bonds so issued, and to give and exchange the said bonds for the debts of the respective companies so merged or consolidated : *Provided*, That the bonds so issued shall not exceed in amount the whole of the debts

of such companies so merged, and that said bonds shall n‹
bear a rate of interest of more than seven per centum p‹
annum.

SEC. 2. That the bonds so issued may be given in lie‹
exchange, and satisfaction of and for all bonds, mortgages, ‹
other debts or claims against the companies thus merged an
consolidated, upon such terms as may be agreed upon by an
between the holders of such debts or claims and the compan
into which such merger or consolidation has taken place.

## A SUPPLEMENT TO AN ACT RELATING TO FENCE‹ APPROVED APRIL 14th, 1851.

*Approved 23d March, 1865. (P. L., 1865, pages 42 and 43.)*

SECTION 1. That if any person or persons, from and afte
the passage of this act, shall maliciously or wantonly breal
or throw down any post and rail or other fence erected fo
the enclosure of land, or shall carry away, break, or destroy
any post, rail, or other material of which such fence wa
built, enclosing any lots or fields within the Commonwealth
such person or persons so offending shall be guilty of a mis
demeanor, and on conviction shall be sentenced to pay a fin‹
not exceeding fifty dollars, one-half thereof to be paid to th‹
informer, on conviction of the offender or offenders, the othe‹
half to the support of the poor of such county, township
borough, or ward where the offense has been committed
with costs of prosecution, or to undergo an imprisonment no‹
exceeding six months, or both or either, at the discretion o
the court.

SEC. 2. That all acts or parts of acts inconsistent herewith
are hereby repealed.

## A SUPPLEMENT TO THE GENERAL LAW RELATING TO RAILROAD COMPANIES, APPROVED 19th FEBRUARY, 1849.

*Approved 24th March, 1865. (P. L., 1865, page 43.)*

SECTION 1. That any company incorporated under any law of this Commonwealth, and having authority to construct a railroad or railroads within the same, under the provisions of the general railroad act of the 19th February, one thousand eight hundred and forty-nine, shall be and is hereby authorized, from time to time, to receive subscriptions for and issue such additional shares of capital stock as may be necessary to construct and fully equip, with suitable locomotive-engines and rolling stock, such railroad or railroads; the par value of which additional shares shall be the same as that of the then existing shares of said company, and the stock so issued shall stand, in all respects, upon the footing of the original stock thereof.

SEC. 2. That the number of directors to be elected by any railroad company incorporated by any law of this Commonwealth may be increased (if deemed expedient) to any number exceeding thirteen.

---

## AN ACT SUPPLEMENTARY TO AN ACT REGULATING RAILROAD COMPANIES, APPROVED THE NINETEENTH DAY OF FEBRUARY, A. D. 1849.

*Approved 24th March, 1865. (P. L., 1865, pages 49, 50, and 51.)*

SECTION 1. That it shall and may be lawful for any railroad company or corporation organized under the laws of this Commonwealth, and operating a railroad, either in whole within or partly within and partly without this State, under authority of this and any adjoining State, to merge and consolidate its capital stock, franchises, and property of any other railroad company or companies or corporations, organized and operated under the laws of this or any other State, whenever the two or more railroads of the companies or corporations

so to be consolidated shall or may form a continuous line
railroad with each other or by means of any intervenir
railroad: *Provided*, That railroads terminating on the banl
of any river, which are or may be connected by ferry (
otherwise, shall be deemed continuous under this act: *Ai
provided further*, That nothing in this act contained shall l
taken to authorize the consolidation of any company (
corporation of this Commonwealth with that of any othe
State whose laws shall not also authorize the like consolidatio

SEC. 2. Said consolidation shall be made under the col
ditions, provisions, restrictions, and with the powers hereafte
in this act mentioned and contained, that is to say—

*First.*—The directors of the several corporations proposin
to consolidate may enter into a joint agreement, under th
corporate seal of each company, for the consolidation of sai
companies and railroads, and prescribing the terms and cor
ditions thereof, the mode of carrying the same into effect, th
name of the new corporation, the number and names of th
directors and other officers thereof, and who shall be the firs
directors and officers, and their places of residence, the numbe
of shares of the capital stock, the amount or par value c
each share, and the manner of converting the capital stock c
each of the said companies into that of the new corporatior
and how and when directors and officers shall be chosen, witl
such other details as they shall deem necessary to perfect sucl
new organization and the consolidation of said companies o
railroads.

*Second.*—Said agreement shall be submitted to the stock
holders of each of the said companies or corporations, at ¿
meeting thereof, called separately, for the purpose of takin{
the same into consideration; due notice of the time and plac(
of holding such meeting, and the object thereof, shall b(
given by written or printed notices addressed to each of the
persons in whose names the capital stock of said companie:
stands on the books thereof, and delivered to such person:
respectively, or sent to them by mail, when their post-offic(
address is known to the company, and also by a genera'
notice published in some newspaper in the city, town, oi
county where such company has its principal office or place

of business; and at the said meeting of stockholders the agreement of the said directors shall be considered, and a vote by ballot taken for the adoption or rejection of the same, each share entitling the holder thereof to one vote; and said ballots shall be cast in person or by proxy; and if two-thirds of all the votes of all the stockholders shall be for the adoption of said agreement, then that fact shall be certified thereon by the secretary of the respective companies, under the seal thereof; and the agreement so adopted, or a certified copy thereof, shall be filed in the office of the secretary of the Commonwealth, and shall from thence be deemed and taken to be the agreement and act of consolidation of the said companies; and a copy of said agreement and act of consolidation, duly certified by the secretary of the Commonwealth, under the seal thereof, shall be evidence of the existence of said new corporation.

SEC. 3. Upon the making and perfecting the agreement and act of consolidation, as provided in the preceding section, and filing the same, or a copy, with the secretary of the Commonwealth, as aforesaid, the several corporations, parties thereto, shall be deemed and taken to be one corporation, by the name provided in said agreement and act, possessing within this Commonwealth all the rights, privileges, and franchises, and subject to all the restrictions, disabilities, and duties of each of such corporations so consolidated.

SEC. 4. Upon the consummation of said act of consolidation as aforesaid, all and singular the rights, privileges, and franchises of each of said corporations, parties to the same, and all the property, real, personal, and mixed, and all debts due on whatever account, as well as of stock subscriptions and other things in action, belonging to each of such corporations, shall be taken and deemed to be transferred to and vested in such new corporation, without further act or deed; and all property, all rights of way, and all and every other interest shall be as effectually the property of the new corporation as they were of the former corporations, parties by said agreement; and the title to real estate, either by deed or otherwise, under the laws of this Commonwealth, vested in either of such corporations, shall not be deemed to revert, or

be in any way impaired by reason of this act : *Provided,* Th
all rights of creditors and all liens upon the property of eith
of said corporations shall be preserved unimpaired, and tl
respective corporations may be deemed to continue in exis
ence to preserve the same ; and all debts, liabilities, and duti
of either of said companies shall thenceforth attach to sa
new corporation, and be enforced against it to the same exte
as if said debts, liabilities, and duties had been incurred
contracted by it.

SEC. 5. Such new company shall, as soon as convenie
after such consolidation, establish such offices as may t
desirable, one of which shall be at some point in this Con
monwealth, on the line of its road, and may change the sam
at pleasure, giving public notice thereof in some newspap
published on the line of said road.

SEC. 6. Suits may be brought and maintained against suc
new company in any of the courts of this Commonwealth fc
all causes of action, in the same manner as against other rai
road companies therein.

SEC. 7. That portion of the road of such consolidate
company in this Commonwealth, and all its real estate an
other property, shall be subject to like taxation, and assesse
in the same manner and with like effect as property of othe
railroad companies within this Commonwealth.

SEC. 8. Any stockholder of any company hereby authorize
to consolidate with any other, who shall refuse to convert hi
stock into the stock of the consolidated company, may, a
any time within thirty days after the adoption of the sai
agreement of consolidation by the stockholders, as in this ac
provided, apply, by petition, to the court of common pleas o
the county in which the chief office of said company may b
kept, or to a judge of said court in vacation, if no such cour
sits within said period, on reasonable notice to said company
to appoint three disinterested persons to estimate the damage
if any, done to such stockholder by said proposed consolida
tion, and whose award, or that of a majority of them, wher
confirmed by the said court, shall be final and conclusive, anc
the persons so appointed shall also appraise said stock o
such stockholder, at the full market value thereof, withou

regard to any depreciation or appreciation in consequence of the said consolidation, and the said company may, at its election, either pay to the said stockholder the amount of damages so found and awarded, if any, or the value of the stock so ascertained and determined, and upon the payment of the value of the stock, as aforesaid, the said stockholder shall transfer the stock so held by him to said company, to be disposed of by the directors of said company or be retained for the benefit of the remaining stockholders ; and in case the value of said stock, as aforesaid, is not so paid within thirty days from the filing of the said award and confirmation by said court and notice to said company, the damages so found and confirmed shall be a judgment against said company, and collected as other judgments in said court are by law recoverable.

(This act supplies but does repeal in direct terms the act of 16th May, 1861.)

---

## SUPPLEMENT TO AN ACT REGULATING LATERAL RAILROADS.

*Approved 18th April, 1865.  (P. L., 1865, page 64.)*

SECTION 1. That the act entitled "An act regulating lateral railroads," passed May fifth, one thousand eight hundred and thirty-two, and the several supplements thereto, shall be construed to authorize the construction of a single or double track railroad, with the necessary sidings, wharves, schutes, machinery, fixtures, and appurtenances, for the transfer and delivery of limestone, iron ore, coal, and other minerals from said lateral railroad on to any public or locomotive road, the damages to the owners of the land to be ascertained and paid in the same manner as under the general railroad law: *Provided*, That not any of said roads shall exceed five miles in length.

## AN ACT TO ENTITLE THE STOCKHOLDERS OF AN RAILROAD COMPANY INCORPORATED BY THIS COM MONWEALTH ACCEPTING THIS ACT TO ONE VOT FOR EACH SHARE OF STOCK.

*Approved 20th May, 1865.  (P. L., 1865, page 847.)*

SECTION 1. That at all general meetings or elections of th stockholders of any railroad company incorporated by th Commonwealth accepting this act and held after such accep ance, each share of stock shall entitle the holder thereof t one vote: *Provided,* That nothing herein contained shall affec stock held by municipal corporations, or any other provisior of the charter of such company, except such as relat exclusively to the number of votes to which the holders ( the shares of stock therein may be entitled.

## AN ACT RELATING TO THE USE OF TUNNELS ANI BRIDGES BY RAILROAD COMPANIES.

*Approved 21st June, 1865.  (P. L., 1865, pages 849 and 850.)*

WHEREAS, Railroad companies incorporated by or author ized to run within the State of Pennsylvania have erected an constructed, or may erect and construct, for the use of thei roads, bridges, and tunnels, and at an expense vastly beyon the proportionate cost of a like distance of any other portio of their lines;

AND WHEREAS, Other railroad companies have or may b authorized to connect their roads with and use the railroad of the company so constructing such tunnels or bridges;

AND WHEREAS, It is proper that the companies so usin should pay for such use a sum in some degree proportionat to the cost of such tunnel or bridge so used; therefore,

SECTION 1. That in each and every case in which any rail road company has been or is authorized to connect with an use the railroad of any other company, and in the exercise o such right shall use any bridge or tunnel constructed by an other railroad company, then, and in each and every sucl case, it shall be lawful for the company, the road, bridge, or tunnel of which it is so used, to charge a sum equal to one-half the interest, at the rate of seven per cent. per annum, upon the cost of the bridge, tunnel, and part of the road so used, and one-half of the cost of repairing, working, and maintaining the same: *Provided always*, That if the company so using the said roadway, bridge, or tunnel shall transport or have transported thereon a greater amount of freight and passengers than are transported thereon by the company owning the same, then and in such case it shall be lawful for the company so owning such roadway, bridge, or tunnel to require payment of such amount of interest at the rate aforesaid, and of the expenses of repairing, working, and maintaining the same, as shall be in proportion to the amount of business so done thereon by the company using the same: *And provided further*, That nothing herein contained shall be construed to affect the right of any company to enter into a contract with respect to such use, nor to affect any contract already made.

---

## AN ACT AUTHORIZING THE PURCHASE BY RAILROAD COMPANIES OF BRANCH OR CONNECTING ROADS.

*Approved 21st June, 1865. (P. L., 1865, page 852.)*

SECTION 1. That when any railroad shall be sold and conveyed by virtue of any mortgage or deed of trust, or under and by virtue of any process or decree of any court of this State, or of the Circuit Court of the United States, it may be lawful for any company of which the railroad connects therewith to purchase and pay for the same, to issue their own stock for such amount as the purchasers may deem the full and fair value thereof, and to hold and enjoy the railroad so purchased, with all the rights, privileges, and franchises, and with the same rights to charge for tolls, transportation, and car service, and subject to the same restrictions as were held, enjoyed, and limited by and in respect to the company of which the road may be so sold.

AN ACT RELATING TO THE ORGANIZATION AND MEET
INGS OF CERTAIN CORPORATIONS INCORPORATE
UNDER THE LAWS OF THIS COMMONWEALTH.

*Approved 27th November, 1865. (P. L., 1866, page 1228.)*

SECTION 1. That in all cases where any company has bee incorporated under the laws of this State, and a majority · the directors, corporators, or stockholders thereof are citizei of any other State, said corporation may be organized ar all the meetings of such corporators, directors, or stockholde held in such place, whether in this State or elsewhere, as suc majority may from time to time appoint: *Provided,' howeve* That the annual election for officers of such corporation sha be held in the State of Pennsylvania, at such time and plac and upon such notice by publication in the newspapers ( this State, as the by-laws of such corporation may from tim to time determine.

———

AN ACT RELATIVE TO DUTIES AND POWERS O
CONSTABLES AND RAILROAD CONDUCTORS IN TH
COUNTIES OF ERIE, CRAWFORD, LUZERNE, SUSQUE
HANNA, AND PIKE.

*Approved 12th March, 1866. (P. L., 1866, pages 182 and 183.)*

SECTION 2. It shall be the duty of the constables, and ( the several police constables, officers, or detectives, appointe by the proper authorities in the counties aforesaid, and the are hereby authorized and required to arrest any profession; thief, pickpocket, or burglar who may be found at any steam boat landing, railroad depot, church, banking institutioi broker's office, place of public amusement, auction-room, ( common thoroughfare, in the city of Erie, in Corry, in th county of Erie, and in Meadville or Titusville, in the count of Crawford, and carry them forthwith to the mayor of th city or burgess of the borough, or a police magistrate, t be appointed by the mayor, burgess, or city or town counc respectively; and if it shall be proven, to the satisfaction (

the mayor, burgess, or other police magistrate, by sufficient
testimony, that the person so arrested was attending or fre-
quenting such place or places for an unlawful purpose, he or
she shall be committed by the said mayor, burgess, or police
magistrate to the jail of the proper county, for a term not
exceeding ninety days, at hard labor, or, at his discretion,
require the person to give security for his or her good
behavior, for a period not exceeding one year, and require
the person to pay the costs incident to his or her arrest,
examination, and commitment.

SEC. 3. That the conductors on the several railroads, while
passing through either of the counties aforesaid, shall have
like power to arrest any one who may be found stealing or
picking the pockets of passengers or others, or committing
any breach of the peace on the cars, and detain him or her
till reaching any one of the places, Erie, Corry, Meadville, or
Titusville, and then deliver him or her to a constable or other
police authority, to be taken before one of the authorities
mentioned in the preceding section, to be dealt with in like
manner as is there provided for real or suspicious offenders;
and the several magistrates before named shall have power to
order the detention of the person or persons so arrested, for a
period not exceeding ten days, if it shall be deemed necessary
to obtain the requisite testimony of absent witnesses to establish
their guilt.

---

AN ACT SUPPLEMENTARY TO AN ACT PASSED THE
TWENTY-FIRST DAY OF FEBRUARY, ANNO DOMINI
ONE THOUSAND SEVEN HUNDRED AND SIXTY-SEVEN,
RELATIVE TO VAGRANTS.

*Approved 21st March, 1866. (P. L., 1866, pages 259 and 260.)*

SECTION 1. That if any person shall be found by any
constable, police officer, or detective, staying or loitering in
or around any steamboat landing, railroad depot, gambling or
drinking saloon, restaurant, banking-house, broker's office, or

any place of public amusement, crowded thoroughfare, o
other place of public resort, in any city or incorporate
borough within the counties of Erie, Crawford, Venango, an
Warren, having no apparent business, trade, or occupation
and without any visible avocation or means of subsistence, i
shall be the duty of said officer to arrest such person, an
take him or her, as soon as may be, before the mayor of an
city, the burgess of any borough, or any convenient magis
trate of the place where the arrest is made; and upon du
proof of the fact, by one or more witnesses or by confession
and upon the party arrested failing to furnish any reasonabl
or satisfactory account of his or her name, residence, character
or business at that place, he or she shall be deemed and take
to be a vagrant, and shall be subject to all the existing law
respecting vagrants now in force in this Commonwealth; an
the mayor of any city and the burgess of every borougl
within the said counties are hereby vested with full authorit
and jurisdiction to execute all the provisions of this act an
all existing laws relative to vagrants.

SEC. 2. That the burgess and town council of each of th
boroughs in said counties shall have power to appoint one o
more special policemen or detectives, whenever they shal
deem it necessary for the protection of their citizens o
strangers against the depredations of thieves, burglars, pick
pockets, gamblers, or other disorderly persons, and appropri
ate public funds of said boroughs or levy tax for payment o
the same, who, after being duly sworn to discharge the dutie
thereof, shall have and exercise all the powers of constable
in the execution of all process in criminal cases and under thi
act, and shall be entitled to the same fees and perquisites a
are now allowed to constables for similar services

SEC. 3. That on the application of any railroad compan
having depots or stations at any places not incorporated int
boroughs, or upon application of a respectable number of th
inhabitants of any borough, when the burgess and counci
have neglected or refused to make the appointment, it shal
be lawful for the courts of quarter sessions of the severa
counties named to appoint special policemen and detective
for such localities, who shall be sworn and give bail, i

required by the court, and shall hold their said offices one year, unless the appointment be sooner revoked by the court.

SEC. 4. That after the arrest of any such person as is hereinbefore described, and upon the oath or affirmation of the arresting officer or other person that he has reason to suspect and does suspect such person of being a gambler, burglar, thief, or pickpocket, it shall be lawful for the mayor, burgess, or justice before whom such person is brought, to direct the officer, in his presence, or that of some disinterested person named by him, to search the person, the baggage, and place of residence or resort of such suspected person, and return to the presiding magistrate everything he may find or take deemed confirmatory of such suspicion, and everything not so deemed shall be left with or returned to the owner; and if, upon said examination and search, such mayor, burgess, or other magistrate shall be satisfied such suspected person is a professional gambler, thief, pickpocket, or burglar, he shall have power so to render his judgment, and then to sentence such party to pay a fine of any sum not exceeding one hundred dollars and the costs of prosecution, and to undergo imprisonment in the county jail for any period not exceeding three months, or to require such party to enter into recognizance and give bail for his or her appearance at the next court of quarter sessions, in such sum as he may fix; and upon the failure of any such party to comply with said sentence or give the required recognizance and bail, to commit him or her to the jail of the county; of all of which doings the said magistrate shall keep a record, and transmit a certified copy of the same to the clerk of the quarter sessions at or before the next succeeding term.

SEC. 5. If any person shall feel him or herself aggrieved by the final adjudication of any mayor, burgess, or justice, under this act, he shall have the right to sue out a writ of *habeas corpus* before any judge of the county in which he shall be so arrested, and have a rehearing of his case, or by giving satisfactory security, in the usual form, shall have the right to have a writ of *certiorari* to remove the proceedings to the next court of quarter sessions for review, which shall suspend the further execution of the judgment or sentence until the case is heard and finally determined by the court.

SUPPLEMENT TO AN ACT ENTITLED "AN ACT REGU
LATING RAILROAD COMPANIES," APPROVED FEBRUARY
NINETEENTH, ANNO DOMINI ONE THOUSAND EIGHT
HUNDRED AND FORTY-NINE.

*Approved 17th April, 1866.* (*P. L., 1866, page 106.*)

SECTION 1. That no suit or action shall be brought against any
railroad company incorporated by the laws of this Common
wealth, for damages for right of way or use and occupancy
of any lands by said company for the use of their railroad
unless such suit or action shall be commenced within five
years after said lands shall have been entered upon for the
purpose of constructing said road, and within three years after
said road shall be in operation: *Provided*, That any person
who would be sooner barred by this act shall not be thereby
barred for two years from the date hereof.

---

## AN ACT RELATING TO RAILROADS.

*Approved 17th April, 1866.* (*P. L., 1866, page 106.*)

SECTION 1. That whenever any judge or judges of election
appointed in accordance with the provisions of the fifth section
of the general act regulating railroad companies, approved
February nineteenth, one thousand eight hundred and forty
nine, shall fail to attend the meeting of stockholders, and
whenever any board of directors shall neglect or refuse to
appoint such judges, then and in such case it shall be con-
sistent for the stockholders of any railroad company, at their
annual meeting, to supply any vacancy, or to select proper
persons to conduct the election for officers of the corporation
for the ensuing year.

---

## AN ACT COMPELLING RAILROAD AND OTHER CORPO-RATIONS TO PAY COUNSEL FEES OF PLAINTIFFS IN CERTAIN CASES.

*Approved 3d May, 1866.* (*P. L., 1866, page 116.*)

SECTION 1. That in all cases where railroad or other corporations, not municipal, shall be liable, either as principals

or guarantors, to pay the interest on bonds, the validity of which bonds shall have been established by a court of competent jurisdiction, and such corporations subject the holders of such bonds to the necessity of bringing suits to recover the said interest, the said corporation shall, in addition to the ordinary costs of suit, pay the fees of plaintiff's counsel, not exceeding ten per cent. on the amount recovered.

---

## AN ACT RELATING TO THE QUALIFICATIONS OF DIRECTORS OF RAILROAD COMPANIES.

*Approved 7th January, 1867.* (*P. L., 1867, page 1368.*)

SECTION 1. That from and after the passage of this act all citizens of the United States shall be eligible to election to the office of director of any railroad company chartered under the laws of this Commonwealth, although they may not be residents of the State of Pennsylvania: *Provided,* That they shall be stockholders of the company to be directors of which they may be so elected: *And provided further,* That a majority of the board of directors of every such railroad company shall be citizens of Pennsylvania.

---

## AN ACT TO EXTEND THE PROVISIONS OF THE ACT CONCERNING THE SALE OF RAILROADS, CANALS, TURNPIKES, BRIDGES, AND PLANK ROADS TO SALES MADE OR TO BE MADE UNDER OR BY VIRTUE OF A POWER OF SALE IN MORTGAGE OR DEED OF TRUST, WITHOUT JUDICIAL PROCESS OR DECREE.

*Approved 19th February, 1867.* (*P. L., 1867, page 28.*)

SECTION 1. That all the provisions of the act entitled "An act concerning the sale of railroads, canals, turnpikes, bridges, and plank roads," approved the eighth day of April, Anno

Domini one thousand eight hundred and sixty-one, sha
extend and apply to sales and conveyances heretofore (
hereafter made under or by virtue of a power of sale con
tained in any mortgage or deed of trust, without any pro
cess or decree of court in the premises; and the perso
or persons, for or on account of whom such railroad, cana
turnpike, bridge, or plank road shall have been or hereafte
may be purchased shall have and enjoy all the rights an
privileges granted and conferred by the said act upon th
person or persons purchasing under judicial process c
decree, as in said act mentioned.

---

## AN ACT MAKING IT AN OFFENSE FOR RAILROAD COR PORATIONS WITHIN THIS COMMONWEALTH TO MAKI ANY DISTINCTION WITH THEIR PASSENGERS ON AC COUNT OF RACE OR COLOR, AND PUNISHING SAII CORPORATIONS AND THEIR AGENTS AND EMPLOYEE: FOR THE COMMISSION OF SUCH OFFENSE.

*Approved 22d March, 1867.   (P. L., 1867, pages 38 and 39.)*

SECTION 1. That on and after the passage of this act an
railroad or railway corporation within this Commonwealtl
that shall exclude, or allow to be excluded by their agents
conductors, or employees, from any of their passenger cars, an
person or persons on account of color or race, or that shal
refuse to carry in any of their cars thus set apart any perso
or persons on account of color or race, or that shall for sucl
reason compel or attempt to compel any person or persons t
occupy any particular part of any of their cars set apart fo
the acommodation of people as passengers, shall be liable, in
an action of debt, to the person thereby injured or aggrieved
in the sum of five hundred dollars, the same to be recovered in
an action of debt as like amounts are now by law recoverable
SEC. 2. That any agent, conductor, or employee of any rail
road or railway corporation within this Commonwealth whc
shall exclude, allow to be excluded, or assist in the exclusion

from any of their cars set apart for the accommodation of passengers, any person or persons on account of color or race, or who shall refuse to carry such person or persons on account of color or race, or who shall throw any car or cars from the track, thereby preventing persons from riding, shall be deemed guilty of a misdemeanor, and, upon conviction thereof, shall pay a fine not exceeding five hundred dollars nor less than one hundred dollars, or be imprisoned for a term not exceeding three months nor less than thirty days, or both, at the discretion of the court.

---

## AN ACT DECLARATORY OF THE STATUTES OF LIMITATION.

*Approved 28th March, 1867. (P. L., 1867, pages 48 and 49.)*

WHEREAS, Doubts have been raised as to the proper construction of the statutes of limitation;

AND WHEREAS, It is just that suits for supposed claims should be speedily brought before the lapse of time destroys the evidence of defense or impairs the recollection of witnesses; therefore,

SECTION 1. That it is hereby declared to be the true intent and meaning of the statutes of limitation, that no suit at law or in equity shall be brought or maintained against any stockholder or director in any corporation or association to charge him with any claim for materials or moneys for which said corporation or association could be sued, or with any neglect of duty as such stockholder or director, except within six years after the delivery of the materials or merchandise, or the lending to or deposit of money with said corporation or association, or the commission of such act of negligence by such stockholder or director.

AN ACT TO AUTHORIZE THE PRESIDENT AND DIRECTOR
OF ANY RAILROAD COMPANY TO DETERMINE B
RESOLUTION THE MANNER IN WHICH AND TH
PERSONS TO WHOM THE INCREASED CAPITAL STOC
THEREOF MAY BE SOLD, AND THE AMOUNTS OF TH
INSTALLMENTS THEREON AND THE TIMES AND MAN
NER OF THEIR PAYMENT.

*Approved 10th April, 1867. (P. L., 1867, page 61.)*

SECTION 1. That in all cases where any railroad compan
is authorized to increase its capital stock, and such increas
has been or may be authorized by the stockholders, it sha
and may be lawful for the president and directors to determin
by resolution in what manner and by whom the same shall b
subscribed or to whom the same shall be issued or sold, an
the amounts of the several installments to be paid thereo
and the times and manner in which the same shall be paid.

———

AN ACT TO REGULATE THE CARRIAGE OF BAGGAG:
BY RAILROAD COMPANIES, AND TO PRESCRIBE TH]
DUTIES AND OBLIGATIONS OF CARRIERS AND PAS
SENGERS IN RELATION THERETO.

*Approved 11th April, 1867. (P. L., 1867, pages 69 and 70.)*

SECTION. 1. That each passenger upon a railroad shall hav
the right to have carried in the car or place provided for tha
purpose, in the train in which he or she may be a passengei
his or her personal clothing, not exceeding, inclusive of th
trunk or box in which it may be contained, one hundre
pounds in weight and three hundred dollars in value.

SEC 2. That no railroad company shall, under any circum
stances, be liable for loss or damage to any baggage or propert
belonging to any such passenger beyond the said sum c
three hundred dollars, unless it shall be proved that the exces
in value thereof over that sum was truly declared to the agent
of the company at the time of its delivery for transportatior
and the sum charged by the railroad company for such trans
portation over and above passage fare was paid: *Providec*

*however,* That the said declaration shall not relieve the claimant from proving the actual value of the articles alleged to have been lost or damaged; but in no event shall there be any recovery beyond the value thus declared.

SEC. 3. That no railroad company providing a car or other place for the deposit of passengers' baggage shall, under any circumstances, be liable for loss of or damage to any articles or property whatsoever not there deposited by the passenger, or which are placed by him or her in the car in which he or she is to be transported.

----

## A FURTHER SUPPLEMENT TO AN ACT ENTITLED "AN ACT REGULATING RAILROAD COMPANIES," APPROVED FEBRUARY 19th, ANNO DOMINI ONE THOUSAND EIGHT HUNDRED AND FORTY-NINE.

*Approved 15th April, 1867.   (P. L., 1867, page 84.)*

SECTION I. That the provisions of the first section of an act passed the seventeenth day of April, Anno Domini one thousand eight hundred and sixty-six, entitled "Supplement to an act entitled 'An act regulating railroad companies,' approved February nineteenth, Anno Domini one thousand eight hundred and forty-nine," shall not apply, or be deemed or taken to have applied, to any action or proceeding pending at the time of the passage of the said act of the seventeenth day of April, Anno Domini one thousand eight hundred and sixty-six, nor in any way to affect the parties to such action or proceeding.

----

## AN ACT IN RELATION TO TAXATION UPON THE STOCK-HOLDERS OF CORPORATIONS.

*Approved 3d January, 1868.   (P. L., 1868, page 1318.)*

SECTION I. That from and after the passage of this act the shares of stock held by any stockholder in any institution or company incorporated under the laws of this State, which in its corporate capacity is liable to and pays into the State

treasury the tax on capital stock imposed by the act approv‹
April twelfth, Anno Domini one thousand eight hundred a›
fifty-nine, entitled "An act to equalize taxation upon corp
rations," shall not be taxable in the hands of said stockhold
personally for State, county, or local purposes; and so mu‹
of the thirty-second section of the act approved April twent
ninth, Anno Domini one thousand eight hundred and forty-fo›
entitled "An act to reduce the State debt and incorporate tl
Pennsylvania Canal and Railroad Company," as imposes a t‹
for State or county purposes upon any stockholder in h
individual capacity as aforesaid, is hereby repealed: *Provide*
That this act shall not be construed to relieve said corporatio›
from any tax now imposed by law, or the real estate belongir
to said corporations from the State, county, or local tax ·
which they are now or may hereafter be subject.

— — — ——

## A SUPPLEMENT TO AN ACT ENTITLED " AN ACT RELA' ING TO CERTAIN CORPORATIONS," APPROVED MARC 13th, ANNO DOMINI ONE THOUSAND EIGHT HUNDRE AND FORTY-SEVEN, AUTHORIZING THE GOVERNOR T APPOINT DIRECTORS FOR CERTAIN CORPORATIONS I CERTAIN CASES.

*Approved 14th February, 1868.* (*P. L.*, *1868, page 40.*)

SECTION 1. That any company heretofore incorporated ar
organized under and subject to the act approved Februai
nineteenth, Anno Domini one thousand eight hundred ar
forty-nine, regulating railroad companies, shall likewise l
subject to the provisions of the act approved March 13t
Anno Domini one thousand eight hundred and forty-seve
entitled "An act relating to certain corporations," in lil
manner as if such company were a railroad or canal compan
except that all persons appointed by the governor shall ha‹
full power and authority to act in the premises without tl
approval or confirmation of the canal commissioners.

## AN ACT TO SECURE FARMERS AGAINST LOSSES CAUSED BY RAILROADS IN ERIE COUNTY.

*Approved 23d March, 1868.  (P. L., 1868, pages 424 and 425.)*

SECTION 1. That it shall be the duty of each company owning or operating a railroad in the county of Erie, to erect, where not already erected, and to keep and maintain on each side of the track or tracks of said road, at all places in said county, except where said road or roads pass through a village, borough, or city, or a public road crosses the same, a suitable fence five feet high, to prevent cattle, sheep, and swine from going upon said tracks; and in case any company referred to in this act shall neglect to perform the duty herein imposed, the company so offending shall be answerable to the owner or owners of any horses, cattle, sheep, or swine, the value of the property injured upon said roads in consequence of such neglect; said company or companies shall further be liable to the penalty of fifty dollars for each place along said roads in said county where the fence or fences required by this act to be built, kept, and maintained are destroyed or broken down and permitted so to remain for a period of three days; the penalty herein imposed to be recovered one-half to the use of the informer and the other half for the use of the school districts of the township in which said offense or offenses shall be committed.

SEC. 2. All damages and penalties in this act to be sued for and recovered as debts of like amount are now by law made recoverable: *Provided,* That this act shall not go into effect until the first day of July, Anno Domini one thousand eight hundred and sixty-eight.

AN ACT TO EXEMPT THE COUNTY OF ALLEGHENY FRO:
THE PROVISIONS OF AN ACT ENTITLED "AN ACT COM
PELLING RAILROAD AND OTHER CORPORATIONS T
PAY COUNSEL FEES OF PLAINTIFFS IN CERTAI
CASES," APPROVED THE THIRD DAY OF MAY, ANN
DOMINI ONE THOUSAND EIGHT HUNDRED AND SIXT\
SIX.

*Approved 25th March, 1868. (P. L., 1868, page 470.)*

SECTION 1. That the county of Allegheny shall be an
hereby is exempted from the provisions and operations of tt
act of assembly entitled "An act compelling railroad ar
other corporations to pay counsel fees of plaintiffs in certa
cases," approved the third day of May, Anno Domini or
thousand eight hundred and sixty-six, and that the sai
county of Allegheny shall not be subject to the provisions
said act, directly or indirectly.

AN ACT FOR THE PROTECTION OF FARMERS AN
OWNERS OF CATTLE, HORSES, SHEEP, AND SWIN
ALONG THE LINE OF RAILROADS IN THE COUNTY O
WARREN.

*Approved 28th March, 1868. (P. L., 1868, page 514.)*

SECTION 1. That for the protection of farmers and ownei
of cattle, horses, sheep, and swine, residing along the line
any railroad now constructed or that may hereafter be cor
structed in the county of Warren, all railroad companie:
when railroads are completed, and on which they are no'
running trains in said county, shall, before the first day
September, one thousand eight hundred and sixty-eight, cor
struct and keep in repair a good and sufficient fence, at lea:
four feet high, along their track, except through incorporate
boroughs; and also construct sufficient cattle-guards at a
road crossings, sufficient to prevent orderly cattle, horse:
sheep, and swine from straying upon any railroad track i
said county; and all railroads that may hereafter be con
structed in said county are hereby required to construct suc
fences and cattle-guards before running trains thereon.

SEC. 2. If any railroad company in said county shall neglect or refuse to comply with the first section of this act, then any person, after giving the president, any director, the superintendent, or chief clerk, fifteen days' notice, may, if said railroad company continue to neglect and refuse to build the fences and cattle-guards as by this act required, build the said fence and cattle-guards, or any portion of the same; and any person so building any fence or cattle-guards in said county, which by this act such railroad companies are required to build, may sue and recover the cost of making such fence or cattle-guards off any railroad company neglecting and refusing to comply with the provisions of this act, together with ten per centum additional to the actual cost of building such fence and cattle-guard, to be sued and recovered in said county of Warren in the same manner as debts of like amount are now recoverable.

---

## AN ACT TO AUTHORIZE INCORPORATED COMPANIES TO INVEST AND REINVEST SURPLUS FUNDS IN MORTGAGES, STOCKS, AND OTHER SECURITIES, AND FIXING THE TIME FOR HOLDING ELECTIONS FOR DIRECTORS.

*Approved 31st March, 1868.* (*P. L., 1868, pages 50 and 51.*)

SECTION 1. That it shall and may be lawful for any and all companies incorporated or organized under the laws of this Commonwealth, including those authorized thereby, to transport merchandise or other property, and also for the directors, managers, or trustees thereof, with the approval of the stockholders, to invest the surplus or other funds or earnings of such companies in mortgages on improved real estate, in ground-rents, in the loans of the United States, in the purchase from holders thereof [of] any of the shares of the capital stock of the respective company, and also in the public debt of the State of Pennsylvania or of the city of Philadelphia, or in other good stocks or securities, and to sell and transfer the same, and to reinvest the proceeds of such sales in securities or stocks of like kind, and to prescribe, by resolution of the

directors or by the by-laws of the company or otherwise, th
mode of making such investments, purchases, and sales, wit
the approval of the stockholders, and the amount or amount
thereof to be purchased, and the price or prices to be paid c
received therefor, and the reinvestment of the proceeds there
of, and to make such compensation as the said director
managers, or trustees may deem proper to any directo
manager, trustee, treasurer, or other agent or officer of suc
company, for the keeping, receiving, paying, investing, c
reinvesting of any of the moneys belonging to the said con
pany, or for any other services performed by him or ther
as agents of the company or otherwise; and that any suc
companies may change and fix the time of holding the:
annual election for directors to such a day as they may selec
a certificate of such change, duly authenticated by the prope
officers of the company, .shall be filed with the auditor
general of this Commonwealth within thirty days after suc
change shall have been made.

---

## AN ACT RELATING TO THE CONSOLIDATION OF RAIL ROAD COMPANIES.

*Approved 2d April, 1868. (P. L., 1868, page 53.)*

SECTION 1. That whenever any merger or consolidation c
two or more railroad companies shall have taken place c
been made, by virtue of any act of assembly of this Commor
wealth, prior to the sixteenth day of May, one thousand eigh
hundred and sixty-one, the company into which such merge
shall have taken place shall have all the powers and authori
ties, and be subject to all the duties and liabilities conferre·
upon railroad companies into which such merger shall hav
been made, under and by virtue of the act passed May six
teenth, one thousand eight hundred and sixty-one, entitle·
"An act relating to railroad companies," and the severa
supplements thereto, regulating the conditions and restriction
upon which such consolidation and merger shall be made.

AN ACT RELATING TO RAILROAD COMPANIES AND COM-
MON CARRIERS, DEFINING THEIR LIABILITIES, AND
AUTHORIZING THEM TO PROVIDE MEANS OF INDEM-
NITY AGAINST LOSS OF LIFE AND PERSONAL INJURY.

*Approved 4th April, 1868.* (*P. L., 1868, pages 58 and 59.*)

SECTION I. That when any person shall sustain personal injury or loss of life while lawfully engaged or employed on or about the roads, works, depots and premises of a railroad company, or in or about any train or car therein or thereon, of which company such person is not an employee, the right of action and recovery in all such cases against the company shall be such only as would exist if such person were an employee : *Provided,* That this section shall not apply to passengers.

SEC. 2. That in all actions now or hereafter instituted against common carriers, or corporations owning, operating, or using a railroad as a public highway, whereon steam or other motive-power is used, to recover for loss and damage sustained and arising either from personal injuries or loss of life, and for which, by law, such carrier or corporation could be held responsible, only such compensation for loss and damage shall be recovered as the evidence shall clearly prove to have been pecuniarily suffered or sustained, not exceeding, in case of personal injury, the sum of three thousand dollars, nor in case of loss of life, the sum of five thousand dollars.

SEC. 3. That it shall be lawful for such carrier or corporation to insure the lives and persons of passengers against loss or injury from accidental causes, and however happening, while in their charge, and for that purpose to issue and sell, to such passengers applying for the same, tickets or policies of insurance, specifying the name of the insured, the premium charged, the particular trip or time covered by the policy, and the amount insured, not exceeding (except at the option of the said carrier or corporation) the sum of twenty-five dollars for each week of disability for a period not longer than twenty-six weeks in case of personal injury, nor more than ten thousand dollars in case of death; and all premiums so received shall be kept separate and apart from the other

receipts of said carrier or corporation, and shall not be liable
for any other claim, debt, or demands against such carrier or
corporation than those arising out of said policies; and the
amount of said premium, and the securities in which the same
are invested for the benefit and protection of such policy-
holders, shall be reported to the auditor-general annually, as
a part of the operations of such carrier or corporation, as is
now provided for by the act entitled " An act requiring railroad companies to make uniform reports to the auditor-
general," approved the fourth day of April, one thousand
eight hundred and fifty-nine: *Provided, nevertheless*, That it
shall be lawful for any such carrier or corporation, in lieu
of issuing tickets of insurance as aforesaid, to keep on sale at
their ticket office the policies of insurance or indemnity
against personal injury or death resulting from accidental
causes issued by insurance companies incorporated for any
such purposes as shall have an actual *bona fide* cash capital,
invested in securities approved by the governor, State treasurer, and auditor-general of this Commonwealth, of at least
two hundred thousand dollars: *Provided*, That a recovery
upon any policy issued or sold under the provisions of this
act shall be no bar to a recovery under the provisions of the
second section of this act.

Sec. 4. That all acts or parts of acts inconsistent herewith
be and the same are hereby repealed; and any provisions in
the acts incorporating such common carriers or corporations
inconsistent herewith shall be repealed upon the acceptance
of the provisions of this act by such carriers or corporations ;
and upon the acceptance of the provisions hereof by any
carrier or corporation, the same shall become a part of its act
of incorporation.

---

### AN ACT TO AUTHORIZE THE FORMATION AND REGU-
### LATION OF RAILROAD CORPORATIONS.

*Approved 4th April, 1868. (P. L., 1868, pages 62 and 65.)*

Section 1. That any number of citizens of Pennsylvania,
not less than nine, may form a company for the purpose of

constructing, maintaining, and operating a railroad for public use in the conveyance of persons and property, or for the purpose of maintaining and operating any unincorporated railroad already constructed for like public use, and for that purpose may make and sign articles of association, in which shall be stated the name of the company, the number of years the same is to continue, the places from and to which the road is to be constructed or maintained and operated, the length of such road as near as may be, and the name of each county in the State through or into which it is made or intended to be made, the amount of the capital stock of the company, which shall not be less than ten thousand dollars for every mile of road constructed or proposed to be constructed, and the number of shares of which said capital stock shall consist, and the name and places of residence of a president, and not less than six nor more than twelve directors of the company, who shall manage its affairs for the first year and until others are chosen in their places; each subscriber to such articles of association shall subscribe thereto his name, place of residence, and the number of shares of stock he agrees to take in said company; on compliance with the provisions of the second section of this supplement, such articles of association shall be acknowledged by at least three of the directors before some officer competent to take acknowledgments of deeds in the county where the principal office is designed to be located, and may be filed in the office of the secretary of the Commonwealth, who shall endorse thereon the day on which they were filed, and record the same in a book to be provided by him for that purpose; and thereupon the said articles of association shall become and be a charter for the said company, and the persons who have so subscribed such articles of association, and all persons who shall become stockholders in such company, shall be a corporation by the name specified in such articles of association or charter, and shall possess the powers and privileges following, to wit:—

*First.*—To have succession by its corporate name for the period limited in its articles of association.

*Second.*—To sue and be sued, complain and defend, in any court of law or equity.

*Third.*—To make and use a common seal and alter the same at pleasure.

*Fourth.*—To hold, purchase, and convey such real and personal estate as the purposes of the corporation shall require, not exceeding the amount limited in the articles of association.

*Fifth.*—To appoint such subordinate officers and agents as the business of the corporation shall require, and to allow them a suitable compensation.

*Sixth.*—To make by-laws, not inconsistent with any existing law, for the management of its property and regulation of its affairs and for the transfer of its stock.

SEC. 2. Such articles of association shall not be filed and recorded in the office of the secretary of the Commonwealth until at least nine thousand dollars of stock for every mile of railroad proposed to be made is subscribed thereto, and ten per centum paid thereon, in good faith and in cash, to the directors named in said articles of association, nor until there is endorsed thereon, or annexed thereto, an affidavit, made by at least three of the directors named in said articles, that the amount of stock required by this section has been in good faith subscribed, and ten per centum paid in cash thereon as aforesaid, and that it is intended in good faith to construct or to maintain and operate the road mentioned in such articles of association; which affidavit shall be recorded with the articles of association as aforesaid.

SEC. 3. A copy of any article of association filed and recorded in pursuance of this act, or of the record thereof, with a copy of the affidavit aforesaid endorsed thereon or annexed thereto, and certified to be a copy by the secretary of the Commonwealth or his deputy, shall be evidence of the incorporation of such company and of the facts therein stated.

SEC. 4. When such articles of association and affidavit are filed and recorded in the office of the secretary of the Commonwealth, the directors named in said articles of association shall, in case the whole of the capital stock is not before subscribed, keep open books of subscription at their general office, and at such other places as they may deem expedient, to fill up the capital stock of the company, giving such notice as they may deem expedient, and shall continue to receive subscriptions until the whole capital stock is subscribed; at the time of subscribing, every subscriber shall pay to the directors ten per centum of the amount subscribed by him in money, and no subscription shall be received or taken without such payment.

SEC. 5. Whenever the foregoing provisions have been complied with, the persons named as corporators in such articles of association are fully authorized to carry into effect the objects named therein, as fully as any corporation heretofore created under any special act of the legislature, and said corporation thus created shall be entitled to exercise all the rights, powers, and privileges, and be subject to all the restrictions and liabilities of the act regulating railway companies, approved the nineteenth day of February, one thousand eight hundred and forty-nine, and the several supplements thereto, as fully and effectually as if said powers were specially incorporated in said charter; and the said company shall commence the proposed railroad, if not more than fifty miles in length, with at least one track, within two years from their organization as aforesaid, and prosecute the work on the same with due diligence, and complete and open the same within five years, and shall have an additional six months to complete their road for each twenty-five miles more than the fifty miles aforesaid: *Provided*, That the road shall be opened for use, in all cases, when fifty miles in length of track are laid.

SEC. 6. Whenever any railroad company created or incorporated under the provisions of this act shall, in the opinion of the directors thereof, require an increased amount of capital stock in order to complete and equip their road and carry out the full intent and meaning of their charter, they shall, if authorized by a majority of the stockholders, at a meeting called for that purpose, file with the secretary of the Commonwealth a certificate setting forth the amount of such desired increase, and thereafter such company shall be entitled to have such increased capital as is fixed by such certificate: *Provided*, That the original amount of stock and increased capital shall in no case exceed the sum of sixty thousand dollars per mile.

Sec. 7. The number of managers of any company incorporated in pursuance of this act shall be a president, and not less than six nor more than twelve directors, as shall be fixed by the corporators thereof at their first meeting to choose directors of said company, a majority of whom shall be citizens of this Commonwealth.

Sec. 8. The president and directors of any railroad company created under this act shall have power to borrow money, not exceeding the amount of capital stock subscribed, and issue the bonds of the company therefor, in such amounts as shall not exceed double the amount actually paid up of the capital stock subscribed, the proceeds whereof shall be actually expended in the construction and equipment of their road; these bonds to be payable at such time, not exceeding fifty years after the date thereof, and at such place and at such rate of interest, not exceeding seven per centum, as said directors may deem best, and may secure the payment of said bonds and interest by a mortgage on the said road and franchises.

Sec. 9. Any company incorporated under this act shall have authority to construct such branches from its main line as it may deem necessary to increase its business and accommodate the trade and travel of the public.

Sec. 10. Companies formed under the provisions of this act shall have the right to construct roads so as to cross at grade the track or tracks of any other railroad in this Commonwealth: *Provided, however,* That the cost of making and keeping such crossing in repair shall be borne by the company whose road crosses the track or tracks of another: *And provided further,* That the company whose road crosses the track or tracks of another shall keep at such crossing as many persons as may be requisite to give the necessary signals to prevent accidents.

Sec. 11. Companies whose roads shall be constructed under the provisions of this act shall have the right to connect their roads with roads of a similar character within this Commonwealth, or at the line thereof, upon such terms as may be agreed upon by those who have the management of said roads; and in case of failure of an agreement on the part of those having the management of said roads, then and in that case either of said parties may apply to the court of common pleas within the jurisdiction in which said connection is proposed to be made, whose duty it shall be to appoint a jury of three disinterested men, who shall determine and fix said terms, which, when approved by said court, shall be conclusive.

SEC. 12. This act shall not be so construed as to authorize the formation of street passenger railway companies to construct passenger railways, under or by virtue of its provisions, in any city or borough of this Commonwealth, nor to authorize any corporation formed under this act to enter upon and occupy any street, lane, or alley in any incorporated city in this Commonwealth, without the consent of such city having been first obtained.

SEC. 13. All acts or parts of acts inconsistent herewith are hereby repealed, so far as they may affect any corporation that may be organized under this act; and the legislature hereby reserves the right to alter, amend, or repeal this act at any time, in such manner, however, as to do no injustice to corporators.

---

## AN ACT TO SECURE FARMERS AND OTHERS AGAINST LOSSES OF HORSES, CATTLE, SHEEP, AND SWINE BY RAILROADS IN THE COUNTY OF CENTRE.

*Approved 9th April, 1868.  (P. L., 1868, pages 779 and 780.)*

SECTION 1. That it shall be the duty of each company owning or operating a railroad in the county of Centre, to erect, where not already erected, and to keep and maintain on each side of the track or tracks of said road, at all places in said county, except where said road or roads passes or pass through a village, borough, or city, or a public road crosses the same, a suitable fence, five feet high, and to build, erect, and maintain such suitable cattle-guard or guards, at all crossings on said railroad, as will prevent horses, cattle, sheep, and swine from going upon said tracks; and in case any company owning or operating said road or roads shall refuse or neglect to perform the duties herein imposed, the company or companies so offending shall be answerable to the owner or owners of any horses, cattle, sheep, or swine to the full value of the property injured upon said road or roads in consequence of such neglect. Said company or companies shall be further liable to the penalty of fifty dollars for each place along said road or roads in said county where the fence or fences required by this act to be built, erected, kept, and maintained are destroyed or broken down and permitted so to remain for a period of ten days; the penalty herein imposed to be recovered one-half to the use of the informer and the other half for the use of the public schools of said county of Centre.

Sec. 2. All damages and penalties in this act to be sued for and recovered as debts of like amount are now by law made recoverable: *Provided*, That this act shall not go into effect until the first day of August, Anno Domini one thousand eight hundred and sixty-eight.

---

## AN ACT RELATIVE TO INCORPORATED COMPANIES.

*Approved 10th April, 1868. (P. L., 1868, pages 80 and 81.)*

Section 1. That it may be lawful, from and after the passage of this act, for any corporation chartered or existing by the laws of this State to determine by the vote of its stockholders, at a meeting duly called for that purpose, the number of directors that shall thereafter govern their affairs: *Provided always*, That said number shall in no event exceed fifteen nor less than five directors: *And provided further*, That a majority of said directors and officers shall be and remain residents of the State of Pennsylvania during the discharge of their duties: *And provided further*, This act shall in no way be construed as interfering with or impairing any of the obligations of the corporation accepting its provisions due or to become due to this Commonwealth.

A SUPPLEMENT TO AN ACT ENTITLED "AN ACT TO
SECURE FARMERS AGAINST LOSSES CAUSED BY RAIL-
ROADS IN ERIE COUNTY," APPROVED ON THE TWENTY-
THIRD DAY OF MARCH, ANNO DOMINI ONE THOUSAND
EIGHT HUNDRED AND SIXTY-EIGHT, EXEMPTING CER-
TAIN LANDS FROM ITS OPERATIONS, AND TO PROVIDE
FOR CASES WHERE FARMERS MAY BE HARMED BY
SAID RAILROAD COMPANIES.

*Approved 13th April, 1868. (P. L., 1868, page 1022.)*

SECTION 1. That the provisions of an act entitled "An act
to secure farmers against losses caused by railroads in Erie
county," approved on the twenty-third day of March, Anno
Domini one thousand eight hundred and sixty-eight, shall not
apply to or upon lands in said county in regard to which contracts exist by virtue of which the owners thereof are bound
to build and maintain fences thereon along the line of the railroad passing through or along the same: *Provided,* That in
all cases where fences along the line of any railroad are
destroyed by fire caused by the running of trains, or by the
employees of any railroad, the said railroad company shall
be liable to the penalties specified in the first and second sections of an act entitled "An act to secure farmers against
losses caused by railroads in Erie county," approved the
twenty-third day of March, Anno Domini one thousand eight
hundred and sixty-eight.

---

AN ACT TO AUTHORIZE RAILROAD COMPANIES LEASING
OR USING OTHER RAILROADS TO PROVIDE FOR THE
PAYMENT OF LIENS THEREON.

*Approved 14th April, 1868. (P. L., 1868, page 100.)*

SECTION 1. That whenever any railroad in this Commonwealth which has been or may hereafter be used or leased by
a railroad company whose railroad may connect therewith,
under any contract, lease, or agreement, shall be or may hereafter become subject, in whole or in part, to the lien of a
mortgage or other incumbrance securing or intended to secure
the payment of bonds or other obligations given or to be

given by or on behalf of the owner or owners of such railroa
so leased or used as aforesaid, it shall and may be lawful fc
such railroad company so leasing and using such railroad t
indorse, guarantee, or otherwise become liable for or assum
the payment of the principal and interest of the said bonds c
other evidence of indebtedness, in such manner and upon suc
terms as may be mutually agreed upon by the parties theret(
or by the officers and directors of the respective companies.

## AN ACT RELATIVE TO THE ASSESSMENT OF DAMAGE CAUSED BY THE CONSTRUCTION OF RAILROADS I] NORTHUMBERLAND COUNTY.

*Approved 14th April, 1868. (P. L., 1868, pages 1108 and 1109.)*

SECTION I. That all proceedings for the assessment (
damages caused to real estate by the construction of railroad
shall be had in the county in which the said real estate i
situate, and not elsewhere; and all laws heretofore passe
authorizing the removal of such proceedings to the courts (
other counties are hereby repealed, so far as regards Northum
berland county.

## AN ACT TO REVISE, AMEND, AND CONSOLIDATE TH] SEVERAL LAWS TAXING CORPORATIONS, BROKER$ AND BANKERS.

*Approved 1st May, 1868. (P. L., 1868, pages 108 and 114.)*

SECTION I. That hereafter no institution or company incoi
porated by or under any law of this Commonwealth, genera
or special, or of any other State, and authorized to do busines
in this State, shall go into operation without first having th
name of the institution or company, the date of incorporatioi
the place of business, the amount of capital paid in, and th
names of the president and treasurer of the same registered i
the office of the auditor-general; and any such institution o
company which shall neglect or refuse to comply with th
provisions of this section shall be subject to a penalty (
five hundred dollars, which penalty shall be collected, on a

account settled by the auditor-general and State treasurer, as taxes on capital stock are settled and collected.

(Repealed, but supplied by act of April 24th, 1874.)

SEC. 2. That hereafter it shall be the duty of the president or treasurer of every company incorporated by or under any law of this Commonwealth, except banks and savings institutions, and of all companies incorporated by any other State and lawfully doing business in this Commonwealth, who are taxable under the laws of this State, to make report in writing to the auditor-general annually, in the month of November, stating specifically the amount of capital paid in, the date, amount, and rate per centum of each and every dividend declared by their respective corporations during the year ending with the first Monday of said month ; and in all cases where any such company shall fail to make and declare any dividend during the year ending as aforesaid, the treasurer and secretary thereof, after being duly sworn or affirmed to do and perform the same with fidelity, according to the best of their knowledge and belief, shall, between the first and fifteenth days of November of each year in which no dividend has been declared as aforesaid, estimate and appraise the capital stock of such company at its actual value in cash, and when the same shall have been so estimated and appraised, they shall forthwith forward a certificate thereof to the auditor-general, accompanied by a copy of their said oath or affirmation, by them signed, and attested by the magistrate or other person qualified to administer the same.

(Repealed, but supplied by act of April 24th, 1874.)

SEC. 3. That if the said officers of any such company or corporation shall neglect or refuse to furnish the auditor-general, on or before the thirty-first day of December in each and every year, with the report aforesaid, or the report and appraisement, as the case may be, as required by the second section of this act, it shall be the duty of the accounting officers of the Commonwealth to add ten per centum to the tax of said corporation for each and every year for which such report or report and appraisement were not so furnished, which percentage shall be settled and collected with the said tax in the usual manner of settling accounts and collecting

such taxes : *Provided*, That if said officers of any such co
pany or corporation shall fail to comply with the provisic
of the second section of this act for three successive years, 1
auditor-general may, if he deems it conducive to the pub
interest, report the fact to the governor, who shall thereup·
by proclamation, declare the charter of said company or c·
poration forfeited and their chartered privileges at an end.

(Repealed, but supplied by act of April 24th, 1874.)

SEC. 4. That the capital stock of all companies whatev
incorporated by or under any law of this Commonwealth,
incorporated by any other State and lawfully doing businι
in this Commonwealth, or that may be hereafter incorporatι
except banks and savings institutions and foreign insurar
companies licensed in ·pursuance of the general acts in relati
thereto, shall be subject to and pay a tax into the treasury
the Commonwealth, annually, at the rate of one-half mill
each one per cent. of dividend made or declared by such co
pany ; and in case of no dividend being made or declared
such company, then three mills upon a valuation of the capi
stock of the same, made in accordance with the provisions
the second section of this act : *Provided*, That compan
liable to tax on dividends, in addition to tax on capital stoι
prior to the act approved April twelfth, one thousand eiξ
hundred and fifty-nine, entitled " An act to equalize taxati
·upon corporations," shall, from the said date, be exempt frι
any tax on dividends : *Provided further*, That building assoc
tions, plank road or turnpike companies, shall not be liaι
for any tax to the Commonwealth when such companies ma
or declare no dividends.

(Repealed, but supplied by act of April 24th, 1874.)

SEC. 5. That the amount of tax on capital stock impos
by the preceding section of this act shall be retained a
deducted, by the treasurer or other officer having charge
any company or corporation as aforesaid, from the divider
or profits made or declared as aforesaid, and he is here
authorized and required, on or before the fifteenth day
January then next, to transmit to the treasury of the Co
monwealth the amount of said tax ; and if, in case where
dividend has been made or declared, the funds of su

ompany, subject to the control of the treasurer, at the period
vhen the value of said capital stock shall be appraised as
equired by the second section of this act, shall be insufficient
o pay the tax aforesaid, it shall be the duty of the said treas-
irer or other officer forthwith to give notice to the stock-
iolders of such company of the amount required on each
hare of stock by them respectively held to enable the said
reasurer to pay the tax aforesaid; and if any such stock-
iolder shall neglect or refuse to pay the amount so required
or the period of thirty days from the time of such notice, the
aid treasurer shall, after giving two weeks' public notice
hereof in one or more newspapers published in or nearest to
he county in which said company or its principal place of
usiness is located, proceed to sell at public sale, and transfer
o the purchaser, so many shares of the stock of such
ielinquent stockholder as may be necessary to pay his portion
of the tax required to be paid as aforesaid; and if any com-
any incorporated as aforesaid shall neglect or refuse to pay
he tax hereinbefore required to be paid, the directors, man-
igers, or treasurers thereof for the time being shall be jointly
ind severally liable, in their individual capacity, for the payment thereof, and the same may be sued for and recovered,
under the direction of the State treasurer, as debts of like
amount are recoverable.

SEC. 6. That every private banker and broker, and every
unincorporated banking and saving institution and express
company, and all corporations incorporated by or doing
business in this Commonwealth, except those liable to a tax
on tonnage under the provisions of this act, and foreign
insurance companies licensed in pursuance of the several acts
in relation thereto, except banks and savings institutions
incorporated by this State, shall annually, upon the first day
of November of each year, make report to the auditor-general,
under oath or affirmation, setting forth the entire amount of
net earnings or income received by said individuals, company,
or corporation from all sources during the preceding year;
and upon such net earnings or income the said individuals,
company, or corporation, as the case may be, shall pay to the
treasurer, for the use of the State, within sixty days thereafter,

three per centum upon such annual net earnings or income,
addition to the taxes imposed by the preceding sections
this act; and in case any corporation, company, or individu
shall neglect or refuse to make the report required by th
section to the auditor-general on or before the thirty-fir
day of December, such corporation, company, or individu
shall be liable to a penalty of ten per centum for such negle(
which shall be added to the amount of tax found due in tl
settlement of their account.

( Repealed by act 21st March, 1873.)

Sec. 7. That the president, treasurer, cashier, or oth
financial officer of every railroad company, steamboat compan
canal company, and slack-water navigation company, and a
other companies now or hereafter doing business in this Stat
and upon whose works freight may be transported, wheth(
by such company or by individuals, and whether suc
company shall receive compensation for transportation, f(
transportation and toll, or shall receive tolls only, exce]
turnpike, plank road, and bridge companies, shall, within thir1
days after the first days of January, April, July, and Octob(
of every year, make return in writing to the auditor-genera
under oath or affirmation, stating fully and particularly th
number of tons of freight carried over, through, or upon th
works of said company for the three months immediatel
preceding each of the above-mentioned days; and each (
said companies, except as aforesaid, shall, at the time of makin
such return, pay to the State treasurer, for the use of th
Commonwealth, on each two thousand pounds of freight s
carried, tax at the following rates, viz.:—*First.* On the produc
of mines, quarries, and clay beds, in the condition in which sai
products may be taken therefrom, two cents. *Second.* On hew
timber, animal food, including live stock, also on the product
of the forest, vegetable and other agricultural products, th
value of which has not been increased by labor, three cent
*Third.* On all other articles, five cents. When the same freigl
shall be carried over and upon different but continuous line
of transportation, said freight shall be chargeable with tax a
if it had been carried but upon one line; and the whole ta
shall be paid by such one of said companies upon whos

works the freight originated, but in such case the tax shall be borne by the several corporations upon whose works the said tonnage was transported, each in proportion to the distance carried, as may be adjusted among themselves; corporations whose lines of improvement are used by others for the transportation of freight, and whose only earnings arise from tolls charged for such use, are authorized to add the tax hereby imposed to said toll and collect the same therewith; but in no case shall tax be twice charged on the same freight carried on or over the same line of improvements.

(Repealed by act of April 24th, 1874.)

SEC. 8. That in addition to the taxes provided for as aforesaid, every railroad, canal, and transportation company liable to a tax upon tonnage, under the preceding section of this act, shall pay to the Commonwealth a tax of three-fourths of one per centum upon the gross receipts of said company; the said tax shall be paid semi-annually, upon the first days of July and January, and for the purpose of ascertaining the amount of the same, it shall be the duty of the treasurer or other proper officer of said company to transmit to the auditor-general, at the dates aforesaid, a statement, under oath or affirmation, of the amount of gross receipts of the said company derived from all sources during the preceding six months; and if any such company shall neglect or refuse, for a period of thirty days after such tax becomes due, to make said return or to pay the same, the amount thereof, with an addition of ten per centum thereto, shall be collected for the use of the Commonwealth, as other taxes are recoverable by law from said companies: *Provided*, That the revenue derived under this section shall be applied to the payment of principal and interest of the debt contracted under the act of the fifteenth of May, Anno Domini one thousand eight hundred and sixty-one, entitled "An act to create a loan and to provide for arming the State."

(Repealed by act 31st March, 1873, as to companies liable to tonnage tax; but companies exempt from tax on tonnage by special law to pay a tax of three-fourths of one per cent. on gross receipts.)

(Repealed by act of April 24th, 1874.)

Sec. 9. That every railroad, canal, or transportation compan
doing business in this State which possesses the right to min
anthracite coal, or to purchase and sell the same, or to lea:
from or to other parties the land or mines from which sai
coal is taken, shall, quarterly, on the first days of Januar;
April, July, and October, make report, under oath or affirmatio1
stating the amount of coal mined by them from propert
owned and leased by them, and also the amount of co;
purchased by them, or mined from property owned by thei
that may be leased to other parties, during the precedin
three months, and shall pay to the State treasurer, for the u:
of the Commonwealth, within thirty days thereafter, a tax (
four cents upon each and every ton of anthracite coal :
purchased or mined: *Provided*, That the amount of co;
consumed in the transaction of their business shall not t
included in their return: *And provided further*, That sai
corporations shall be exempt from the payment of the ta
upon tonnage, imposed by the seventh section of this ac
upon all coal upon which a tax shall be paid under th
provisions of this section, and also from the tax on n(
earnings or income imposed by the sixth section of this ac
and also from the tax upon gross receipts imposed by th
eighth section of this act, so far as their net earnings an
gross receipts are derived from the mining, transportatio1
and sale of the said coal: *And provided also*, That if an
corporation shall fail to make the return required by th;
section, within thirty days after the time herein specified, the
shall be liable to a penalty of ten per centum for such neglec
the said penalty to be added to the amount of tax found du
under the provisions of this section, upon settlement made b
the auditor-general and State treasurer in accordance wit
law.

(Repealed by act of April 24th, 1874; but re-enacted b
same act.)

Sec. 10. That it shall be the duty of the cashier of ever
bank and savings institution incorporated under the laws (
this State, to collect annually from every shareholder of sai
bank or savings institution a tax of one per centum upo
the par value of the shares held by said shareholder, an

to pay the same into the State treasury on or before the first day of July in every year; and the said shares shall be exempt from all other taxation under the laws of this Commonwealth.

(The act 3d January, 1868, P. L., 1318, provided that the shares of stock held by any stockholder in any institution or company incorporated under the laws of this State, which in its corporate capacity is liable to and pays into the State treasury the tax on capital stock imposed by the act approved April 12th, Anno Domini 1859, entitled "An act to equalize taxation on corporations," shall not be taxable in the hands of said stockholders personally for State, county, or local purposes; and so much of the thirty-second section of the act approved April 29th, Anno Domini 1844, entitled "An act to reduce the State debt and incorporate the Pennsylvania Canal and Railroad Company," as imposes a tax for State or county purposes upon any stockholder in his individual capacity, as aforesaid, is hereby repealed: *Provided*, That this act shall not be construed to relieve said corporations from any tax now imposed by law, or the real estate belonging to said corporations from the State, county, or local tax to which they are now or may hereafter be subject.)

SEC. 11. That the president, treasurer, or cashier of every company, except bank or savings institution incorporated under the laws of this Commonwealth, doing business in this State, which pays interest to its bondholders or other creditors, shall, before the payment of the same, retain from said bondholders or creditors a tax of five per centum upon every dollar of interest paid as aforesaid; and shall pay over the same semi-annually, on the first days of July and January in each and every year, to the State treasurer, for the use of the Commonwealth; and every president, treasurer, or cashier as aforesaid, shall, annually, on the thirty-first day of each December, or within thirty days thereafter, report to the auditor-general, under oath or affirmation, stating the entire amount of interest paid by said corporation to said creditors during the year ending on that day; and thereupon the auditor-general and State treasurer shall proceed to settle an account with said corporation as other accounts are now

settled by law; and in the settlement of said accounts th
persons aforesaid shall be allowed the same commission o
compensation as is now allowed by law to county treasurers
and in case the said president, treasurer, or cashier shal
neglect or refuse to make the report required by thi
section within sixty days after the time specified, he shal
forfeit to the State the amount of his commission for sucl
failure or neglect: *Provided*, That the principal sums from th
interest of which the said tax is deducted shall not b
assessed and taxed for State purposes in the valuation c
personal property, or returned by county commissioners t
the board of revenue commissioners.

(Repealed by act 21st March, 1873. Same tax imposed oi
the company without right to retain tax by section four o
said act, but repealed by act April 24th, 1874.)

SEC. 12. That in the settlement of all accounts for taxes du
the Commonwealth, under the preceding sections of this act
by corporations or individuals, the auditor-general and Stat
treasurer shall charge interest upon the balance or balance:
found due the Commonwealth by such corporations o
individuals, at the rate of twelve per centum per annum ,fron
the time said taxes became due and payable to the tim
of the settlement of the same; and all balances due th
Commonwealth by the corporations or individuals aforesaid
on accounts settled agreeably to the provisions of the act o
March thirtieth, one thousand eight hundred and eleven
or any other act of assembly, shall bear interest from sixt
days after date of settlement, at the rate of twelve pe
centum per annum, until the same are paid: *Provided*, Tha
the payment of interest, as aforesaid, shall not relieve sai
corporations or individuals from any of the penalties pre
scribed for neglect and refusal to furnish reports to th
auditor-general.

SEC. 13. That the auditor-general and State treasurer, o
any agent appointed by them, are hereby authorized to examin
the books and papers of any corporation, association, company
private banker, or broker, to verify the accuracy of any retur
made to them, or either of them, under the provisions of thi
act.

SEC. 14. That the revenue derived from tax on net earnings or income, under the sixth section of this act, and from tonnage, under the seventh section, and from coal mined, under the ninth section, shall, so far as it is necessary, be first applicable to the payment of the ordinary expenses of government, and the residue not needed for such purpose shall be transferred to the sinking fund, as directed by the act of the twenty-second of April, one thousand eight hundred and fifty-eight.

(Sections 12, 13, and 14 are supplied by act of April 24th, 1874, and, though differently worded, are not repealed.)

SEC. 15. That hereafter every company incorporated by or under any general or special law of this Commonwealth, except railroad, canal, turnpike, bridge, or cemetery companies, and companies incorporated for literary, charitable, or religious purposes, shall pay to the State treasurer, for the use of the Commonwealth, a bonus of one-quarter of one per centum upon the amount of capital stock which said company is authorized to have, in two equal installments, and a like bonus upon any subsequent increase thereof. The first installment shall be due and payable upon the incorporation of said company, or upon the increase of the capital thereof, and the second installment one year thereafter; and no company, as aforesaid, shall have or exercise any corporate powers until the first installment of said bonus is paid; and the governor shall not issue letters patent to any company until he is satisfied that the first installment of said bonus has been paid to the State treasurer; and no company incorporated by any special act of assembly shall go into operation or exercise any corporate powers or privileges, nor shall said act be enrolled among the laws of the State, until said first installment of bonus has been paid as aforesaid.

SEC. 16. The following acts of assembly and parts thereof, so far as the same are altered and supplied by this act, be and the same are hereby repealed:—

Section first of the act approved June eleventh, one thousand eight hundred and forty, to create additional revenue, to be applied towards the payment of interest and extinguishment of the debts of the Commonwealth.

Section thirty-three of the act approved April twenty-ninth one thousand eight hundred and forty-four, to reduce th State debt and to incorporate the Pennsylvania Canal and Railroad Company.

Sections seventy-one and seventy-two of the act approved May seventh, one thousand eight hundred and fifty-five, to provide for the ordinary expenses of government, the repair of the public canals and railroads, and other general and special appropriations.

An act approved April twenty-first, one thousand eigh hundred and fifty-eight, for the better securing to th Commonwealth the payment of taxes due by incorporated companies.

An act approved April twelfth, one thousand eight hundred and fifty-nine, to equalize taxation upon corporations.

The first, second, third, fifth, and sixth sections of an ac approved April thirtieth, one thousand eight hundred and sixty-four, imposing additional taxes for State purposes, and to abolish the revenue board.

The first, second, and third sections of the act approved February twenty-third, one thousand eight hundred and sixty-six, to amend the revenue laws of the Commonwealth.

An act approved April ninth, one thousand eight hundred and sixty-seven, regulating interest on public accounts.

An act approved March twenty-second, one thousand eigh hundred and sixty-seven, to increase the revenues of the Commonwealth.

---

## AN ACT RELATING TO TONNAGE TAX ON COKE ANI CRUSHED ROCK SAND.

*Approved 26th February, 1869. (P. L., 1869, page 5.)*

SECTION 1. That from and after the passage of this act the rate of tonnage tax to be paid by railroad and other trans portation companies on coke and crushed rock sand shall no be greater than the rate fixed by law upon the product o mines.

AN ACT SUPPLEMENTARY TO AN ACT RELATING TO
CERTAIN CORPORATIONS, APPROVED THE TWENTY-
THIRD DAY OF APRIL, A. D. 1861.

*Approved 17th March, 1869. (P. L., 1869, page 11.)*

SECTION 1. That it shall and may be lawful for any railroad
company or companies created by or existing under the laws
of this Commonwealth, from time to time to purchase and
hold the stock and bonds, or either, or to agree to purchase
or guarantee the payment of the principal or interest, or
either, of the bonds of any other railroad company or companies chartered by it or existing under the laws of any
other State.

---

AN ACT TO AUTHORIZE AN INCREASE IN THE NUMBER
OF DIRECTORS OR MANAGERS OF RAILROAD COMPA-
NIES, AND TO GIVE STOCKHOLDERS THE POWER TO
LOCATE THE GENERAL OFFICE OF SUCH COMPANIES.

*Approved 17th March, 1869. (P. L., 1869, pages 11 and 12.)*

SECTION 1. That the directors or managers of any railroad
company incorporated by or under the laws of this Commonwealth be and they are hereby authorized to add to their
number, by selecting from the body of the stockholders, from
time to time, an additional member or members, who shall
act as a vice-president or additional vice-president of such
corporation, and who shall have such powers and receive
such compensation as the board of directors or managers,
by its by-laws or by resolution, may establish and direct:
*Provided, however,* That the number of directors or managers
of such corporation shall not be thereby increased beyond
seventeen.

SEC. 2. That it shall be lawful for any such corporation,
by resolution of its stockholders, to determine where the
general office of such company shall be located, and where
the meetings of its board of directors or managers, and
also the meetings of its stockholders, and where also its
elections for directors or managers shall be held: *Provided
always,* That no place shall be selected which is not within

the limits of this Commonwealth: *And provided also*, Th
this act shall only apply to such railroad corporations
shall, by resolution of its president and board of directo
or managers, duly accept the same.

---

AN ACT TO ENABLE RAILROAD, CANAL, AND SLAC]
WATER NAVIGATION COMPANIES TO STRAIGHTE:
WIDEN, DEEPEN, AND OTHERWISE IMPROVE THE]
LINES OF RAILROADS, CANALS, AND SLACK-WATE
NAVIGATION, AND THE BRIDGES, AQUEDUCTS, PIER
AND STRUCTURES THEREOF.

*Approved 17th March, 1869.* (*P. L., 1869, pages 12 and 13.*)

SECTION I. That it shall and may be lawful for any rai
road, canal, and slack-water navigation company now (
hereafter incorporated by or under any law of this Commoı
wealth, to straighten, widen, deepen, enlarge, or otherwiː
improve the whole or portions of their lines of railroad
canals, and slack-water navigation, and the bridges, cros
ings, sidings, aqueducts, piers, and structures thereof, ar
make new feeders, whenever, in the opinion of the board
directors of any such company, the same may be necessaı
for the better securing the safety of persons and property ar
increasing the facilities and capacity for the transportation
traffic thereon, and for such purposes to purchase, hold, ar
use, or enter upon, take, and appropriate land and materia
*Provided*, That before any such company shall enter upon (
take possession of any such lands and material, they shɛ
make ample compensation to the owner or owners thereof (
parties interested therein, or tender adequate security therefc
SEC. 2. That where any such company cannot agree wiı
the owner or owners, or parties interested in such land ar
materials, for the compensation proper for the damage doı
or likely to be done, or where, by reason of the absence (
legal incapacity of any such owner or owners or partiₑ
interested therein, no such compensation can be agreₑ
upon, the same shall be ascertained and paid in the mannₑ
provided in the eleventh section of the act regulating railroa
companies, approved February nineteenth, Anno Domini oı
thousand eight hundred and forty-nine.

A SUPPLEMENT SUPPLEMENTAL TO AN ACT PROVIDING FOR THE CONSTRUCTION OF LATERAL RAILROADS AND FOR OTHER PURPOSES, APPROVED THE FIFTH DAY OF APRIL, ANNO DOMINI ONE THOUSAND EIGHT HUNDRED AND FORTY-NINE, EXTENDING THE SAME TO NORTHUMBERLAND COUNTY.

*Approved 3d April, 1869. (P. L., 1869. pages 697 and 698.)*

SECTION I. That the provisions of the second section of the act providing for the construction of lateral railroads and for other purposes, and approved the fifth day of April, Anno Domini one thousand eight hundred and forty-nine, be and the same are hereby made to extend to the county of Northumberland.

---

A FURTHER SUPPLEMENT TO AN ACT REGULATING LATERAL RAILROADS, APPROVED THE FIFTH DAY OF MAY, ANNO DOMINI ONE THOUSAND EIGHT HUNDRED AND THIRTY-TWO.

*Approved 6th April, 1869. (P. L., 1869, page 17.)*

SECTION I. That it shall be at the option of the petitioners, or the legal representatives of the petitioners, for any lateral railroad located or to be located under the act to which this is a supplement, upon payment of all costs, at any time before ground shall be broken, and within two years from the confirmation of the right of way, to abandon the right of construction; and, as evidence thereof, shall file their declaration of that intent in writing in the court having jurisdiction, which court may set aside and terminate all previous proceedings, upon terms equitable and just to all parties in interest.

---

AN ACT RELATING TO THE SETTLEMENT OF PUBLIC ACCOUNTS.

*Approved 8th April, 1869. (P. L., 1869, page 19.)*

SECTION I. That the auditor-general, State treasurer, and attorney-general be authorized to revise any settlement made

with any person or body politic by the auditor-general whe
it may appear, from the accounts in his office or from othe
information in his possession, that the same has been erron
ously or illegally made, or to resettle the same according t
law, and to credit or charge, as the case may be, the amour
resulting from such resettlement upon the current accounts (
such person or body politic.

---

AN ACT SUPPLEMENTARY TO AN ACT RELATING T(
RAILROAD COMPANIES, APPROVED MAY SIXTEENTH
ANNO DOMINI ONE THOUSAND EIGHT HUNDRED ANI
SIXTY-ONE.

*Approved 10th April, 1869. (P. L., 1869, pages 24 and 25.)*

SECTION 1. That whenever any merger of the corporate
rights, powers, and franchises of a railroad company shal
hereafter be made into any other railroad company, unde
authority of the act relating to railroad companies, approvec
May sixteenth, Anno Domini one thousand eight hundrec
and sixty-one, it shall and may be lawful for said companie:
to specify in the joint agreement for such consolidatior
and merger what corporate rights, powers, obligations
duties, and franchises created by the charter, or existing
under or in pursuance of or by force of any act of assembly
relating to either of said companies, shall be transferred
to or become vested in or shall continue in the company
into which said merger is made; and the said consolidated
company shall be subject to and be regulated and governed
only by the corporate rights, powers, duties, obligations, and
franchises so specified in and vested by said agreement; and
upon the filing of the same in the office of the secretary of the
Commonwealth, it shall thereupon be deemed and taken to be
its act of incorporation for all purposes whatsoever: *Provided,*
*however,* That the consolidated company so formed shall not
acquire by said agreement any powers, franchises, or privileges
that were not theretofore granted to them, or either of them,
by law; and due notice of any such merger shall first be given,
by publication, to the stockholders of the respective companies,

and shall not be valid or effective until ratified or approved
by them, as required by said act of May sixteenth, Anno
Domini one thousand eight hundred and sixty-one; and
all laws and parts of laws inconsistent with this act, and with
the corporate and other rights which may be defined in and
acquired under any agreement of consolidation or merger
made in pursuance hereof, be and the same are hereby
repealed.

---

## A SUPPLEMENT TO "AN ACT RELATING TO CERTAIN CORPORATIONS," APPROVED THE TWENTY-THIRD DAY OF APRIL, ANNO DOMINI ONE THOUSAND EIGHT HUNDRED AND SIXTY-ONE.

*Approved 10th April, 1869.* (*P. L., 1869, pages 25 and 26.*)

SECTION 1. That when, in pursuance of the act to which
this is a supplement, any railroad company shall make, or has
made, a contract with any other railroad company chartered
by another State, but authorized by law to extend its road into
this State, by which it shall obtain a right to connect the roads
of the two companies, or run its cars and engines thereon or
on any other railroad, it shall not be lawful for any person, in
any manner, or by color of any authority, to interfere with or
interrupt the enjoyment of said right, according to the terms
of the contract, until the right so to interfere shall be finally
established by the highest judicial tribunal of the State in
which the railroad, for the use of which the contract was
made, is located.

SEC. 2. That if any company chartered by this State, or
authorized by law to extend its road into this State, shall be
interfered with, interrupted, or enjoined, contrary to the provisions of the first section of this supplement, and thereby
prevented from enjoying the rights stipulated for in such
contract, it shall be lawful for the company so interfered with,
interrupted, or enjoined, to apply, by bill in equity, to the
Supreme Court, or any judge thereof, setting forth the facts;
whereupon it shall be the duty of the court or judge, if

satisfied that the complainant has been so interfered witl
interrupted, or enjoined, to issue a writ of injunction, withou
security, against the railroad company with which the con
plainant contracted, forbidding it, its agents or employees an
all other persons, to exercise any corporate privileges or us
its own railroad within this State until the further order of tl
said court or judge.

SEC. 3. That thenceforward such complaint shall procee
as other cases in equity; and if, on first hearing, said cou
shall be of opinion that the interference, interruption, or ii
junction complained of was without sufficient cause, it sha
decree a continuance of the injunction theretofore granted, s
long as the interruption or injunction complained of sha
continue.

## AN ACT REQUIRING A MAJORITY OF THE DIRECTOR OR MANAGERS OF CORPORATIONS TO CONSTITUTE QUORUM.

*Approved 15th April, 1869. (P. L., 1869, page 29.)*

SECTION 1. That whenever the number of directors or mai
agers of any corporation may be increased under authority ‹
law, a majority of the whole number shall be necessary t
constitute a quorum; and all laws inconsistent with this a‹
be and the same are hereby repealed.

## AN ACT TO AUTHORIZE RAILROAD AND CANAL COMPA NIES TO AID IN THE DEVELOPMENT OF THE COAl IRON, LUMBER, AND OTHER MATERIAL INTEREST OF THIS COMMONWEALTH.

*Approved 15th April, 1869. (P. L., 1869, pages 31 and 32.)*

SECTION 1. That it shall and may be lawful for railroad an
canal companies to aid corporations authorized by law t
develop the coal, iron, lumber, or other material interests ‹
this Commonwealth, by the purchase of their capital stoc
and bonds, or either of them, or by the guarantee of or agre‹
ment to purchase the principal and interest, or either, of suc

bonds: *Provided*, That this act shall not apply to the stock and bonds of any corporation possessing mining or manufacturing privileges in the county of Schuylkill.

---

## AN ACT TO REPEAL AN ACT ENTITLED "AN ACT TO AUTHORIZE THE SALE OF THE PROPERTY OF ANY INCORPORATED COMPANY UPON THE BONDS SECURED BY A MORTGAGE GIVEN BY IT, WITH LIKE EFFECT AS IF SOLD UPON THE MORTGAGE."

*Approved 15th April, 1869.  (P. L., 1869, page 32.)*

SECTION 1. That the act entitled "An act to authorize the sale of the property of any incorporated company upon the bonds secured by a mortgage given by it, with like effect as if sold upon the mortgage," approved the tenth day of April, Anno Domini one thousand eight hundred and sixty-seven, be and the same is hereby repealed.

---

## AN ACT TO CONFIRM THE ACKNOWLEDGMENTS OF DEEDS, MORTGAGES, OR OTHER INSTRUMENTS OF WRITING HERETOFORE MADE BY CORPORATIONS.

*Approved 17th April, 1869.  (P. L., 1869, page 68.)*

SECTION 1. That the provisions of the third section of an act entitled "An act authorizing notaries public in this State, and in any States or territory in the United States, to take acknowledgments of deeds and letters of attorney, and to confirm acknowledgments heretofore made," approved the twenty-second day of April, Anno Domini one thousand eight hundred and sixty-three, be and the same is hereby extended to all deeds, mortgages, or other instruments of writing informally acknowledged by any corporation since the passage of said act: *Provided*, That no case heretofore judicially decided shall be affected by this act.

A SUPPLEMENT TO AN ACT ENTITLED "AN ACT FO: THE PROTECTION OF FARMERS AND OWNERS O CATTLE, HORSES, SHEEP, AND SWINE ALONG TH LINE OF RAILROADS IN WARREN COUNTY," APPROVE: MARCH TWENTY-EIGHTH, ONE THOUSAND EIGH' HUNDRED AND SIXTY-EIGHT, AND EXTENDING TH: SAME TO THE COUNTIES OF BRADFORD, McKEAN AND VENANGO.

*Approved 17th April, 1869. (P. L., 1869, pages 1125 and 1126.)*

SECTION 1. That if any company referred to in said ac shall neglect to perform the duties imposed by said act, th company so offending shall be answerable to the owners c cattle, horses, sheep, or swine, to the value of the propert injured upon said roads in consequence of such neglect.

SEC. 2. The provisions of said act and this supplement b and the same are hereby extended to the counties of Brad ford, McKean, and Venango, and that the several courts o said county shall have like jurisdiction.

---

AN ACT TO ENABLE COURTS OF COMMON PLEAS OF THI! COMMONWEALTH TO CHANGE THE NAME, STYLE, ANI TITLE OF CORPORATIONS.

*Approved 20th April, 1869. (P. L., 1869, pages 82 and 83.)*

SECTION 1. That it shall be lawful for the several courts o common pleas of this Commonwealth to change the name style, and title of any corporation within their respectivє counties, with the same proceedings and in the same manneı as they are now authorized to improve, amend, and alteı charters : *Provided,* That no proceedings for such purpose shal. be entertained by the courts until notice of such application is given to the auditor-general, and proof of such fact is pro· duced to the courts; and upon final decree in such proceeding before using such name, the parties in interest shall file with the auditor-general a copy of the decree making such change.

SEC. 2. That the third section of the act approved fourth April, one thousand eight hundred and forty-three, giving authority to courts of quarter sessions to change the name style, and title of corporations, be and the same is hereby repealed.

## A SUPPLEMENT TO THE ACT TO REVISE, AMEND, AND CONSOLIDATE THE SEVERAL LAWS TAXING CORPORATIONS, BROKERS, AND BANKERS, APPROVED MAY ONE, ONE THOUSAND EIGHT HUNDRED AND SIXTY-EIGHT.

*Approved 24th April, 1869. (P. L., 1869, pages 94 and 95.)*

WHEREAS, The legislature, in repealing the various laws in force, so far as they were supplied by the act to which this is a supplement, to wit, the acts of April twenty-one, one thousand eight hundred and fifty-eight; April twelve, one thousand eight hundred and fifty-nine; April nine, one thousand eight hundred and sixty-seven; March twenty-two, one thousand eight hundred and sixty-seven; and portion of the acts of June eleven, one thousand eight hundred and forty; April twenty-nine, one thousand eight hundred and forty-four; May seven, one thousand eight hundred and fifty-five; April thirty, one thousand eight hundred and sixty-four; and February twenty-three, one thousand eight hundred and sixty-six, inadvertently failed to make positive provision for the collection and payment of the taxes falling due and payable under those laws: to remedy which—

SECTION 1. That the general repeal of those laws or parts thereof shall read "so far as the same are altered and supplied, except so far as shall be necessary to enforce the collection and payment of all taxes assessed or falling due and payable under said acts or any of them."

---

## A FURTHER SUPPLEMENT TO THE ACT ENTITLED "AN ACT TO ENABLE CITIZENS TO HOLD TITLE WHICH HAD BEEN HELD BY ALIENS AND CORPORATIONS," APPROVED THE NINTH DAY OF JANUARY, ANNO DOMINI ONE THOUSAND EIGHT HUNDRED AND SIXTY-ONE.

*Approved 26th April, 1869. (P. L., 1869, page 96.)*

SECTION 1. That the provisions of the act entitled "An act to enable citizens to hold title which had been held by aliens and corporations," approved the ninth day of January, Anno Domini one thousand eight hundred and sixty-one, be and hereby are extended to all sales and conveyances of real estate which had been made prior to the passage of this act.

## AN ACT AUTHORIZING CORPORATIONS TO INCREASE THEIR BONDED OBLIGATIONS AND CAPITAL STOCK.

*Approved 29th December, 1869. (P. L., 1870, pages 1374 and 1375.)*

SECTION 1. That it shall and may be lawful for any corporation created by or existing under the laws of this Commonwealth to increase its bonded obligations and secure the same by mortgage, and also to increase its capital stock, from time to time, to any amount not exceeding fifty per cent. of the amounts heretofore authorized, and to sell or dispose of the same on such terms and conditions as to said corporation may seem proper: *Provided, however,* That this act shall not apply to any corporation until it is duly accepted by it, whereupon it shall be taken and deemed to be a part of its act of incorporation and be made under its authority; and a certificate, duly attested by the president and treasurer of said company, under its corporate seal, setting forth the acceptance of the act, with the amounts and character of the increase, shall be filed in the auditor-general's office of the Commonwealth, and a copy thereof be filed with the secretary of State: *And provided further,* That on all such increase the State shall be entitled, *pro rata,* to the same bonus or tax that is now assessed by law on like amounts of the existing capital of the respective corporations.

## AN ACT TO PREVENT THE INJURY OR DESTRUCTION OF BAGGAGE WITHIN THE LIMITS OF THE STATE OF PENNSYLVANIA.

*Approved 12th February, 1870. (P. L., 1870, page 15.)*

SECTION 1. That any baggage-master, express agent, stage driver, hackman, or other person whose duty it is to handle, remove, or take care of the baggage of passengers, who shall willfully or recklessly injure or destroy any trunk, valise, box, package, or parcel, while loading, transporting, unloading,

delivering, or storing the same, shall be guilty of a misdemeanor, and on conviction thereof shall be sentenced to pay
a fine not exceeding one hundred dollars: *Provided*, That the
provisions of this act shall not be so construed as to release
railroad or other transportation companies from their liabilities
under existing laws.

---

## AN ACT TO AUTHORIZE RAILROAD COMPANIES TO LEASE OR BECOME LESSEES AND TO MAKE CONTRACTS WITH OTHER RAILROAD COMPANIES, CORPORATIONS, AND PARTIES.

*Approved 17th February, 1870.  (P. L., 1870, page 31.)*

SECTION 1. That it shall and may be lawful for any railroad
company or companies created by or existing under the laws
of this Commonwealth, from time to time to lease or become
the lessees, by assignment or otherwise, of any railroad or railroads, or enter into any other contract with any other railroad
company or companies, individuals, or corporations, on such
terms and conditions as may be agreed upon, whether the
road or roads embraced in such lease, assignment, or contract
may be within the limits of this State or created by or existing
under the laws of any other State or States; and any railroad
company or companies of this Commonwealth may agree to
guarantee, in whole or in part, the payments and covenants of
any such lease, assigned lease, or contract: *Provided, however,*
That such road or roads, so embraced in any such lease,
assignment, contract, or guarantee, shall be connected either
directly or by means of intervening line with the railroad or
railroads of said company or companies of this Commonwealth
so entering into such lease, assignment, contract, or guarantee,
and thus forming a continuous route or routes for the transportation of persons and property: *Provided, further,* That the
provisions of this act shall in no wise, nor by any construction
whatever, apply to the Pittsburg and Connellsville Railroad
Company.

## AN ACT TO AUTHORIZE CANAL COMPANIES TO BUILI LATERAL RAILROADS.

*Approved 28th March, 1870.* (*P. L., 1870, pages 41 and 42.*)

SECTION 1. That it shall be lawful for any canal compan₂ now or hereafter incorporated by or under the laws of thi Commonwealth, to construct and operate lateral railroads anᵤ branches therefrom, not exceeding, respectively, ten miles iⁱ length, with the necessary appurtenances, from suitable point on the line of their canals to any mines, quarries, or othe desirable points for the procurement of traffic for said canals and shall have and enjoy, and be subject to all and singular th₍ provisions and restrictions of an act of assembly regulatin₎ railroad companies, approved the nineteenth day of February one thousand eight hundred and forty-nine, and the supple ments thereto, necessary for the location, construction, anᵤ operation of the said roads and branches.

---

## AN ACT TO AUTHORIZE AND DIRECT THE ATTORNEY GENERAL, UPON COMPLAINT MADE BY PARTIES WHOSI INTERESTS ARE THEREBY AFFECTED, TO INSTITUTI PROCEEDINGS, ACCORDING TO LAW, AGAINST CORPO RATIONS ALLEGED TO HAVE VIOLATED DUTIES IM POSED UPON THEM BY LAW.

*Approved 1st April, 1870.* (*P. L., 1870, pages 45 and 46.*)

SECTION 1. That in all cases in which heretofore any privi leges or immunities have been granted to any corporation b₎ any act of the general assembly of the Commonwealth, upoɪ terms and conditions in such act prescribed, for the knowin₎ and intentional neglect or refusal to perform and comply witɪ which terms and conditions a forfeiture or determination of sucɪ privileges and immunities is provided for in the act, it shal be the duty of the attorney-general of the Commonwealth upon complaint made to him by any party whose rights o: interests are affected by such neglect or refusal, to institutᵤ forthwith procedings, in a court of competent jurisdiction, tᴄ ascertain the fact of such neglect or refusal; and if sucɪ

neglect or refusal shall be adjudged by such court to have
occurred, then and in such case all the rights, privileges,
powers, and immunities granted to said corporation upon
such terms and conditions shall forthwith cease and determine; and thereupon the governor of the Commonwealth
shall provide such organization as may be needful to manage
any such property, until otherwise directed by the legislature:
*Provided, however,* That all expenses incident to the management thereof shall be paid from its own proceeds; and nothing
in this act contained shall be deemed as authorizing any
liability against or expenditure by the Commonwealth of
Pennsylvania: *Provided,* That when proceedings under the
provisions of this act are commenced in any court other than
the Supreme Court, the right of appeal to the Supreme Court
shall exist to either party, as in other cases: *Provided further,*
This act shall not apply to bridge companies.

---

## A SUPPLEMENT TO THE ACT ENTITLED "AN ACT RELAT-ING TO EXECUTIONS," APPROVED THE SIXTEENTH OF JUNE, ANNO DOMINI ONE THOUSAND EIGHT HUNDRED AND THIRTY-SIX.

*Approved 7th April, 1870.  (P. L., 1870, pages 58 and 59.)*

SECTION 1. That in addition to the provisions of the sixty-
second section of the act of the sixteenth day of June, Anno
Domini one thousand eight hundred and thirty-six, relating
to executions, and in lieu of the provisions or proceedings
by sequestration under said act, plaintiff or assigns, in any
judgment against any corporation not excepted by said act,
may have execution *fieri facias* issued from the court wherein
said judgment is entered, which shall command the sheriff
or other officer to levy the sum of said judgment, with
interest and costs of suit, of any personal, mixed, or real
property, franchises, and rights of such corporation, and
thereupon proceed and sell the same, excepting lands held
in fee, which latter shall be proceeded against and sold in
the manner provided in cases for the sale of real estate;

the proceedings on judgment under the aforesaid provision of this supplement shall be without stay of execution: *Pn vided*, That the purchaser or purchasers of any or all of sai property, real, personal, or mixed, together with the franchise and rights, shall take the same clear of all encumbrance: excepting any mortgage or mortgages which may legall exist at the time of levy thereupon, the lien of which sha not be affected in any manner by said sale.

SEC. 2. That by virtue of any execution issued under thi act, the levy may extend to the property, franchises, and right of said corporation, in any and every county of this Commor wealth wherein the same may be, and shall be endorsed o said writ; the levy and sale thereof shall be as effective a though all said property, franchises, and rights were locatec used, levied upon, and sold in the county wherein said writ c execution was issued, and shall fully divest the defendants c all interest therein.

---

## AN ACT REQUIRING RAILROAD, CANAL, NAVIGATION AND TELEGRAPH COMPANIES TO MAKE UNIFORM RE PORTS TO THE AUDITOR-GENERAL.

*Approved 9th April, 1870.* (*P. L., 1870, page 61.*)

SECTION 1. That the auditor-general of this Commonwealt be and is hereby directed to make out, and cause to b printed, a blank form for the annual reports of the sever; railroad, canal, navigation, and telegraph corporations of th State, referred to in the second section of this act; and th said auditor-general shall forward, by mail or otherwise, on c before the first day of October in each year, to each of th said corporations, copies of the said form; and when the san shall have been received from the several aforesaid corpor; tions, he shall cause the same to be filed in his office, copic of which shall be transmitted to the legislature on or befoi the fifteenth day of February in each year.

SEC. 2. That it is hereby made the duty of each railroa canal, navigation, and telegraph company whose works c lines are in whole or in part within the limits of this State, to make out and return to the auditor-general an annual report, within thirty days after the expiration of their financial year, according to a form to be prescribed by the said auditor-general, embracing in detail the operations and affairs of the said corporations during the financial year, and such other information as the auditor-general shall direct; said report to be attested by the oath or affirmation of the president, superintendent, or sequestrator, and the treasurer of the company: *Provided,* That companies whose financial year end after December thirty-first shall make approximate reports to December thirty-first, and forward the same on or before the thirty-first day of January.

SEC. 3. That every such railroad, canal, navigation, and telegraph corporation which shall refuse or neglect to make such report as before provided, shall be liable to a penalty of five thousand dollars to the use of the Commonwealth, for every such refusal or neglect, to be sued for and recovered as debts of like amount are or may be by law recoverable.

SEC. 4. That all acts or parts of acts of assembly inconsistent with the provisions of this act be and they are hereby repealed; saving, however, to the Commonwealth the right to collect any penalty heretofore incurred.

---

## A SUPPLEMENT TO AN ACT REGULATING RAILROAD COMPANIES, APPROVED FEBRUARY NINETEENTH, ONE THOUSAND EIGHT HUNDRED AND FORTY-NINE.

*Approved 14th April, 1870. (P. L., 1870, page 73.)*

SECTION 1. That it shall and may be lawful for any two or more railroad companies incorporated by or under any law of this Commonwealth to jointly endorse or guaranty the bonds or other obligations of any other railroad company for the payment of money, and such company or companies so endorsing or guaranteeing may take such securities and indemnity from the company whose bonds or obligations may thus be endorsed or guaranteed as aforesaid, as may be agreed upon by the several companies respectively, to and with each

other, either jointly or separately; and it shall further be lawfi
for such companies, so endorsing or guaranteeing as aforesaic
to apportion and limit their liability as between themselve
or as between themselves and the company or companie
whose bonds or obligations may be endorsed or guarantee(
as may be respectively agreed upon.

---

A SUPPLEMENT TO AN ACT ENTITLED "AN ACT RE
LATING TO RAILROAD AND CANAL COMPANIES," AI
PROVED APRIL ELEVENTH, ONE THOUSAND EIGH
HUNDRED AND SIXTY-FOUR.

*Approved 14th April, 1870.  (P. L., 1870, page 75.)*

SECTION I. That it shall be lawful for any canal or naviga
tion company incorporated by this Commonwealth, to pui
chase and hold the stock and bonds, and to lease the roa
and property of, or become consolidated and merged with, an
railroad company so incorporated, and for any such railroa
company to purchase and hold the stock and bonds, and t
lease the canal, navigation, and property of, or become coi
solidated and merged with, any such canal or navigatio
company in the same manner as such purchases, lease
consolidation, and merger are now allowed by law by an
between railroad companies, and all the provisions of exis
ing acts relative to such purchases, leases, consolidation, an
merger by and between railroad companies are, wheneve
applicable, hereby extended so as to embrace the purchase
leases, consolidation, and merger hereby authorized.

---

JOINT RESOLUTION FOR THE PROTECTION OF TH
RIGHTS OF CORPORATIONS CHARTERED BY THIS COM
MONWEALTH.

*Approved 14th April, 1870.  (P. L., 1870, page 1334.)*

SECTION I. That the attorney-general of this Commoi
wealth be instructed to commence proceedings against a
corporations which have constructed or may hereafter coi
struct railroad or telegraph lines within this State witho·

authority of law: *Provided*, That this act shall not apply to telegraph lines used by corporations solely for their private purposes.

---

## AN ACT FURTHER SUPPLEMENTARY TO AN ACT REGU-LATING RAILROAD COMPANIES, APPROVED THE NINE-TEENTH DAY OF FEBRUARY, ANNO DOMINI ONE THOUSAND EIGHT HUNDRED AND FORTY-NINE.

*Approved 26th April, 1870. (P. L., 1870, page 1274.)*

SECTION 1. That it shall and may be lawful for any railroad company or corporation duly organized under the laws of this State, for the purpose of constructing a railroad, either wholly within, or partly within and partly without, this State, under authority of this and any adjoining State, to merge and con-solidate its capital stock, franchises, and property with any other railroad company or companies or corporations organ-ized under the laws of this or any other State, whenever the two or more railroads of the companies or corporations so to be consolidated shall or may form, when constructed, a con-tinuous line of railroad with each other, or by means of any intervening railroad; and such consolidation may be effected in accordance with the laws of this Commonwealth, either under special or general statutes of other States.

---

## AN ACT RELATIVE TO CHANGES OF VENUE.

*Approved 28th April, 1870. (P. L., 1870, page 1293.)*

SECTION 2. That it shall and may be lawful for either party in any suit or action, real or personal, now pending or that may hereafter be brought in any of the courts of this Com-monwealth, by or against any incorporated company, to remove the same into the court of any other adjacent county indicated by the president judge of the court in which the suit was originally brought; which suits so removed shall be proceeded in by the proper court, in like manner and subject to like rules and proceedings as if it had remained in the court in which it was originally commenced, and upon fin judgment *testatum* executions may issue as in other case *Provided*, That the party so removing shall first take ar subscribe an oath or affirmation, to be filed of record with tl cause, that such removal is not made for the purpose of dela but because he firmly believes a fair and impartial trial cann be had in the county in which such suit is brought or orig nated.

---

### AN ACT TO AUTHORIZE CORPORATIONS TO SUBSCRIE FOR OR PURCHASE THE CAPITAL STOCK, AND TO PUl CHASE THE BONDS OF THE AMERICAN STEAMSHl COMPANY OF PHILADELPHIA.

*Approved 17th February, 1871. (P. L., 1871, page 56.)*

SECTION I. That it shall and may be lawful for priva corporations, created by or doing business in this Commo wealth, to subscribe for or to purchase the capital stock ai bonds of the American Steamship Company of Philadelph:

---

### AN ACT SUPPLEMENTARY TO THE ACTS RELATING 1 LATERAL RAILROADS.

*Approved 17th February, 1871. (P. L., 1871, page 56.)* .

SECTION I. That in all proceedings now pending or whi may hereafter be instituted, to procure the right to constru lateral railroads, or for the acquisition of wharves or landinɡ or for either of said purposes, the appeal to court from t report of the viewers shall extend, not only to the assessme of damages, but to the question of the necessity of the pr posed lateral railroad, wharf, or landing, and shall also exte1 to the question whether such landing or wharf is necessary the owner thereof, for his own uses or purposes; and if tl jury shall so find, the same shall not be taken from him.

AN ACT TO DECLARE THE MEANING OF AN ACT COM-
PELLING RAILROAD AND OTHER CORPORATIONS TO
PAY COUNSEL FEES OF PLAINTIFF IN CERTAIN CASES,
APPROVED MAY THIRD, ONE THOUSAND EIGHT HUN-
DRED AND SIXTY-SIX.

*Approved 16th March, 1871. (P. L., 1871, page 231.)*

SECTION I. That the true intent and meaning of an act entitled "An act compelling railroad and other corporations to pay counsel fees of plaintiffs in certain cases," approved May third, one thousand eight hundred and sixty-six, is and is hereby declared to be that corporations named in said act shall only be liable to pay the plaintiff's counsel fees in case said corporations have contested the validity of the bonds for the recovery of the interest on which suit has been brought, and such validity has been established by a court of competent jurisdiction.

---

AN ACT RELATING TO NON-USED AND ABANDONED
FRANCHISES OF TURNPIKE, PLANK ROAD, CANAL, AND
SLACK-WATER NAVIGATION COMPANIES, OR PUBLIC
HIGHWAYS, PROVIDING WHAT SHALL CONSTITUTE
EVIDENCE OF ABANDONMENT.

*Approved 22d March, 1871. (P. L., 1871, pages 231 and 232.)*

SECTION I. That whenever any turnpike, plank road, canal, or slack-water navigation, or public highway of any company or corporation incorporated by the laws of this Common-wealth for the purpose of making, operating, or using the same, has been or shall have been, for the period of five successive years or upwards, decayed, out of repair, and unused for the purposes mentioned in the charter of such company, the same shall be deemed and held to be abandoned, together with all the easements and servitudes incident thereto; and all the rights, privileges, and franchises of such company in respect to the same shall cease and determine; and such condition and non-user for the period aforesaid may be given in evidence in any suit or proceeding wherein the facts of such abandonment may be material, and shall be conclusive proof thereof: *Provided*, That this act shall not apply to any such company, heretofore incorporated, unless the right is reserved in its charter to resume its corporate privileges and franchises in case of the misuse or abuse thereof: *Provided*, That the provisions of the bill shall not apply to any canal in the counties of Schuylkill, Wyoming, Bradford, and Berks, nor to any turnpike or plank road in the county of Carbon.

---

## A SUPPLEMENT TO THE ACT OF APRIL FOURTH, ONE THOUSAND EIGHT HUNDRED AND SIXTY-EIGHT, RELATIVE TO THE FORMATION AND REGULATION OF RAILROAD CORPORATIONS.

*Approved 28th April, 1871.  (P. L., 1871, pages 246 and 247.)*

SECTION 1. That any number of persons, not less than three all of whom must become stockholders, may form a company for the purpose of constructing, maintaining, and operating a railroad for public use, as provided for in the act to which this is a supplement: *Provided*, Said railroad shall not be of a greater length than five miles; and its stockholders may exercise all the powers granted in the act to which this is a supplement, under such rules and regulations as they may adopt, in the election of officers and the appointment of agents for carrying on the business of the corporation, not inconsistent with the act to which this is a supplement.

SEC. 2. That any corporation formed under the act to which this is a supplement, having constructed a road, or having partially constructed one, of no greater length than that fixed by this act, electing to organize under the provisions hereof shall have the power to do so if a majority of its stock so determines, and shall, within thirty days, file in the office of the secretary of the Commonwealth a certificate of its action and a copy of its articles of association, under forms fixed by said secretary; and any corporation failing, refusing, or neglecting so to do shall be subject to a fine of fifty dollars, to be collected as other fines are by the proper officers of the Commonwealth.

---

A SUPPLEMENT TO AN ACT TO ENABLE RAILROAD, CANAL, AND SLACK-WATER NAVIGATION COMPANIES TO STRAIGHTEN, WIDEN, DEEPEN, AND OTHERWISE IMPROVE THEIR LINES OF RAILROADS, CANALS, AND SLACK-WATER NAVIGATION, AND THE BRIDGES, AQUE-DUCTS, PIERS, AND STRUCTURES THEREOF, APPROVED THE SEVENTEENTH DAY OF MARCH, ANNO DOMINI ONE THOUSAND EIGHT HUNDRED AND SIXTY-NINE.

*Approved 2d May, 1871. (P. L., 1871, page 248.)*

SECTION 1. That in addition to the remedies and proceedings provided by the second section of the act to which this is a supplement, all and singular the provisions of the second and third sections of the act of assembly approved the ninth day of April, Anno Domini one thousand eight hundred and fifty-six, entitled "A supplement to an act entitled 'An act regulating railroad companies,' approved the nineteenth day of February, Anno Domini one thousand eight hundred and forty-nine," and of the first section of the act of assembly approved the twenty-seventh day of April, Anno Domini one thousand eight hundred and fifty-five, entitled "An act extending the right of trial by jury to certain cases," are hereby made applicable to all cases arising and proceedings instituted under the said act to which this is a supplement.

---

AN ACT RELATING TO LEASES OR CONTRACTS FOR THE USE OF CANALS OR OTHER NAVIGATION WORKS BY RAILROAD COMPANIES.

*Approved 3d May, 1871. (P. L., 1871, pages 248 and 249.)*

SECTION 1. That the authority conferred upon railroad companies by the act approved the seventeenth day of February, Anno Domini one thousand eight hundred and seventy,

entitled "An act to authorize railroad companies to lease o
become lessees and to make contracts with other railroac
companies, corporations, and parties," shall extend to and em
brace leases, assignments of lease, or other contracts relatin;
to canal and other navigation works, situated either in this o
any other State : *Provided*, That neither the provisions of th(
said act approved the seventeenth day of February, on(
thousand eight hundred and seventy-one, nor of this act
shall authorize the leasing or merging of or entering int(
contracts with the Susquehanna Canal Company, or the pur
chase in whole or in part of the said canal, its capital stocl
loans, or securities by any railroad company.

## AN ACT FOR THE COLLECTION OF MINERAL STATISTICS

*Approved 9th May, 1871.* (*P. L., 1871, pages 261 and 263.*)

SECTION I. That in addition to the information now requirec
to be furnished to the auditor-general by the several railroac
and canal companies of this Commonwealth, each of said railroad and canal companies, when their railroad or canal passe:
through any of the coal regions of this State, shall report foi
the year one thousand eight hundred and seventy-one, anc
annually, as soon after the first day of January in each year
or the close of the fiscal year of said companies, as the
information can be procured under oath of one of the officer:
of said company, to the auditor-general, the quantity of coa'
of each kind and of coke, in tons of two thousand pound:
each, received for transportation at each station on every
such railroad and at each coal-shipping point on said canal
distinguishing in said report the quantities received direcl
from the mines from that received from other railroad oi
canals, giving the name of said connecting railroad or canals
in such a manner that the amount of the production of coa]
on the line of said railroad or canal may be correctly ascertained; the Monongahela Slack-water Navigation Company,
and all other slack-water navigation companies engaged in
conveying coal or coke, are also hereby required to make

returns in the same manner as is hereinbefore required of railroad and canal companies.

SEC. 2. It shall also be the duty of each of said railroad companies to report the quantity of coal purchased or mined for their own use in this State by them during each year, and which was produced along the line of said railroad, and stating at what place or places the same was mined, and which was not included in the reports of coal received for transportation before mentioned of said railroad, or of any other railroad or canal.

SEC. 3. It shall be the duty of all coal-mining companies or firms and individuals working mines, and of all State and county officers, to furnish to the auditor-general, in answer to his letters or circulars, all information in their possession in regard to the quantity of coal mined that is sent to market direct by any navigable river, or used by any rolling-mill, blast furnace, salt works, or otherwise, and which is not transported on any railroad, canal, or slack-water navigation company, and also to inform him when and of whom correct information as to the coal production of any such locality can be procured; and further, to inform him of all accidents in mines in counties where there is no mine inspector appointed by law, and how the same was caused.

SEC. 4. It shall be the duty of the auditor-general, on receiving said reports and such other authentic information as he shall collect, to collate said reports and information, and make a report, giving the results only, in tabular form, showing the quantity of coal mined during each year in each county and in each important coal-producing region, in a perspicuous form, separating the several kinds of coal into anthracite, semi-bituminous, bituminous, and splint or block coal, suitable for smelting iron, giving also from time to time the statistics of each region, from the beginning of its coal trade, so far as it can be ascertained; he shall also specially report the number of accidents resulting in death or injury in coal mines in those counties where there is no mine inspector, classifying them according to the cause thereof, whether occasioned by fire, explosions, falls of roof or coal in shafts or slopes, or other causes, under ground or at the surface.

SEC. 5. The auditor-general shall also, in the same manner collect statistics, collate, classify, and report, at the same time the quantities of petroleum, salt, iron ore, zinc, and othe mineral productions of the Commonwealth; also, the pig iroi and merchant or wrought iron manufactured in the Common wealth.

SEC. 6. Eight thousand copies of said report of the auditor general, together with his suggestions on the workings o existing laws and his propositions as to new enactments shall be published for distribution, annually, as soon as it i prepared, with the title of the "Mineral Statistics of Pennsyl vania;" and one copy thereof shall be sent by mail, by the auditor-general, to each person who shall have furnishec him with information as aforesaid, and the balance shall be delivered to the legislature for distribution.

SEC. 7. Any railroad or canal or slack-water navigatior company, or coal-mining company, firm, or individual en- gaged in mining, or any county officer, who shall neglect or refuse, for thirty days, to make report or give the informatior required by this act, shall be liable to a penalty of one hundred dollars, to be recovered by order of the auditor- general, in an action of debt, in which the Commonwealth shall be plaintiff, by the district attorney of the proper county the one-half thereof to go to said district attorney and the other half for the use of the poor of the proper poor district

---

AN ACT RELATING TO CERTAIN RAILROAD, CANAL, AND INCORPORATED COMPANIES AUTHORIZED TO CON- STRUCT RAILROADS, AND AUTHORIZING SUCH COM- PANIES TO PURCHASE AND HOLD STOCK AND BONDS, TO LEASE ROADS AND PROPERTY OF, AND CONSOLI- DATE WITH, EACH OTHER IN THE COUNTIES OF SUS- QUEHANNA, WYOMING, WAYNE, AND LUZERNE.

*Approved 18th May, 1871.* (*P. L., 1871, pages 942 and 943.*)

SECTION 1. That it shall be lawful for any railroad, canal, or navigation company incorporated by or exercising within this Commonwealth, and under and in pursuance of the laws

thereof, corporate privileges, within the counties of Susquehanna, Wyoming, Wayne, and Luzerne, to purchase and hold
the stock and bonds, and to lease the road and property of, or
become consolidated and merged with, any other incorporated
company authorized by the laws of this Commonwealth to
construct a railroad or possessing railroad privileges, and for
any such [any] incorporated company so authorized to construct a railroad or, possessing railroad privileges, to purchase
and hold the stock and bonds, and to lease the road, canal,
and property of, or become consolidated and merged with,
any such railroad, canal, or navigation company, in the same
manner as such purchases, leases, consolidation, and merger
are now provided or allowed by law and by and between
railroad companies incorporated by this Commonwealth; and
all the provisions of existing acts relative to such purchases,
leases, consolidation, and merger by and between railroad
companies incorporated by this Commonwealth are, whenever or so far as applicable, hereby extended so as to
embrace the purchases, leases, consolidations, and mergers
hereby authorized, and so that the authority by this act
conferred may be effectually and lawfully exercised; and
when any merger and consolidation shall be made in accordance with the provisions of this act, all the property, rights,
franchises, and privileges of the company so merged shall, by
virtue of such merger, be thereby transferred to and vested
in the company into which such merger shall be made: *Provided*, That any consolidated company formed by merging of
two or more companies, under the provisions of this act, shall
not charge any higher rates for transportation than the rates
now allowed by law over the respective roads so merged.

----

## AN ACT TO AUTHORIZE MARRIED WOMEN OWNING CAPITAL STOCK OF ANY RAILROAD COMPANY TO SELL AND TRANSFER THE SAME.

*Approved 2d June, 1871.* (*P. L.*, *1871, page 283.*)

SECTION I. That it shall and may be lawful for any married
woman, owning any share or shares of the capital stock of
any railroad company, to sell and transfer the same with like
effect as if she were unmarried.

## AN ACT RELATING TO LEGAL PROCEEDINGS BY ANI AGAINST CORPORATIONS.

*Approved 19th June, 1871.*  (*P. L., 1871, pages 1360 and 1361.*)

SECTION 1. That in all proceedings in courts of law o: equity of this Commonwealth, in which it is alleged that th( private rights of individuals or the rights or franchises o other corporations are injured or invaded by any corporatioı claiming to have a right or franchise to do the act from whicl such injury results, it shall be the duty of the court in whicl such proceedings are had to examine, inquire, and ascertaiı whether such corporation does, in fact, possess the right oı franchise to do the act from which such alleged injury tc private rights or to the rights and franchises of other corpo· rations results, and if such rights or franchises have not beer conferred upon such corporation, such courts, if exercising equitable power, shall, by injunction, at suit of the privatє parties or other corporations, restrain such injurious acts; anc if the proceedings be at law for damages, it shall be lawful therein to recover damages for such injury, as in other cases.

SEC. 2. When such legal proceedings relate to crossings oı lines of railroads by other railroads, it shall be the duty oı courts of equity of this Commonwealth to ascertain and define by their decree the mode of such crossing which will inflict the least practical injury upon the rights of the company owning the road which is intended to be crossed, and if, in the judgment of such court, it is reasonably practicable to avoid a grade-crossing, they shall by their process prevent a crossing at grade.

## A SUPPLEMENT TO AN ACT ENTITLED "AN ACT RELA- TIVE TO CHANGES OF VENUE."

*Approved 21st February, 1872.*  (*P. L., 1872, page 19.*)

SECTION 1. That all the expenses incurred in the trial of any suits by the county to which they may be removed under the provisions of the act entitled "An act relative to the change of venue," approved April twenty-eighth, Anno Domini one thousand eight hundred and seventy, shall be paid by the county from which such suits have been removed.

## AN ACT TO PREVENT TRESPASSING UPON RAILROAD CARS IN THE COUNTY OF BERKS.

*Approved 21st February, 1872. (P. L., 1872, page 131.)*

WHEREAS, Minors and other persons frequently enter upon and into and be upon railroad cars in the county of Berks, contrary to the rules of the corporations owning such cars, and for the purpose of being, riding, and traveling thereon without any payment of fare, and by entering upon and leaving such cars serious and fatal accidents have occurred; therefore,

SECTION 1. That any person being in or upon or entering in or upon any railroad car in the county of Berks, whether the same be passenger, freight, coal, or other car, with the intention of being, riding, or traveling in or upon such car, contrary to the rules of the person, persons, or corporation owning the same, and with the intention of being in or upon, riding, or traveling upon such car without paying fare, shall forfeit and pay a penalty of not more than five dollars, which penalty shall be paid to the treasurer of the school district in which said offense was committed, for the use of said district.

SEC. 2. Any constable or police officer having knowledge of the violation of this act may forthwith arrest such offender, and take him before any judge, alderman, or justice of the peace, or such offender may be arrested by a warrant or *capias* issued by such magistrate, upon information duly made on oath or affirmation; and said magistrate shall proceed to hear and determine the matter in issue, and if he shall convict the person so charged with the violation of the provisions of this act, he shall proceed to pronounce the forfeiture which he shall adjudge against the person so convicted; and if the person so convicted refuse or neglect to satisfy such forfeiture immediately, with costs, or produce goods and chattels whereon to levy the said forfeiture, together with costs, then the said justice shall commit the offender to the Berks county prison for a period not exceeding ten days.

(Extended to several other counties, 27th February, 1873.)

## AN ACT RELATING TO STRAIGHTENED OR IMPROVE] LINES OF RAILROAD.

*Approved 3d April, 1872. (P. L., 1872, pages 35 and 36.)*

SECTION 1. That it shall be lawful for the president an‹ directors of any railroad company to retain the possession an‹ use, either in whole or part, of any portion of the origina railroad for which an improved or straightened line has bee substituted, if in their opinion the abandonment of the sai‹ portion would be inconvenient or injurious to the interests ‹ the public and of the railroad company.

## AN ACT TO AUTHORIZE CORPORATIONS TO ISSUE PREFERRED STOCK.

*Approved 3d April, 1872. (P. L., 1872, pages 37 and 38.)*

SECTION 1. That it shall be lawful for any company now o hereafter incorporated by or under any general law of thi Commonwealth to issue, with the consent of a majority ii interest of its stockholders, preferred stock of the company not exceeding at any time one-half of the capital stock o the corporation, the holders of which preferred stock shal be entitled to receive such dividends thereon, not exceedin; twelve per cent. per annum, as the board of directors of sai‹ company may prescribe, payable out of the net earnings ‹ the company; and the holders of said preferred stock shal not be liable for any debts of the company.

## AN ACT EXEMPTING THE COUNTIES OF LANCASTER VENANGO, AND BERKS FROM ALL THE PROVISION: OF AN ACT ENTITLED "AN ACT RELATING TO CHANGE: OF VENUE," APPROVED APRIL TWENTY-EIGHTH ANNO DOMINI ONE THOUSAND EIGHT HUNDRED ANI SEVENTY.

*Approved 3d April, 1872. (P. L., 1872, page 839.)*

SECTION 1. That from and after the passage of this act th‹ counties of Lancaster, Venango, and Berks shall be exemp from all of the provisions of an act entitled "An act relating to changes of venue," approved April twenty-eighth, Anno Domini one thousand eight hundred and seventy.

---

AN ACT SUPPLEMENTAL TO AN ACT ENTITLED "A SUP-PLEMENT TO ACTS RELATING TO INCORPORATIONS BY THE COURTS OF COMMON PLEAS," APPROVED ON THE NINTH DAY OF APRIL, ANNO DOMINI ONE THOU-SAND EIGHT HUNDRED AND FIFTY-SIX.

*Approved 4th April, 1872. (P. L., 1872, pages 40 and 41.)*

SECTION I. That the "proper county" intended by said act, approved as aforesaid, may be, at the option of any corporation praying for permission to dissolve in the way and manner in said act designated, either the county in which the principal operations of the corporations are conducted or that county in which its principal office or place of business is located: *Provided,* That notice of said application shall be given by publication in two papers in the county in which the principal operations are conducted and that in which the principal office is located.

---

AN ACT RELATING TO FOREIGN EXECUTORS, ADMIN-ISTRATORS, GUARDIANS AND REPRESENTATIVES OF DECEDENTS AND WARDS.

*Approved 8th April, 1872. (P. L., 1872, pages 44 and 45.)*

SECTION I. That it shall and may be lawful for any executor, administrator, or other person representing the estate of any decedent, or for any guardian or other legal representative of the estate of a minor, acting under letters testamentary or of administration or other authority, granted by or under the laws of any other State or territory of the United States, or of any kingdom, state, sovereignty, or country, to transfer any or all shares of stock and registered loan, or either, of any incorporated company of this Commonwealth, standing in the

name of any decedent minor, or *cestui que trust*, and to receiv
the dividends and interest, or either thereof, whenever a dul;
authenticated copy of the will or other grant of authorit;
under which such transfer or receipt is proposed to be mad
shall have been filed in the office of the register of wills fo
the county in which such incorporated company has its trans
fer office or principal place of business; and all transfers c
stock or loans or receipts for dividends or interest heretofor
made by foreign executor, administrator, guardian, and other
acting as aforesaid, are hereby validated.

---

AN ACT FOR THE APPOINTMENT OF A RECEIVER II
CASES WHERE CORPORATIONS HAVE BEEN DISSOLVEI
BY JUDGMENT OF OUSTER, UPON PROCEEDINGS OI
QUO WARRANTO.

*Approved April 4th, 1872. (P L., 1872, pages 46 and 47.)*

SECTION 1. That whenever any corporation incorporate;
under the laws of this Commonwealth shall have been dis
solved by judgment of ouster, upon proceedings of *qu
warranto* in any court of competent jurisdiction, all the estate
both real and personal, of which such corporation are in an;
way seized or possessed shall pass to and vest in the persoi
who at the time of such dissolution are the officers of sucl
corporation, in trust, to hold the same for the benefit of th
stockholders and creditors of the corporation.

SEC. 2. The Supreme Court, or any judge thereof sitting a
*nisi prius*, shall, upon the petition of any stockholder o
creditor of such corporation, appoint a receiver, who shal
have all the powers of a receiver appointed by a court c
chancery, to take possession of all the estate, both real an;
personal, thereof, and make distribution of the assets amon;
the persons entitled to receive the same according to law
*Provided*, That written notice, as may be directed by the cour;
shall be given to the persons, or a majority of them, who wer
at the time of the dissolution officers of the corporation, c
the intention, time, and place of presenting such petition
*And provided further*, That it shall be the duty of sucl

receiver to give notice of his appointment, time, and place of meeting to all the stockholders of such corporation, and to advertise the same as the court may direct.

SEC. 3. That the provisions of this act shall also apply to any corporation that has been heretofore dissolved by judgment of ouster upon proceedings of *quo warranto* in any court of competent jurisdiction, the affairs of which have not been settled and adjusted.

---

## AN ACT FOR THE BETTER PROTECTION OF THE WAGES OF MECHANICS, MINERS, LABORERS, AND OTHERS.

*Approved 9th April, 1872. (P. L., 1872, pages 47 and 49.)*

SECTION 1. That all moneys that may be due, or hereafter become due, for labor and services rendered by any miner, mechanic, laborer, or clerk, from any person or persons, or chartered company employing clerks, miners, mechanics, or laborers, either as owners, lessees, contractors, or underowners of any works, mines, manufactory, or other business where clerks, miners, or mechanics are employed, whether at so much per diem or otherwise, for any period not exceeding six months immediately preceding the sale and transfer of such works, mines, manufactories, or business, or other property connected therewith, in carrying on said business, by execution or otherwise, preceding the death or insolvency of such employer or employers, shall be a lien upon said mine, manufactory, business, or other property in and about or used in carrying on the said business or in connection therewith, to the extent of the interest of said owners or contractors, as the case may be, in said property, and shall be preferred and first paid out of the proceeds of the sale of such mine, manufactory, business, or other property as aforesaid: *Provided*, That the claim of such miner, mechanic, laborer, and clerk thus preferred shall not exceed two hundred dollars: *And provided further*, That this act shall not be so construed as to impair contracts existing or liens of record vested prior to its passage: *And provided further*, That no such claim shall be a lien upon any real estate, unless the same be filed in the prothonotary's office of the county in which such real estate is situated, within three months after the same becomes due and owing, in the same manner as mechanics' liens are now filed.

SEC. 2. In all cases of executions, landlords' warrants attachments, and writs of a similar nature hereafter to be issued against any person or persons or chartered company engaged as before mentioned, it shall be lawful for such miners, laborers, mechanics, or clerks to give notice in writing of their claim or claims, and the amount thereof, to the officer executing either of such writs, at any time before the actual sale of the property levied on; and such officers shall pay to such miners, laborers, mechanics, and clerks, out of the proceeds of sale, the amount each is justly and legally entitled to receive, not exceeding two hundred dollars.

SEC. 3. In all cases of the death, insolvency, or assignmen of any person or persons or chartered company engaged in operations as hereinbefore mentioned, or of, executions issued against them, the lien of preference mentioned in the first section of this act, with the like limitations and powers, shall extend to every property of said persons or chartered company.

SEC. 4. That no mortgage, or other instrument by which a lien is hereafter credited, shall operate to impair or postpone the lien and preference given and secured to the wages and moneys mentioned in the first section of this act: *Provided* That no lien of mortgage or judgment entered before such labor is performed shall be effected or impaired thereby.

SEC. 5. That in all cases of appeal from the judgment of justice of the peace for wages or moneys mentioned in the first section of this act, the party appellant, his agent or attorney, shall make oath or affirmations that it is not for the purpose of delay that such appeal is entered, but because he firmly believes injustice has been done; the bail required in cases of appeal from the judgments of justices of peace and from the awards of arbitrators for the wages and money mentioned in the first section of this act shall be bail absolute in double the amount of said judgments and awards, and th probable amount of costs accrued and likely to accrue in such cases, with one or more sufficient sureties conditioned for the payment of the amount of the debt, interest, and cost that shall be legally recovered in such case against the appellant.

SEC. 6. That all laws or parts of laws inconsistent herewith be and the same are hereby repealed.

---

AN ACT AMENDING THE PROVISO IN SECTION FIVE OF AN ACT TO PREVENT FRAUDS UPON TRAVELERS, AP-PROVED THE SIXTH DAY OF MAY, ANNO DOMINI ONE THOUSAND EIGHT HUNDRED AND SIXTY-THREE.

*Approved 10th April, 1872. (P. L., 1872, page 51.)*

SECTION 1. That the proviso in section five of an act to prevent frauds upon travelers, approved the sixth day of May, Anno Domini one thousand eight hundred and sixty-three, be and the same is hereby amended so that the same shall read as follows: *Provided,* That this act shall not prohibit any person who has purchased a ticket from any agent authorized by this act, with the *bona fide* intention of traveling upon the same the whole distance between the points named in the said ticket, from selling the unused part of the same to the company that sold the same; and it shall be the duty of the said company to pay for such unused portion of ticket the difference between the actual fare to point used and the amount paid for such ticket.

---

AN ACT RELATING TO THE STOCK AND BONDS OF RAIL-ROAD AND CANAL COMPANIES MERGED OR PROPOSING TO MERGE AND HELD BY EXECUTORS, GUARDIANS, OR TRUSTEES.

*Approved 12th April, 1872. (P. L., 1872, page 61.)*

SECTION 1. That it shall and may be lawful for any executor, guardian, or trustee holding the stock and bonds, or either, of any railroad or canal company which may be authorized to merge and consolidate with, or which has become merged

and consolidated with, any other railroad or canal company, t(
agree for and in respect to the said stock and bonds, or eithei
so held by them, to the terms and conditions of such propose(
or actual merger, and to accept in lieu or exchange for sai(
stock and bond, or either, (but to be held in like trusts,) th(
stock and bonds, or either, of the company so merging o
formed by such merger and consolidation.

---

## AN ACT AUTHORIZING MINING AND MANUFACTURINC COMPANIES, OR OTHER ORGANIZED COMPANIES OF INDIVIDUALS, TO GIVE, AND BANKS OR OTHER ORGAN IZED COMPANIES OR INDIVIDUALS TO TAKE AND HOLI MORTGAGES ON REAL ESTATE, TO SECURE PAYMEN1 OF NOTES, BILLS, AND RENEWALS THEREOF.

*Approved 17th February, 1873. (P. L., 1873, page 35.)*

SECTION 1. That it shall be lawful for mining and manufacturing companies organized under any special or general law
of this Commonwealth, or for any other organized company oi
individual, to execute and deliver, and for all banks organizec
under any law of this Commonwealth, or any other organizec
company, individual, or individuals, to take and hold mortgages on real estate, to secure payment of such notes, bills
and other negotiable or other paper, and renewals thereof
belonging to or made by said companies, as the said banks
companies, individual, or individuals shall agree to and
execute, from time to time, for discount or otherwise : *Provided,* That such mortgage shall operate as a lien from the
date of the record of such instrument.

---

## AN ACT TO EXTEND TO CERTAIN COUNTIES AN ACT EN-TITLED "AN ACT TO PREVENT TRESPASSING UPON RAILROAD CARS IN THE COUNTY OF BERKS," APPROVED THE TWENTY-FIRST DAY OF FEBRUARY, ANNO DOMINI ONE THOUSAND EIGHT HUNDRED AND SEVENTY-TWO.

*Approved 27th February, 1873. (P. L., 1873, page 181.)*

SECTION 1. That the provisions of an act entitled "An act
to prevent trespassing upon railroad cars in the county of

Berks," approved the twenty-first day of February, Anno Domini one thousand eight hundred and seventy-two, be and the same is hereby extended to the counties of York, Hunt-'ingdon, Union, Philadelphia, Westmoreland, Perry, Bucks, Montour, and Schuylkill.

---

## AN ACT TO PREVENT RAILROAD COMPANIES AND OTHER CORPORATIONS NOW OR HEREAFTER CREATED UNDER THE LAWS OF THIS COMMONWEALTH FROM CONSTRUCTING ANY RAILROAD OR OTHER WORKS WITHIN, OVER, OR UPON THE LANDS, TENEMENTS, OR HEREDITAMENTS BELONGING OR APPERTAINING TO THE PENNSYLVANIA STATE LUNATIC HOSPITAL, SITUATE IN DAUPHIN COUNTY.

*Approved 1st March, 1873. (P. L., 1873, page 38.)*

WHEREAS, The constructing of any railroad through the grounds of said hospital would be detrimental to the interests of those for whose benefit and improvement the same was built, and dangerous to them when taking exercise and recreation within the grounds thereof; therefore,

SECTION 1. That it shall not be lawful for any railroad company or other corporation now or hereafter created under the laws of this Commonwealth, and the same are hereby forbidden and prohibited from entering in or upon or from constructing or building any railroad or other works within, upon, or over any lands, tenements, or. hereditaments belonging or appertaining to the said the Pennsylvania State Lunatic Hospital.

---

## AN ACT TO AUTHORIZE CORPORATIONS TO SECURE THE PAYMENT OF THEIR BONDS AND OBLIGATIONS BY A MORTGAGE UPON THEIR PROPERTY, RIGHTS, AND FRANCHISES.

*Approved 13th March, 1873. (P. L., 1873, page 45.)*

SECTION 1. That it shall be lawful for any railroad corporation of this Commonwealth to secure the payment of any and all bonds and obligations which they have heretofore made and issued, or may hereafter make and issue, by a mortgage bearing a rate of interest not exceeding seven per centum per annum, upon the whole or any part of their prop-erty, rights, and franchises, subject to any prior encumbrances thereon; *Provided*, That this act shall not be construed to empower any railroad company to issue bonds in excess of the capital stock actually paid in.

---

## AN ACT RELATING TO THE REVENUES OF THE COM-MONWEALTH.

*Approved 21st March, 1873. (P. L., 1873, page 46.)*

WHEREAS, In order to meet the increased expense resulting from the late war, and to extinguish the loan of three millions of dollars created for that purpose, as well as to place the credit of the Commonwealth on a secure basis, it became necessary to establish an anomalous and somewhat burden-some system of taxation;

AND WHEREAS, The revenue raised by taxing the capital or the industry of the State ought not to exceed the amount necessary to meet the ordinary expenses of government and reduce the debt at a reasonable rate;

AND WHEREAS, In the act of February twenty-third, eighteen hundred and sixty-six, imposing a tax on the gross receipts of railroads and carrying companies, as well as in the revised tax laws of eighteen hundred and sixty-eight, it was clearly expressed to be for the purpose of extinguishing the loan created by the act of May fifteen, Anno Domini one thou-sand eight hundred and sixty-one, known as the war loan, which purpose is now substantially accomplished; therefore,

SECTION 1. That all laws or parts of laws now in force in this Commonwealth under and by virtue of which taxes for State purposes are levied and assessed upon horses, mares, geldings, mules, and cattle, shall be and they are hereby repealed, so far as they give authority to impose State taxes on the same: *Provided*, That this section shall not take effect until the next meeting of the board of revenue commissioners of this Commonwealth.

SEC. 2. That so much of the sixth section of the act entitled "An act to revise, amend, and consolidate the several laws taxing corporations, brokers, and bankers," approved May first, Anno Domini one thousand eight hundred and sixty-eight, as imposes a tax upon the net earnings or income of incorporated companies liable to the tax on capital stock under the fourth section of said act, be and the same is hereby repealed, said repeal to take effect from and after the first day of November, Anno Domini one thousand eight hundred and seventy-two: *Provided*, That this act shall not be construed to release any taxes which accrued prior to the first day of November aforesaid, nor in any way to affect suits heretofore or hereafter brought in the name of the Common-wealth for the collection of such taxes, and the penalties and interest attached thereto, nor to release private bankers, brokers, or incorporated companies having no taxable capital stock, but for such purposes the section hereby repealed shall continue in full force and effect.

SEC. 3. That so much of the eighth section of the act last aforesaid as imposes a tax upon the gross receipts of railroad, canal, and transportation companies, be and the same is hereby repealed, said repeal to take effect from and after the first day of July next: *Provided*, That any company which has been exempt from the tax on tonnage by any special law shall be liable to pay the tax of three-fourths of one per centum upon their gross receipts; and that this act shall not be construed to release any taxes upon gross receipts accruing prior to the first day of July next, nor in any way to affect suits heretofore or hereafter instituted in the name of the Commonwealth for the collection of such taxes, and the penalties and interest attached thereto.

SEC. 4. That every company, except bank or savings insti-tutions, incorporated under the laws of this Commonwealth, and authorized to issue bonds or other evidences of indebted-ness, and which pays interest to its bondholders or other creditors, shall pay to the State treasurer, for the use of the Commonwealth, semi-annually, on the first days of July and January in each and every year, beginning with the first day of July, Anno Domini one thousand eight hundred and seventy-three, a tax equal to five per centum upon every dollar of interest paid as aforesaid; and it shall be the duty o any company aforesaid to make semi-annual reports to the auditor-general, under oath, showing the total amount of the indebtedness of said company, and the amount of interest paic to their bondholders or other creditors.

That the eleventh section of the act approved May first, eighteen hundred and sixty-eight, entitled " An act tc revise, amend, and consolidate the several laws taxing cor- porations, brokers, and bankers," is hereby repealed, said repeal to date from and after the first day of July next, saving however, to the Commonwealth the right to collect any taxes accruing under said section prior to the date of repeal afore- said.

(Section 4 repealed by act of April 24th, 1874.)

---

### AN ACT TO PROVIDE FOR A PERMANENT CENTENNIAL EXPOSITION BUILDING FOR THE PEOPLE OF THE COMMONWEALTH, IN THE CITY OF PHILADELPHIA.

*Approved 27th March, 1873. (P. L., 1873, page 50.)*

SECTION 1. That the sum of one million dollars be and the same is hereby appropriated for the erection of a permanent centennial exposition building for the people of this Common- wealth, and for the use of the centennial anniversary of American independence, under the direction of the United States centennial board of finance, incorporated by act of congress, to be paid, however, only as hereinafter provided No larger sum than shall be received into the State treasury on account of the centennial anniversary fund hereinafter provided for shall be paid by the State treasurer on account of the permanent centennial exposition building during the present year, and not exceeding three hundred thousand dollars shall be paid of the amount hereby appropriated during the year Anno Domini one thousand eight hundred and seventy-four, and not more than three hundred thousand dollars during the year Anno Domini one thousand eight hundred and seventy-five, and the residue of one million dollars shall be paid on or before the fourth day of July, Anno Domini one thousand eight hundred and seventy-six: *Provided*, That the moneys herein appropriated are in no event to be drawn from or out of the revenue of the Commonwealth which, under the Constitution and laws of the State, are set apart for payment of the State debt; and if, from any cause, the revenue especially provided as a centennial anniversary fund, by the fifth section of this act, shall be insufficient to provide the whole moneys hereinbefore appropriated, no more money than the sum of two hundred and fifty thousand dollars shall be paid from the State treasury to the purposes aforesaid.

SEC. 2. Before any part of the money hereby appropriated shall be paid, satisfactory evidence shall be furnished to the State centennial supervisors hereinafter named that at least one million dollars of *bona fide* responsible private subscriptions shall have been made within the city of Philadelphia to the capital stock of the said United States centennial board of finance, which shall be officially certified to the governor by the said supervisors, and a sum not less than five hundred thousand dollars shall have been appropriated by the municipal authorities of the city of Philadelphia, to be applied to the erection of the permanent centennial exposition building hereinafter provided for, and a contract shall have been executed by the said centennial board of finance, and the centennial board of finance incorporated by act of congress, with the State centennial supervisors hereinafter named, the commissioners of Fairmount Park, and the representatives of the city of Philadelphia, as the authorities of said city shall appoint for the purpose, stipulating that a permanent fire-proof building shall be erected in Fairmount Park as part of the centennial exposition buildings, to cost not less than one million five hundred thousand dollars, which building shall remain in Fairmount Park perpetually, as the property of the people of this Commonwealth, for the preservation and exhibition of national and State relics and works of art, industry, mechanicism, and products of the soil, mines, *et cetera*, of this State, and that it shall be kept open perpetually, after the year Anno Domini one thousand eight hundred and

seventy-six, for the improvement and enjoyment of the peopl
of this Commonwealth, under such regulations as the Fair
mount Park commissioners and the State centennial super
visors and the proper representatives of the city of Philadel
phia shall from time to time prescribe ; but such regulation
shall at all times afford equal facilities and privileges to a
the people of this Commonwealth, without regard to locality
condition, or race, which contract shall be approved by th
governor of the State before it shall be deemed valid; afte
the centennial anniversary exposition shall have closed, th
said park commissioners and State supervisors and the prope
representatives of the city of Philadelphia may admit int
said building the works of art, products of industry, *et ceter*
from any other state or government, under such regulation
as may be deemed just and proper, but there shall be n
discrimination between the several States of this Union no
between the governments of the world.

SEC. 3. Alexander Henry, J. Gillingham Fell, and Joh
O. James, of the city of Philadelphia, William M. Lyon an
John H. Shoenberger, of the county of Allegheny, Georg
R. Messersmith, of Franklin county, William Bigler, of th
county of Clearfield, Ario Pardee, Sr., of the county of Lu
zerne, and John H. Ewing, of the county of Washington, b
and they are hereby appointed State centennial supervisor
who shall, in addition to the powers and duties hereinbefor
prescribed, formally approve the design, plans, and specifica
tions for said permanent centennial exposition building, an
report the same, with their approval, to the governor; an
they shall formally approve any contract or contracts for th
erection of said building, and for materials for the same, an
also report such contract or contracts, with their approval, t
the governor; and no part of the money hereby appropriate
shall be paid until such design, plans, specifications, and con
tract or contracts shall have been officially approved by sai
supervisors and so certified to and approved by the governo
When said supervisors shall certify to the governor that th
labor done and materiaĺs furnished for said building amoun
to the sum of one hundred thousand dollars, the governo
shall draw his warrant on the State treasurer in favor of th

treasurer of the centennial board of finance for fifty thousand dollars, and thereafter, whenever the said supervisors shall certify to the governor that the additional work done and materials furnished amount to the sum of one hundred thousand dollars, and that the money previously paid has been fully and properly applied, he shall draw his warrant in like manner for fifty thousand dollars, if so much shall remain unpaid, in accordance with the stipulation for the annual payments contained in the first section of this act; and when said supervisors shall certify that said centennial exposition building is complete, that the full sum of one million five hundred thousand dollars has been expended on the same, and that the previous payments have been fully and properly applied, the residue of one million dollars shall be paid as hereinbefore directed, but no larger amount shall be paid during any one year than is provided in the first section of this act.

SEC. 4. Said board of State centennial supervisors shall elect one of their number as president and shall appoint a secretary, who shall keep a record of the proceedings of the board, and file a complete duplicate of the same with the governor at the close of each year; any vacancy occurring in the board shall be filled by the said board, but no person shall be chosen to fill any such vacancy without receiving five votes; and any of said supervisors may be removed at any time by the governor on address of a majority of both branches of the legislature; said boards shall not exercise any authority or control over the centennial exposition building during the centennial anniversary exposition, but said permanent building shall, during such exposition, be under the same control and direction of the United States centennial commission as the other buildings erected by said centennial board of finance.

SEC. 5. That in order to provide revenue to enable the State to meet the appropriation hereinbefore made on or before the first day of July, Anno Domini one thousand eight hundred and seventy-three, all street passenger railway companies now incorporated in the city of Philadelphia shall make return to the State treasurer, under oath of the proper officers, stating the gross receipts of each of said companies from the passage of this act until said return is made, and like quarterly return shall be made by said companies thereafter until the first da' of April, Anno Domini one thousand eight hundred an seventy-seven, inclusive; and with each report there shall b be paid by said street passenger railway companies to th State treasurer three per centum of such gross receipts, whicl revenue shall be placed by the State treasurer to the credit c the centennial anniversary fund; and all moneys paid by sai State treasurer on account of the appropriations hereinbefor made shall be paid out of said centennial anniversary fund unti the same is exhausted, and the residue, if any required to be paid during any one year, shall be paid out of any moneys ii the treasury not otherwise appropriated. On the first day o April, Anno Domini one thousand eight hundred and seventy seven, the tax upon the gross receipts of said railroad com panies shall cease and determine. Any of said street passenge railway companies which shall, within thirty days after th passage of this act, file with the State treasurer an officia acceptance of its provisions, shall thereupon, each and even of them, be released from any penalty or penalties to whicl they or any of them might be liable under any proceeding ir law or equity for any violation of the provisions of thei charters respectively prior to the passage of this act; anc the faith of the State is hereby pledged to such accepting companies that the legal rate of fares said companies are nov authorized to collect shall not be reduced by legislative enact ment before the first day of April, Anno Domini one thousanc eight hundred and seventy-seven. Any street passenge railway companies incorporated after the passage of this ac shall also report their gross receipts and pay the tax on the same from and after they commence to carry passengers, a: hereinbefore provided.

## AN ACT DECLARING CERTAIN ACTS RELATING TO ANY RAILROAD COMPANY WITHIN THE BOROUGH OF SUSQUEHANNA DEPOT, SUSQUEHANNA COUNTY, TO BE UNLAWFUL.

*Approved 10th April, 1873. (P. L., 1873, page 593.)*

SECTION 1. That it shall be unlawful for any person or persons to be found· loitering, remaining, or congregating in or about the depot, freight-house, offices, shops, or other buildings, or upon the cars or engines, or on the railroad tracks, yard, or other grounds used for railroad purposes belonging to any railroad company and located within the borough of Susquehanna Depot and county of Susquehanna, without lawful business.

SEC. 2. And it shall and may be lawful to arrest such offender or offenders, and for the burgess of said borough, or any justice of the peace of the county aforesaid within said borough, to convict such offender or offenders summarily, in the same manner as provided by the act of assembly relating to vagrants passed February twenty-first, Anno Domini one thousand seven hundred and sixty-seven, and thereupon to impose upon any such offender or offenders a fine not exceeding ten dollars and the costs of prosecution ; and in case any such offender so convicted as aforesaid shall refuse or neglect to pay the fine so imposed and the costs of prosecution as aforesaid, he shall be committed by the said burgess or justice of the peace imposing the same to the common jail of the said county for the period of ten days.

---

## AN ACT TO EXTEND TO THE COUNTY OF DELAWARE AN ACT ENTITLED "AN ACT TO PREVENT TRESPASSING UPON RAILROAD CARS IN THE COUNTY OF BERKS," APPROVED THE TWENTY-FIRST DAY OF FEBRUARY, ANNO DOMINI ONE THOUSAND EIGHT HUNDRED AND SEVENTY-TWO.

*Approved 10th April, 1873. (P. L., 1873, page 624.)*

SECTION 1. That the provisions of an act entitled " An act to prevent trespassing upon railroad cars in the county of

Berks," approved the twenty-first day of February, Ann Domini one thousand eight hundred and seventy-two, l and the same is hereby extended to the county of Delawar( *Provided*, That any commitment under this act shall be t the Delaware county prison.

---

### A SUPPLEMENT TO AN ACT ENTITLED "AN ACT TO AL THORIZE CORPORATIONS TO ISSUE PREFERRED STOCK APPROVED THE THIRD DAY OF APRIL, ANNO DOMIN ONE THOUSAND EIGHT HUNDRED AND SEVENTY-TW(

*Approved 28th April, 1873.* (*P. L.*, *1873, page 79.*)

SECTION 1. That any company authorized by the act t which this is a supplement to issue preferred stock ma issue the same in different classes, to be distinguished in suc manner as the directors of such company may prescribe; an they may give to the various classes such order of preferenc in the payment of the dividends or in the rate of dividenc thereon or in the redemption of the principal thereof as ma be approved by the holders of a majority of the stock of th company; and the company shall have the right to redeer its preferred stock upon such terms as may be prescribed i the issue thereof; and it may specifically appropriate for th payment of the dividends upon any class of stock, or for th redemption of the principal thereof, the revenues from an specific department of its business or the proceeds of an specified portions of its assets or property: *Provided*, That n injustice shall thereby be done to the existing rights of othe stockholder or creditors of the company.

---

### AN ACT TO AUTHORIZE THE REGISTRY OR TRANSFE] OF CERTAIN BONDS.

*Approved 1st May, 1873.* (*P. L.*, *1873, page 87.*)

SEC. 1. That bonds issued or which may be issued by th State of Pennsylvania, or by any county, .city, municipa authority, or corporation therein, payable to bearer, may, at th option and at the expense of the holder thereof, be returned, and new registered bonds, of the same or of a larger denomination, to the aggregate amount thereof, be issued, payable at the same time and place as the bonds so retired, to the order of the holder of said registered bonds, and transferable only by assignment executed before and attested under the hand and seal of some officer authorized by law to take the acknowledgments of deeds, which transfer shall only become operative against the corporations aforesaid when noted on the transfer-book of the party or corporation issuing the bond, and which book of transfer all parties or corporations issuing such bonds are hereby required to keep; and for the interest due or to become due on the bonds so retired as aforesaid, it shall be lawful for the obligors to issue interest certificates, at the same rate of interest, due at the same time and place as the original coupons corresponding with the denominations of the registered bonds, and payable to the order of the holder of said registered bond.

SEC. 2. And it shall further be lawful for any corporate body as aforesaid, which shall issue or may have issued coupon bond or bonds payable to bearer, to register any such original bond or bonds in the name of the holder thereof and upon his or her request and at his or her expense, and stamp or print in large type, or write upon the face thereof, that the same will only be paid to the order of the registered holder thereof; and from and after such stamping, printing, or writing, such bonds shall only be transferable in the manner provided for in the first section of this act, unless the holder shall make them payable to bearer by a properly attested assignment to that effect; such bond shall continue subject to successive registrations, limitations, or transfers to bearer, at the option of each holder; and the word registered stamped, printed, or written upon the coupon of such bonds shall be legal notice that they are no longer payable to bearer, but to the order of the party in whose name the bond to which the coupon is attached shall be registered, unless the last assignment thereon, duly executed, shall be to the bearer, in which event the coupon shall be payable, as in other cases of coupon bonds, to bearer.

SEC. 3. It shall be lawful for the holder or holders of any

such coupon bonds or bond payable to bearer to stamp, prir
or write on the face thereof "Payable to endorsed holder
and to endorse thereon "Pay to order of ———," signing hi
her, or their names thereto in the presence of some offic
authorized to take the acknowledgment of deeds, who sha
attest the same under his hand and seal, and said bond ther
after shall only be payable to the legal holder thereof, or tl
legal representative of such holder; such bond or bonds sha
continue subject to successive transfers in the same manne
and with like force and effect, by the person thus legall
holding the same; and the holder of such bond may stam
print, or write on the coupons thereof, "Endorsed," and suc
stamping, printing, or writing on the face and coupons of suc
bond shall be notice that they are no longer payable to beare
but to the endorsed holder or order or the legal represen
atives thereof, unless the last endorsement shall be to beare
when they shall be payable as other coupon bonds, to beare

SEC. 4. Registrations made, or to be made, of such bon
in the manner herein provided, or in such other manner i
may have been adopted between the makers and holde:
thereof, shall be valid; and the provisions of this act shall n
be construed as repealing special enactments in regard to tl
transfer of bonds of any corporation, nor shall the transfer
any bond or bonds in the manner herein provided impair an
security or the lien of any mortgage which may have bee
given to secure the payment thereof, or the rights, duties, an
powers of any trustee in relation thereto.

---

## AN ACT AUTHORIZING DIRECTORS OF RAILROAD COM PANIES TO ELECT VICE-PRESIDENTS.

*Approved 5th June, 1873. (P. L., 1874, page 331.)*

SECTION I. That it shall be lawful for the directors of an
railroad company incorporated by the laws of this Commoɪ
wealth to elect from among their number a vice-president (
vice-presidents and prescribe their duties.

A SUPPLEMENT TO AN ACT ENTITLED "AN ACT REGU-
LATING LATERAL RAILROADS," APPROVED THE FIFTH
DAY OF MAY, ANNO DOMINI ONE THOUSAND EIGHT
HUNDRED AND THIRTY-TWO, IN THE COUNTY OF
ARMSTRONG.

*Approved 6th June, 1873. (P. L., 1874, page 417.)*

SECTION 1. That the provisions of the act to which this is a supplement shall be extended to embrace owners of furnaces and all kinds of manufacture of iron, so that such owners may erect lateral railroads from their works to their mines, in the same manner as if they were connecting their mines with a railroad.

SEC. 2. That the provisions of said act shall also apply to navigable streams, so that owners of land may construct lateral roads from their mines to all navigable streams under the provisions of the act to which this is a supplement: *Provided,* That the provisions of this act shall only apply to the county of Armstrong.

---

AN ACT TO AUTHORIZE MARRIED WOMEN OWNING
LOANS OF THIS COMMONWEALTH OR OF THE CITY OF
PHILADELPHIA, OR CAPITAL STOCK OF ANY CORPORA-
TION OF THIS COMMONWEALTH, TO SELL AND TRANS-
FER THE SAME.

*Approved 1st April, 1874. (P. L., 1874, page 49.)*

SECTION 1. That it shall and may be lawful for any married woman owning any of the loans of this Commonwealth or of the city of Philadelphia, or any share or shares of the capital stock of any corporation created by or under the laws of this Commonwealth, to sell and transfer the same with like effect as if she were unmarried.

# AN ACT TO PROVIDE FOR THE MANNER OF INCREASIN( THE CAPITAL STOCK AND INDEBTEDNESS OF COR PORATIONS.

*Approved 18th April, 1874. (P. L., 1874, page 61.)*

SECTION 1. That the capital stock or indebtedness of an: corporation may be increased from time to time by the con sent of the persons or bodies corporate holding the large amount in value of the stock of such company, to such amoun as such corporation is by law authorized to increase its capitŁ stock or indebtedness: *Provided,* That no corporation sha increase the amount of its indebtedness beyond the amour of its capital stock subscribed until the amount of its capitŁ stock subscribed shall be fully paid in.

SEC. 2. That any corporation desirous of increasing it capital stock or indebtedness as provided by this act shall, b a resolution of its board of directors, call a meeting of it stockholders therefor, which meeting shall be held at its chit office or place of business in this Commonwealth, and notic of the time, place, and object of said meeting shall be publishe once a week for sixty days prior to such meeting in at leas one newspaper published in the county, city, or boroug wherein such office or place of business is situate.

SEC. 3. At the meeting called pursuant to the second sectio of this act, an election of the stockholders of such corpoi ation shall be taken for or against such increase, which sha be conducted by three judges, stockholders of said corporatioi appointed by the board of directors to hold said electioi and if one or more of said judges be absent, the judge c judges present shall appoint a judge or judges who shall at in the place of the judge or judges absent, and who shall rt spectively take and subscribe an oath or affirmation, before a officer authorized by law to administer the same, well an truly and according to law to conduct such elections to th best of their ability; and the said judges shall decide upon th qualification of voters, and when the election is closed cou the number of shares voted for and against such increase, an declare whether the persons or bodies corporate holding tr

larger amount of the stock of such corporation have con-
sented to such increase or refused to consent thereto, and shall
make out duplicate returns of said election, stating the number
of shares of stock that voted for such increase and the number
that voted against such increase, and subscribe and deliver the
same to one of the chief officers of said company.

SEC. 4. Each ballot shall have endorsed thereon the number
of shares thereby represented, but no share or shares transferred within sixty days shall entitle the holder or holders
thereof to vote at such election or meeting, nor shall any
proxy be received or entitle the holder to vote unless the
same shall bear date and have been executed within three
months next preceding such election or meeting; and it shall
be the duty of such corporation to furnish the judges at said
meeting with a statement of the amount of its capital stock,
with the names of persons or bodies corporate holding the
same, and number of shares by each respectively held, which
statement shall be signed by one of the chief officers of such
corporation, with an affidavit thereto annexed that the same
is true and correct to the best of his knowledge and belief.

SEC. 5. That it shall be the duty of such corporation, if
consent is given to such increase, to file in the office of the
secretary of the Commonwealth, within thirty days after such
election or meeting, one of the copies of the return of such
election provided for by the third section of this act, with a
copy of the resolution and notice calling the same thereto
annexed, and upon the increase of the capital stock or indebt-
ness of such corporation, made pursuant thereto, it shall be
the duty of the president or treasurer of such corporation,
within thirty days thereafter, to make a return to the secretary of the Commonwealth, under oath, of the amount of such
increase, and in case of neglect or omission so to do such corporation shall be subject to a penalty of five thousand dollars,
which penalty shall be collected on an account settled by the
auditor-general and State treasurer as accounts for taxes due
the Commonwealth are settled and collected. And the secretary of the Commonwealth shall cause said return to be
recorded in a book kept for that purpose, and furnish a certified copy of the same to the auditor-general.

SEC. 6. That every corporation shall within sixty days, when requested by the auditor-general, render to him a report under the oath of its president or treasurer, of the amount of capital stock or bond indebtedness issued pursuant to the provisions of this act, showing, in case of stock, to whom issued and the price or consideration received therefor, amount received, and from whom in money, in labor, and in other property, and, if so requested, a detailed statement of the character, value, and situation of the property so received, and in case of refusal or neglect so to do, shall be subject to a penalty of five thousand dollars for each and every thirty days thereafter such corporation shall refuse or neglect to make such report, which penalty or penalties shall be collected on an account or accounts settled from time to time by the auditor-general and State treasurer as accounts for taxes due the Commonwealth are settled and collected.

SEC. 7. That every company, except railroad, canal, turnpike, bridge, or cemetery companies, and companies incorporated for literary, charitable, or religious purposes, which shall increase its capital stock under the provisions of this act, shall pay to the State treasurer, for the use of the Commonwealth, a bonus of one-quarter of one per centum upon the amount of said increase, in two installments, the first to be due upon the filing of the certificate required by the preceding section of this act to be filed in the office of the secretary of the Commonwealth, and the second installment one year thereafter : *Provided*, That nothing in this act shall be construed to reduce the amount of bonus to be paid by any company having in its charter a special provision requiring the payment of a bonus at a higher rate than one-quarter of one per centum.

SEC. 8. All acts and parts of acts inconsistent with the provisions of this act are hereby repealed.

## AN ACT TO ENABLE THE OFFICERS OF DISSOLVED CORPORATIONS TO CONVEY REAL ESTATE HELD BY SUCH CORPORATIONS.

*Approved 20th April, 1874.* (*P. L., 1874, page 110.*)

SECTION 1. That whensoever it has occurred or shall happen that any corporation has been or shall be dissolved, owning lands or other real estate in this Commonwealth at the time of dissolution, whether by decree of court or expiration of time or otherwise, it shall be lawful for the officers last in office, if in life, or any trustee to be appointed for the purpose by the court of common pleas of the county where the real estate is or shall be located, on the petition to such court by majority in amount and value of all the shareholders or corporators, and upon giving security in double the probable value of the real estate to be sold, (said security to be approved by the court), together with such notice as the said court may require to be given to all not represented by petition or answer, by actual service or advertisement, to make conveyance of such real estate in absolute fee simple, under such decree as the said court may make for the sale, either public or private; and the proceeds of sale shall be applied or distributed by the party or parties so making sale, as part of the effects of the defunct corporation, to creditors or shareholders, as the said court may adjudge them to be entitled. And if such corporation had made sale of real estate and had not conveyed the same, such court may decree conveyance in specific execution of such contract in manner aforesaid.

---

## AN ACT TO PROHIBIT FOREIGN CORPORATIONS FROM DOING BUSINESS IN PENNSYLVANIA WITHOUT KNOWN PLACES OF BUSINESS AND AUTHORIZED AGENTS.

*Approved 22d April, 1874.* (*P. L., 1874, page 108.*)

SECTION 1. That from and after the passage of this act no foreign corporation shall do any business in this Commonwealth until said corporation shall have established an office or offices and appoint an agent or agents for the transaction of its business therein.

SEC. 2. It shall not be lawful for any such corporation to do any business in this Commonwealth until it shall have filed in the office of the secretary of the Commonwealth a statement under the seal of said corporation and signed by the president or secretary thereof, showing the title and object of said corporation, the location of its office or offices, and the name or names of its authorized agent or agents therein; and the certificate of the secretary of the Commonwealth, under the seal of the Commonwealth, of the filing of such statement shall be preserved for public inspection by each of said agents in each and every of said offices.

SEC. 3. Any person or persons, agent, officer, or employee of any such foreign corporation who shall transact any business within this Commonwealth for any such foreign corporation without the provisions of this act being complied with shall be guilty of a misdemeanor, and upon conviction thereof shall be punished by imprisonment not exceeding thirty days and by fine not exceeding one thousand dollars, or either, at the discretion of the court trying the same.

---

## AN ACT FOR THE TAXATION OF CORPORATIONS.

*Approved 24th April, 1874.* (*P. L., 1874, page 68.*)

SECTION 1. That hereafter no institution or company incorporated by or under any law of this Commonwealth, general or special, or of any other State and authorized to do business in this Commonwealth, shall go into operation without first having the name of the institution or company, the date of incorporation, the act of assembly under which incorporated, the place of business, the amount of capital paid in, and the names of the president and treasurer of the same, registered in the office of the auditor-general. And any such institution or company which shall neglect or refuse to comply with the provisions of this section shall be subject to a penalty of five hundred dollars, which penalty shall be collected on an account settled by the auditor-general and State treasurer in the same manner as taxes on stock are settled and collected.

SEC. 2. That hereafter it shall be the duty of the president or treasurer of every company now or hereafter incorporated by or under any law of this Commonwealth, except banks and saving institutions, and of every company now or hereafter incorporated by any other State and doing business in this Commonwealth, which is taxable under the laws of this State, to make report in writing to the auditor-general annually, in the month of November, stating specifically the amount of capital paid in, the date, amount, and rate per centum of each and every dividend declared by their respective corporations during the year ending with the first Monday of said month; and in all cases where any such company shall fail to make and declare any dividend upon either its common or preferred stock during the year ending as aforesaid, the treasurer and secretary thereof, after being duly sworn or affirmed to do and perform the same with fidelity according to the best of their knowledge and belief, shall, between the first and fifteenth days of November of each year in which no dividend has been declared as aforesaid, estimate and appraise the capital stock of such company upon which no dividend has been made or declared at its value, not less than the average price which said stock sold for during said year, and when the same shall have been so truly estimated and appraised, they shall forthwith forward to the auditor-general a certificate thereof, accompanied by a copy of their said oath or affirmation, by them signed, and attested by the magistrate or other person qualified to administer the same : *Provided*, That if the auditor-general or State treasurer, or either of them, is not satisfied with the valuation so made and returned, they are hereby authorized and empowered to make a valuation thereof, and to settle an account upon the valuation so by them made, for the taxes, penalties, and interest due Commonwealth thereon; and any corporation dissatisfied with such settlement may appeal therefrom, as is now provided by law for appeals, from the settlement of accounts by the auditor-general and State treasurer.

SEC. 3. That if the said officers of any such company or corporation shall neglect or refuse to furnish the auditor-general, on or before the thirty-first day of December in each and every year, with the report aforesaid or the report and appraisement, as the case may be, as required by the second section of this act, it shall be the duty of the accounting officers of the Commonwealth to add ten per centum to the tax of said corporation for each and every year for which such report or report and appraisement were not so furnished, which precentage shall be settled and collected with the said tax in the usual manner of settling accounts and collecting such taxes: *Provided*, That if said officers of any such company or corporation shall intentionally fail to comply with the provisions of the second section of this act for three successive years, the auditor-general shall report the fact to the governor, who, if he shall be made satisfied such failure was intentional, shall thereupon by proclamation declare the charter of said company or corporation forfeited and its chartered privileges at an end, whereupon the same shall cease, end, and be determined.

SEC. 4. That every railroad company, canal company, steamboat company, slack-water navigation company, transportation company, street passenger railway company, and every other company, now or hereafter incorporated by or under any law of this Commonwealth, or now or hereafter incorporated by any other State and doing business in this Commonwealth, and owning, operating, or leasing to or from another corporation or company any railroad, canal, slack-water navigation, or street passenger railway, or device for the transportation of freight or passengers, or in any way engaged in the transportation of freight or passengers, shall be subject to and pay a tax into the treasury of the Commonwealth, annually, at the rate of nine-tenths of one mill upon its capital stock for each one per cent. of dividend made or declared by such company; and in case of no dividend being made or declared by such company upon either its common or perferred stock, then six mills upon a true valuation of the capital stock of the same upon which no dividend has been made or declared, made in accordance with the provisions of the third section of this act.

SEC. 5. That every company whatever now or hereafter incorporated under any law of this Commonwealth, or now or hereafter incorporated by any other State and doing business in this Commonwealth, except those upon which a tax is imposed by the fourth section of this act, and excepting also banks and savings institutions, building associations, and foreign insurance companies licensed in pursuance of the general acts in relation thereto, shall be subject to and pay a tax into the treasury of the Commonwealth, annually, at the rate of one-half mill upon its capital stock for each one per cent. of dividend made or declared by such company; and in case of no dividend being made or declared by such company upon either its common or preferred stock, then three mills upon a true valuation of the capital stock of the same upon which no dividend has been made or declared, made in accordance with the provisions of the third section of this act.

SEC. 6. That it shall be the duty of the treasurer or other officer having charge of any company upon which a tax is imposed by either of the fourth or fifth sections of this act to transmit the amount .of said tax to the treasury of the Commonwealth within fifteen days from the thirty-first day of December in each and every year; and if any company shall neglect or refuse to pay the tax hereinbefore required to be paid, the directors, managers, or treasurer thereof for the time being shall be jointly and severally liable in their individual capacity for the payment thereof, and the same may be sued for and recovered, under the direction of the State treasurer, as other debts of like amount due the Common-wealth are recoverable: *Provided*, That the remedy against the directors, managers, or treasurer in their individual capacity shall not prevent the Commonwealth from proceeding against the corporation by any process provided by law.

SEC. 7. That every company incorporated or organized by or under any law of this Commonwealth, or incorporated or organized by or under any law of any other State and doing business in this Commonwealth, which possesses the corporate right or privilege to mine or to purchase and sell coal, shall, semi-annually, upon the first days of July and January in each and every year, make report, under oath or affirmation, to the auditor-general of the number of tons of coal mined during the six months preceding the said first day of July and January by such company, and also of the number of tons of coal that shall be mined by any incorporated association, partnership, or individual under any lease, contract, grant, or mining privilege, upon the property of which the company making such report is the owner or lessee or has any mining or coal privilege or interest therein, and also of the number of tons not mined as aforesaid which shall have been purchased during the same period by the said company, and shall pay into the treasury of the Commonwealth an additional tax upon its corporate franchises created by or used within this Commonwealth, at the rate of three cents upon each and every ton of two thousand two hundred and forty pounds of coal so mined or purchased as aforesaid: *Provided*, That the amount of coal consumed in the transaction of its business by any such company shall not be included in its return: *And provided further*, That said tax shall not be payable more than once in respect of the same ton of coal: *And provided also*, That if any such company shall neglect or refuse for a period of thirty days after such tax becomes due to make said return or to pay the same, the amount thereof, with an addition of ten per centum thereto, shall be collected for the use of the Commonwealth as other taxes are recoverable by law from said companies.

SEC. 8. That the taxes imposed by the fourth section of this act, and the revenues derived therefrom, shall be assigned to the sinking fund of this Commonwealth, and all other taxes imposed by this act, and the revenues derived therefrom, shall be applicable to the payment of the ordinary and current expenses of the government.

SEC. 9. That the auditor-general and State treasurer, or any agent appointed by them or either of them, are hereby authorized to examine the books and papers of any corporation, institution, or company, to verify the accuracy of any return made under the provisions of this or any other act of assembly.

SEC. 10. That in the settlement by the auditor-general and State treasurer of all accounts for taxes due the Commonwealth, they shall charge interest upon the balance or balances found due the Commonwealth at the rate of twelve per centum per annum, from the time said balances became due and payable to the time of the settlement of the same, and all balances due the Commonwealth on accounts settled by the auditor-general and State treasurer shall bear interest from sixty days after the date of settlement at the rate of twelve per centum per annum until the same are paid, and any judgment recovered thereon shall bear interest at the rate of twelve per centum per annum until paid, and the payment of interest as aforesaid shall not relieve any corporation from any of the penalties or commissions prescribed by law for neglect or refusal to furnish reports to the auditor-general or to pay any claim due to the Commonwealth from such corporation.

SEC. 11. That all laws or parts of laws inconsistent herewith, and the first, second, third, fourth, seventh, eighth, and ninth sections of an act entitled "An act to revise, amend, and consolidate the several laws taxing corporations, brokers, and bankers," approved ·the first day of May, Anno Domini one thousand eight hundred and sixty-eight, and the fourth section of an act entitled "An act relating to the revenues of the Commonwealth," approved the twenty-first day of March, Anno Domini one thousand eight hundred and seventy-three, be and the same are hereby repealed; saving, reserving, and excepting unto the Commonwealth the right to collect any taxes accrued or accruing under any of said sections or acts prior to the repeal of the same: *Provided, however,* The repeal of the aforesaid first, second, third, fourth, seventh, eighth, and ninth sections of the act entitled "An act to revise, amend, and consolidate the several laws taxing corporations, brokers, and bankers," approved the first day of May, Anno Domini one thousand eight hundred and sixty-eight, and the repeal of the aforesaid fourth section of an act entitled "An act relating to the revenues of the Commonwealth," approved the twenty-first day of March, Anno Domini one thousand eight hundred and seventy-three, shall not have the effect of reimposing any tax heretofore repealed by any of said sections: *Provided further,* That on all payments made of taxes accrued under the aforesaid fourth section of the act approved the twenty-first day of March, Anno Domini one thousand eight hundred and seventy-three, entitled "An act relating to the revenues of the Commonwealth," no interest or penalty shall be charged, and an abatement of five per centum shall be allowed when such payment shall be made within thirty days after the date of the approval of this act, and the repeal of the said fourth section mentioned in this proviso shall take·effect as of the first day of January, Anno Domini one thousand eight hundred and seventy-four, reserving, however, unto the Commonwealth the right to collect any and all taxes accruing under said fourth section prior to the date of repeal as aforesaid.

---

## AN ACT RELATING TO THE TRANSPORTATION OF EX- PLOSIVE OR DANGEROUS MATERIAL.

*Approved 6th May, 1874. (P. L., 1874, page 121.)*

SECTION 1. That if any person shall knowingly deliver or cause to be delivered to any canal, railroad, steamboat, or other transportation company, or to any person, firm, or corpo- ration engaged in the business of transportation, any nitro- glycerine, dualiñ, dynamite, gunpowder, mining or blasting powder, gun cotton, phosphorus, or other explosive material adapted for blasting or for any other purpose for which the articles before mentioned, or any of them, may be used, under any false or deceptive invoice or description, or without informing such person, firm, or corporation in writing, at or before the time when such delivery is made, of the true nature of such, and without having the keg, barrel, can, or package containing the same plainly marked with the name of the explosive material therein contained, together with the word "dangerous" article, such person shall be guilty of a mis- demeanor, and upon conviction thereof shall be sentenced to imprisonment for thirty days and to pay a fine of one hun- dred dollars, and shall be responsible for all damages to persons or property directly or indirectly resulting from the explosion or combustion of any such article.

SEC. 2. It shall and may be lawful for any officer or agent of any person, firm, or corporation engaged in the business of transportation, upon affidavit made of the fact that any pack- age tendered for transportation, not in compliance with the provisions of the first section hereof, is believed to contain explosive material such as aforesaid, to require such package to be opened, and to refuse to receive any such package unless such requirement be complied with; and if such package be opened and found to contain any explosive material, the said package and its contents shall be forthwith removed to any lawful place for the storing of gunpowder; and, after conviction of the offender, or after three months from such removal, the said package, with its contents, shall be sold at public sale, after the expiration of ten days from notice of the time and place of such sale published in one newspaper in the county where such seizure shall have been made; and the proceeds of such sale, after deducting therefrom the expenses of removal, storage, advertisement, and sale, shall be paid into the treasury of the said county.

## A SUPPLEMENT TO AN ACT FOR THE BETTER PROTECTION OF THE WAGES OF MECHANICS, MINERS, LABORERS, AND OTHERS, APPROVED THE NINTH DAY OF APRIL, ANNO DOMINI ONE THOUSAND EIGHT HUNDRED AND SEVENTY-TWO.

*Approved 8th May, 1874.* (*P. L., 1874, page 120.*)

SECTION 1. That the proviso to the fourth section of an act entitled " An act for the better protection of the wages of mechanics, miners, laborers, and others, approved the ninth day of April, Anno Domini one thousand eight hundred and seventy-two," shall not hereafter be so construed as to in any manner apply to coal-lease mortgage or mortgages, or to make the same a lien preferred to the lien of the wages of labor mentioned in said act, but that such claim of wages shall be a lien preferred thereto.

SEC. 2. That the last proviso of the first section of said act, which is as follows :—" No such claim shall be a lien upon any real estate unless the same be filed in the prothonotary's office of the county in which such real estate is situated, within three months after the same becomes due and owing, in the same manner as mechanics' liens are now filed," be and the same is hereby repealed.

SEC. 3. That all acts or parts of acts inconsistent herewith are hereby repealed.

AN ACT RELATIVE TO SERVICE OF PROCESS UPON THE STOCKHOLDERS OF CORPORATIONS IN ACTIONS BROUGHT TO CHARGE THE STOCKHOLDERS FOR DEBTS OF THE CORPORATION OR FOR UNPAID INSTALLMENTS UPON THEIR STOCK.

*Approved 14th May, 1874. (P. L., 1874, page 146.)*

SECTION I. That in all actions or proceedings now or hereafter brought or instituted in any county within this Commonwealth to charge the stockholders of any corporation with any of the debts of such corporation or to enforce payment of installments due upon stock, service of summons or other process may be made upon the stockholders resident within such county in the same manner as writs of summons are now directed to be served, and upon those residing in other counties of this Commonwealth by the sheriff of the county in which they may respectively reside, and upon those non-residents of this Commonwealth by publication for four successive publications in a newspaper published within the county where such action or proceeding is brought or instituted and also in the State in which such non-residents may reside, as the court from which such action or proceedings shall issue may direct, and a copy of such publication shall be mailed to the post-office address of such non-resident stockholders, if such address can be ascertained.

---

AN ACT TO ENFORCE THE SIXTH SECTION OF THE SEVENTEENTH ARTICLE OF THE CONSTITUTION OF THIS COMMONWEALTH, PROVIDING THAT NO PRESIDENT, DIRECTOR, AGENT, OR EMPLOYEE OF ANY RAILROAD OR CANAL COMPANY SHALL BE INTERESTED IN THE FURNISHING OF MATERIAL OR SUPPLIES TO SUCH COMPANY OR IN THE BUSINESS OF TRANSPORTATION AS A COMMON CARRIER OF FREIGHT OR PASSENGERS OVER THE WORKS OWNED, LEASED, CONTROLLED, OR WORKED BY SUCH COMPANY.

*Approved 15th May, 1874. (P. L., 1874, page 178.)*

SECTION I. That no president, director, officer, agent, or employee of any railroad or canal company of this Commonwealth shall hereafter be interested in any contract for the furnishing of materials or supplies to any such railroad or canal company, and it shall not be lawful for such president, director, officer, agent, or employee to institute or maintain any action at law or suit in equity to recover under such contract for his or their interest therein : *Provided, however,* That all rights under *bona fide* contracts made prior to the first day of January, Anno Domini one thousand eight hundred and seventy-four, shall not be in anywise thereby affected.

SEC. 2. No president, director, officer, agent, or employee of any railroad company or canal company of this Commonwealth shall hereafter be engaged in the business of transportation as a common carrier of freight by any express or other freight line, or in the transportation of passengers by any sleeping or parlor car or other line, over the works owned, leased, controlled, or worked by such company, and any profit realized by such president, director, officer, agent, or employee in violation of the provisions of this section shall belong to and be recoverable by such railroad or canal company : *Provided,* Suit therefor shall be commenced within one year after the discovery of such violation.

SEC. 3. Nothing, however, in this act contained shall prevent any president, director, officer, agent, or employee from being a shareholder in any incorporated or joint stock company or association : *Provided, however,* That no director interested as a shareholder as aforesaid shall vote upon any contract for furnishing material or supplies to be entered into with any other incorporated or joint stock company or association in which he is likewise interested as a shareholder, and no contract shall be made by any officers, agent, or employee for furnishing material or supplies with any incorporated or joint stock company or association in which such officer, agent, or employee is likewise interested as a shareholder, unless in pursuance of an order of the board of directors or of a proper disinterested superior officer of such railroad or canal company. Any violation of the provisions of this act shall be punished by a fine not exceeding five hundred dollars.

SEC. 4. This act to take effect January first, one thousand eight hundred and seventy-five.

AN ACT TO PROVIDE FOR THE ADJUSTMENT, SETTLE-
MENT AND COLLECTION OF COMPENSATION FROM
RAILROAD COMPANIES FOR RAILROADS LOCATED OR
THAT MAY BE LOCATED ON COUNTY BRIDGES, AND TO
EMPOWER COUNTY COMMISSIONERS TO MAKE CON-
TRACTS RELATING THERETO.

*Approved 15th May, 1874. (P. L., 1874, page 185.)*

SECTION I. That any railroad company which has heretofore located or may hereafter locate its railroad upon any
county bridge in this Commonwealth is hereby authorized to
contract and agree with the commissioners of said county for
the use, purchase, removal, replacing, or exchange of such
bridge, or for the compensation proper to be paid to said
county by said company for the use and occupancy of said
bridge or such parts thereof as may be used and occupied by
said railroad company, and for that purpose the said commissioners are hereby authorized and empowered to contract
and agree with said company, and empowered to do all such
acts as may be necessary and proper to effectually carry out
such contract; and any such contracts and agreements made
by any county commissioners, and all rights, property, and
privileges granted thereby to any railroad company, are hereby
fully approved, ratified, and confirmed.

SEC. 2. That all moneys due or hereafter becoming due,
and all obligations that have been heretofore or hereafter may
be incurred by said companies, under said agreements and
contracts heretofore made or hereafter to be made, may be
collected and enforced in the same manner as debts of like
amount are now recovered in this Commonwealth.

AN ACT TO AUTHORIZE THE ISSUING OF LETTERS
PATENT TO CERTAIN CORPORATIONS.

*Approved 15th May, 1874. (P. L., 1874, pages 186.)*

SEC. I. That upon the application of the president and
secretary of any corporation heretofore or hereafter created
under any general or special law of this Commonwealth, accompanied by due proof that said corporation has complied

with all the conditions provided by law and the Constitution to enable it to have a corporate existence and transact business, it shall be lawful for the governor to issue letters patent, under the great seal of the Commonweaith, in such form as he may prescribe, to such corporation, declaring it to be and erecting it into a body corporate or politic in deed and in law. ·

---

## AN ACT TO AUTHORIZE CORPORATIONS TO INCREASE THE SECURITY OF THEIR BONDED INDEBTEDNESS.

*Approved 15th May, 1874.* (*P. L., 1874, page 186.*)

SECTION 1. That it shall and may be lawful for any corporation existing by or under the authority of any law of this Commonwealth which shall have mortgaged any part of its estate, corporate property, and.franchises for the security of all or any portion of its bonded indebtedness, to mortgage its remaining estate, corporate property, and franchises, or any part of the same, as a further and additional security for' the same bonded indebtedness: *Provided, however,* That no lien then existing upon such remaining estate, property, and franchises shall be thereby impaired or affected.

---

## AN ACT RELATIVE TO FORFEITURES OF CHARTERS OR GRANTS OF SPECIAL OR EXCLUSIVE PRIVILEGES TO RAILROAD, TURNPIKE, AND PLANK ROAD CORPORATIONS.

*Approved 15th May, 1874.* (*P. L., 1874, page 188.*)

SECTION 1. That railroad corporations heretofore chartered by the legislature subject to the provisions of the general railroad act, approved the nineteenth day of February, one thousand eight hundred and forty-nine, and the several supplements thereto, and all turnpike and plank road companies, duly incorporated and under which a *bona fide* organization has been made and business commenced in good faith and an expenditure of at least five thousand dollars has been made for construction, but whose charters or grants of special or exclusive privileges may have been forfeited or may hereafter be subject to forfeiture by limitation by reason of the limitation of time fixed in such charters or grants of privileges, such forfeiture or limitation fixed for completion shall be remitted or extended, and shall be held and taken to be remitted or extended, if such corporations so organized as aforesaid shall, within one year from the passage of this act or within one year from the expiration of the time limited for completion, elect to prosecute to completion the public works which were originally authorized to be constructed by their charters as aforesaid, and shall at the time of such election consent, in such a manner as shall be prescribed by law, to such charters or grants of special or exclusive privileges, to the provisions of the Constitution of this Commonwealth : *Provided*, That all such public works shall be prosecuted to completion within five years from the date of the election aforesaid.

SEC. 2. The board of directors of any such corporations shall, by resolution, elect to prosecute the public works authorized to be constructed by their charters, and shall cause the same to be recorded on the minutes of the board, and a copy of the same, duly certified, shall be attached to and, with the instrument by which consent is given to subject such charters to the provisions of the Constitution of the Commonwealth, be filed and recorded in the office of the secretary of the Commonwealth.

---

## AN ACT REQUIRING COUNTY COMMISSIONERS, RAILROAD AND OTHER CORPORATIONS TO MAKE ANNUAL REPORTS TO THE SECRETARY OF INTERNAL AFFAIRS IN LIEU OF SIMILAR REPORTS HERETOFORE MADE TO THE AUDITOR-GENERAL.

*Approved 15th May, 1874.* (*P. L., 1874, page 193.*)

SECTION 1. That the county commissioners of each county of the State, including the board of revision of the city of Philadelphia, shall, upon the first day of June, one thousand eight hundred and seventy-four, and upon the same day annually thereafter, make out in tabular form, by assessment districts, a full statement of all property taxable for county purposes, showing the real and personal in separate columns, the amount of tax assessed for county purposes, and also the debt of said county; the same to be enclosed by mail to the secretary of internal affairs at Harrisburg; and in case of refusal or neglect to make such returns, the same may be enforced by mandamus.

SEC. 2. The secretary of internal affairs, in lieu of the auditor-general, shall, after the first day of July, one thousand eight hundred and seventy-five, transmit to the railroad and other corporations named in the act of fourth of April, one thousand eight hundred and fifty-nine, and also in the act of ninth April, one thousand eight hundred and seventy, the blanks required, and upon the reception of such returns he shall arrange the same for publication; and in case of neglect or refusal to make such returns each of such corporations thus refusing shall be subject to the penalties in said acts.

SEC. 3. That hereafter the secretary of internal affairs, in lieu of the auditor-general, shall send out the blanks required by the act of May ninth, one thousand eight hundred and seventy-one, entitled "An act for the collection of mineral statistics," and said secretary shall do and perform all the duties enjoined in said act in regard to the collecting, compiling, and publishing a report of the same number of copies ordered to be published by the auditor-general.

SEC. 4. Until the secretary of internal affairs shall be duly qualified, the returns required by the provisions of the first and third sections of this act shall be made to and the duties thereby- imposed performed by the chief of the bureau of statistics.

## AN ACT TO FACILITATE THE TRANSFER OF STOCKS AND LOANS.

*Approved 23d May, 1874. (P. L., 1874, page 222.)*

SECTION 1. That all certificates of stocks and loans which have been or may hereafter be issued by this Commonwealth or by any municipal or other corporation shall be transferable by the legal owner thereof, without any liability on the part of the transfer agents of the Commonwealth or the municipal or other corporation permitting such transfers to recognize or see to the execution of any trust, whether expressed, implied, or constructive, to which such stocks or loans may be subject, unless when such transfer agents of the Commonwealth or officers of such municipal or other corporation charged with the duty of permitting such transfer to be made shall have previously received actual notice in writing, signed by or on behalf of the person or persons for whom such stocks or loans appear by the certificate thereof to be held in trust, that the proposed transfer would be a violation of such trust.

AN ACT TO ENABLE RAILROADS, CANALS, OR OTHER TRANSPORTATION COMPANIES TO ACCEPT OF THE TERMS OF THE SEVENTEENTH ARTICLE OF THE CONSTITUTION, ADOPTED THE SIXTEENTH DAY OF DECEMBER, ANNO DOMINI ONE THOUSAND EIGHT HUNDRED AND SEVENTY-THREE.

*Approved 5th June, 1874. (P. L., 1874, page 275.)*

SECTION 1. That it shall be the duty of the board of directors of any railroad, canal, or other transportation company in existence on the first day of January, one thousand eight hundred and seventy-four, desiring to accept of the provisions of the seventeenth article of the Constitution of the State, adopted on the sixteenth day of December, one thousand eight hundred and seventy-three, to file in the office of the secretary of the Commonwealth a certificate in writing, signed by the president and secretary and attested by the corporate seal of the company, stating that at a regular or special meeting of said board of directors a resolution, in pursuance of the consent of the stockholders, was adopted, accepting of all the provisions of said article, and all the powers and privileges and limitations and restrictions mentioned therein shall be deemed and taken for all purposes to apply to said corporation. The said certificate shall be recorded in the office of the secretary of the Commonwealth in a suitable book to be by him kept for that purpose.

SEC. 2. No such certificate shall be made by the officers aforesaid without the consent of the stockholders of the corporation, to be obtained by an election to be held in the same manner as prescribed by law for increasing the capital stock of a corporation.

## A SUPPLEMENT TO AN ACT ENTITLED "AN ACT TO AUTHORIZE THE FORMATION AND REGULATION OF RAILROAD CORPORATIONS."

*Approved 8th June, 1874. (P. L., 1874, page 277.)*

SECTION 1. That from and after the passage of this act articles of association, authorized by an act entitled "An act to authorize the formation and regulation of railroad corporations," approved April fourth, Anno Domini one thousand eight hundred and sixty-eight, may be filed and recorded in the office of the secretary of the Commonwealth when five thousand dollars of stock for every mile of railroad proposed to be made is subscribed and ten per centum paid thereon in good faith, in cash, to the director named in said articles of association.

SEC. 2. Section fifth of the act to which this is a supplement is hereby amended so as to allow each company organized under said act one year to complete their road for each twenty-five miles more than the fifty miles required to be finished within two years, as provided in said section.

SEC. 3. On filing of the articles of association provided in this act aforesaid and the act to which this is a supplement, the governor shall issue his letters patent creating the association aforesaid a body corporate, with power to use and enjoy all the powers and privileges conferred by the act aforesaid and the several supplements thereto.

SEC. 4. All acts and parts of acts inconsistent herewith are hereby repealed.

## AN ACT TO AUTHORIZE THE COUNTIES, CITIES, TOWNS, OR TOWNSHIPS OF THIS STATE, RESPECTIVELY, TO ENTER INTO CONTRACTS WITH RAILROAD COMPANIES WHOSE ROADS ENTER THEIR LIMITS, WHEREBY SAID COMPANIES MAY RELOCATE, CHANGE, OR ELEVATE THEIR RAILROADS.

*Approved 9th June, 1874. (P. L., 1874, page 282.)*

SECTION 1. That the proper authorities of any county, city, town, or township of this State, respectively, be and they are hereby authorized and empowered to enter into contracts with any of the railroad companies whose roads enter their limits respectively, whereby the said railroad companies may relocate, change, or elevate their railroads within said limits, or either of them, in such manner as in the judgment of such authorities respectively may be best adapted to secure the safety of lives and property and promote the interest of said county, city, town, or township, and for that purpose the said authorities shall have power to do all such acts as may be necessary and proper to effectually carry out such contracts; and any such contracts made by any railroad company or companies as aforesaid with said authorities, or either of them, are hereby fully ratified and confirmed: *Provided,* That nothing in this proviso contained shall affect any contract made or hereafter to be made with any railroad company from apportioning the expenses of altering and adjusting the grades of existing railroads and intersecting streets in any city or borough so as to dispense with grade crossings.

---

## AN ACT FOR FURTHER REGULATION OF APPEALS FROM ASSESSMENTS OF DAMAGES TO OWNERS OF PROPERTY TAKEN FOR PUBLIC USE.

*Approved 13th June, 1874. (P. L., 1874, page 283.)*

SECTION 1. That in all cases of damages assessed against any municipal or other corporation or individual or individuals invested with the privilege of taking private property for public use, for property taken, injured, or destroyed by the construction or enlargement of their works, highways, or improvements, whether such assessment shall have been made by viewers or otherwise than upon a trial in court, and an appeal is not provided for or regulated by existing laws, an appeal may be taken by either party to the court of common pleas of the proper county within thirty days from the ascertainment of the damages or the filing a report thereof in court pursuant to any general or special act, and not afterwards.

SEC. 2. Any appeal taken pursuant to this act shall be signed by the party or parties taking the same or by his or their agent or attorney, and shall be accompanied by an affidavit of the party appellant or of his or their agent or attorney, that the same is not taken for the purpose of delay, but because the affiant firmly believes that injustice has been done.

SEC. 3. That any party entitled to an appeal under the eighth section of the sixteenth article of the Constitution, or who would be entitled to an appeal in any future case under this act under the same circumstances, shall have the right to to take an appeal from any assessment of damages, or reassessment or ascertainment thereof as aforesaid, made or filed on or after the first day of January of the present year and before the passage of this act; but such appeal shall be taken within thirty days after the passage of this act, and in conformity with the second section thereof.

---

## AN ACT REQUIRING EVERY RAILROAD OR CANAL CORPORATION ORGANIZED IN THIS STATE TO MAINTAIN AN OFFICE THEREIN FOR THE TRANSACTION OF ITS BUSINESS.

*Approved 14th June, 1874. (P. L., 1874, page 289.)*

SECTION 1. That every railroad or canal corporation organized in this State shall maintain an office therein for the transaction of its business, where transfers of its stock shall be made and books kept for the inspection by any stock or bondholder or any other person having any pecuniary interest in such corporation, in which shall be recorded the amount of capital stock subscribed or paid in and by whom, the names of the owners of its stock and the amounts owned by them respectively, the transfers of said stock, and the names and places of residence of its officers.

---

AN ACT TO CARRY INTO EFFECT SECTION EIGHT OF ARTICLE SEVENTEEN OF THE CONSTITUTION, IN RELATION TO GRANTING FREE PASSES OR PASSES AT A DISCOUNT BY RAILROAD OR OTHER TRANSPORTATION COMPANIES.

*Approved 14th June, 1874. (P. L., 1874, page 289.)*

SECTION 1. That no railroad, railway, or other transportation company having accepted the provisions of the seventeenth article of the Constitution, or hereafter organized, shall grant free passes or passes at a discount to any person, except to an officer or employee of the company issuing the same, and any person signing or issuing any such free passes or passes at a discount, except to officers or employees as aforesaid, shall be subject to pay a fine to the Commonwealth not exceeding one hundred dollars: *Provided*, That nothing herein contained shall be held to prevent the use of passes granted previous to the adoption of the present Constitution, the limited time whereof has not expired, nor to prevent the use of passes granted for a valuable consideration under contracts made between corporations and individuals or between one corporation and another.

---

AN ACT TO EXTEND THE TIME FOR THE COMPLETION OF RAILROADS AUTHORIZED TO BE CONSTRUCTED BY RAILROAD OR RAILWAY CORPORATIONS OF THIS COMMONWEALTH UNDER ANY GENERAL LAW.

*Approved 17th March, 1875. (P. L., 1875, page 7.)*

SECTION 1. *Be it enacted, &c.*, That the time for completing all railroads in this Commonwealth, commenced by railroad or railway companies incorporated under or in pursuance of any general law of this Commonwealth, be and the same is hereby extended for the further period of five years from and after the time limited for the completion of the same by any general law under and by virtue of which any such corporation may have been incorporated: *Provided*, Any railroad or railway company enjoying the benefits and privileges of this act shall hereafter hold its charter subject to the provisions of the Constitution of this Commonwealth.

---

A SUPPLEMENT TO AN ACT TO AUTHORIZE THE FORMA-
TION AND REGULATION OF RAILROAD CORPORATIONS,
APPROVED APRIL FOUR, ANNO DOMINI ONE THOUSAND
EIGHT HUNDRED AND SIXTY-EIGHT.

*Approved 18th March, 1875. (P. L., 1875, page 28.)*

SECTION I. *Be it enacted, &c.*, That whenever, under the the provisions of the act approved the fourth day of April, Anno Domini one thousand eight hundred and sixty-eight, entitled "An act to authorize the formation and regulation of railroad companies," any number of citizens of Pennsylvania, not less than nine, may be desirous of forming a company for the purpose of constructing, maintaining, and operating a railroad, having a gauge not exceeding three feet, for public use in the conveyance of persons and property, they may state in the articles of association which they are required to make and sign the capital stock of the company at six thousand dollars, or any greater amount, for every mile of road proposed to be constructed; and that said articles of association may be filed and recorded in the office of the secretary of the Commonwealth when three thousand dollars of stock for every mile of railroad proposed to be made is subscribed, and ten per centum paid thereon in good faith and in cash to the directors named in said articles of association.

A SUPPLEMENT TO AN ACT ENTITLED "AN ACT RELA-
TIVE TO FORFEITURE OF CHARTERS OR GRANTS OF
SPECIAL OR EXCLUSIVE PRIVILEGES TO RAILROAD,
TURNPIKE, AND PLANK ROAD CORPORATIONS," AP-
PROVED MAY FIFTEENTH, ONE THOUSAND EIGHT
HUNDRED AND SEVENTY-FOUR, PRESCRIBING THE
MANNER IN WHICH SAID CORPORATIONS SHALL CON-
SENT TO HOLD THEIR CHARTERS SUBJECT TO THE
PROVISIONS OF THE CONSTITUTION ADOPTED DECEM-
BER SIXTEENTH, ONE THOUSAND EIGHT HUNDRED
AND SEVENTY-THREE.

*Approved 30th March, 1875.* (*P. L., 1875, page 37.*)

Section 1. *Be it enacted, &c.,* That the stockholders of any
railroad corporation, turnpike, or plank road company mentioned in the act of assembly entitled "An act relative to
forfeitures of charters or grants of special or exclusive privileges to railroad, turnpike, and plank road corporations,"
approved May fifteenth, one thousand eight hundred and
seventy-four, shall, in order to obtain the benefit of said act
of assembly, consent, at a special meeting to be called in
accordance with its charter and by-laws, to accept the Constitution of the State adopted December sixteenth, one
thousand eight hundred and seventy-three, and to thereafter
hold its charter subject to all the provisions thereof, and shall
cause an instrument in writing, under the seal of the company,
and signed by the president and secretary, testifying to its
consent as aforesaid, to be filed and recorded in the office of
the secretary of the Commonwealth.

Sec. 2. The action of the stockholders of any railroad
company under this act shall be taken to be of the same force
and effect, for the purpose of also accepting the terms of the
seventeenth article of the said Constitution, as the action of
the directors of such company prescribed in the act of
assembly entitled "An act to enable railroads, canals, or other
transportation companies to accept the terms of the seventeenth article of the Constitution adopted the sixteenth day
of December, Anno Domini one thousand eight hundred
and seventy-three," approved June fifth, one thousand eight
hundred and seventy-four.

# INDEX.

241

P/

BONDS.—Where companies have issued or may issue and dispose of bonds for less than par, not to be deemed usury............................................................. ...........................

    commissioners of Allegheny county to exchange stock of railroad companies for bonds of the county issued for stock.........................................................................

    bond to be filed with petition for appointment of viewers to assess damages for right of way ................. ..................................................................................

    executors and others may exchange bonds of Allegheny county for stock of railroad companies for which bonds were issued.....................................................

    any railroad company may purchase and hold stock and bonds of any other railroad company in the State................................................................. ...........

    bonds may be issued and mortgage given to secure same on any branch, lateral, or diverging railroad.....................................................................................

    bonds may be issued and mortgage given to secure same for payment of debts of consolidated roads...........................................................................

    corporations to pay plaintiff's counsel fees in cases where validity of bonds contested and established............................... .........................................................

    Allegheny county exempted from provision of act 3d May, 1866, for payment of plaintiff's counsel fees.................................................................... ...........................

    may be issued for borrowed money and mortgage given to secure same, under general railroad law of 4th April, 1868...............................................................

    and stock of any railroad company of this or any other State may be purchased and held by companies of this State..............................................................

    and stock of coal, iron, and lumber companies may be purchased or guaranteed by any railroad or canal company.......................................................................

    act of 10th April, 1867, authorizing sale of corporate property on a bond same as on mortgage, repealed..................................................................................

    bonded debt and capital stock may be increased by any corporation fifty per cent.........

    any two or more railroad companies may jointly endorse or guarantee bonds of any other railroad company.......................................................................................

    any canal or navigation company may purchase and hold stock and bonds of any railroad company................................................................................

    private corporations may subscribe for and purchase stock and bonds of American Steamship Company..........................................................................

    act 3d May, 1866, for payment of counsel fees, to mean only cases where validity of bonds contested and established............. .......................................................

    companies in Susquehanna, Wyoming, Wayne, and Luzerne counties may purchase and hold stock and bonds of any other railroad company.......................................

    executor, &c. holding stock and bonds of any company authorized to consolidate may exchange them for stock and bonds of consolidated company.............................

    and obligations of any railroad corporation may be secured by mortgage upon property, rights, and franchises.....................................................................

    interest on bonds and evidences of debt subject to State tax of five per cent...................

    may be registered in name of holder and transferable only on company's books.............

    may be further secured by mortgage on remaining estate, property, and franchises........

BONUS OR TAX to be paid to State—one-fourth of one per cent. on stock increased......

BOOKS AND PAPERS may be examined by auditor-general and State treasurer or an agent, to verify returns made................................................................................162,

BRADFORD COUNTY.—Act 28th March, 1868, for protection of farmers and owners of cattle, &c., and supplement extended to Bradford and other counties......................

    act 22d March, 1871, for determination of rights when highway abandoned, not to extend to Bradford county........................................................................................

BRANCHES may be constructed from main line by companies, under general railroad law of 4th April, 1868.................................................................................

BREACH OF PEACE.—Conductors may arrest persons committing breach of peace on cars passing through Erie, Crawford, Warren, and Venango counties........................

BRIDGES to be constructed by proprietors of lateral railroads to enable all persons to pass over railroads at public roads................................ ...........................................

    to be constructed by proprietors of lateral railroads to enable occupants of land to pass over railroads on their lands ...............................................................................

# 255